ISLAMIC PHILOSOPHY

ISLAMIC PHILOSOPHY

BY

M. SAEED SHEIKH

Head, Department of Philosophy
Government College, Lahore

FOREWORD BY

Professor M. M. SHARIF

THE OCTAGON PRESS
LONDON

First published 1962
First Impression in this Edition 1982

ISBN: 90086050 2

Photoset and printed in Great Britain by
Redwood Burn Limited, Trowbridge, Wiltshire

CONTENTS

	Page
Dedication	vi
Foreword	vii
From the Preface to the First Edition	ix

CHAPTERS:

1.	Muʿtazilism	1
2.	Ashʿarism	14
3.	Historical Origin and Sources of Sufism	21
4.	Philosophy of the Ikhwān al-Ṣafā'	32
5.	Al-Kindi	42
6.	Abū Bakr al-Rāzi	50
7.	Al-Fārābi	57
8.	Ibn Sīna	67
9.	Al-Ghazāli	85
10.	Ibn Bājjah	117
11.	Ibn Ṭufayl	123
12.	Ibn Rushd	131
13.	Ibn Khaldūn	140

Select Bibliography	152
Index	163

To
AL-KINDI
The First Arab Philosopher of Islam

FOREWORD

The author of this work, which makes a valuable contribution to the literature produced in Pakistan, Mr Saeed Sheikh, is Professor of Philosophy in the Government College, Lahore, and has lectured on Muslim Philosophy for more than a decade. In my opinion, Mr Saeed Sheikh is just the right person to have written a short study of Muslim thought.

Nearly one-third of the book gives us an account of the four principal philosophical movements of the early medieval period—*Mu'tazilism, Ash'arism, Sufism* and the *Ikhwān al-Ṣafā'*. The rest of it deals with the group of thinkers who were known during the same period as the 'Philosophers,' i.e., thinkers under the influence of Greek philosophy.

Mr Saeed's account of the philosophy of each movement and each thinker consists of the most lucid and precise statement I have come across in any short history of Islamic philosophy.

The book contains a comprehensive bibliography, useful notes and a detailed index, the utility of which for the students of philosophy and Islamic studies and those general readers who want to extend their studies in Muslim thought further is evident.

As this work can make an excellent text-book, Mr Saeed Sheikh has placed under great obligation the teachers and students of the colleges and universities in which Muslim philosophy and Islamic studies are included in the syllabus.

M.M. SHARIF

FROM THE PREFACE TO THE FIRST EDITION

The present work grew out of private notes substantially completed in 1952 and used thereafter for some years as a basis for class lectures on the History of Muslim Philosophy. I had no intention to get these scattered notes published in the form of a book without elaborate revision and supplementation till there arose an urgency to do so. As a result of the recommendations of the National Education Commission, Muslim Philosophy has been introduced as a subject of study by the various Universities of Pakistan at the undergraduate level. Not many text-books on the subject are, however, available: demand for them both from the students and teachers is persistent. This handbook is primarily a small contribution towards meeting this demand, though it is believed also to interest the general reader.

The book makes no claim to originality. I have frequently consulted and freely drawn upon the valuable contributions of the learned Orientalists and other reputed scholars and to these I have often referred to in the Notes. I make full acknowledgement of my debt to them all.

I may add that though I have freely utilised the Orientalists' contribution to Muslim philosophy I have not always accepted their views uncritically. In particular I have challenged implicitly in many parts of my book the view that Muslim philosophy is simply a juxtaposition of incongruent elements and not a new reconstruction or that the Muslim philosophers' reception of Greek philosophy was merely a passive imitation and not a creative assimilation. My conviction has been that in their daring philosophical experiment of reconciling the divine with the human, i.e., the fundamentals of Islamic religion with the philosophic and scientific traditions found in their cultural environment, Muslim philosophers came to have many fresh insights and made new advances in the sphere of religio-philosophical thought. It is futile to ignore or minimise the novelty and fecundity of the Muslim thinkers and their genuine contribution to human knowledge. That in Muslim philosophers there are many close parallels to modern and even contemporary philosophy, is a clear proof of this. I have not hesitated to point out in my *exposés* of the thought-systems of al-Fārābi, Ibn Sīna, al-Ghazāli, Ibn Khaldūn and others, the remarkable anticipations in them, among others, of Descartes' Methodological Doubt and *cogito ergo sum*, Spinoza's Idealism, Cartesians' Occasionalism, Leibnitz's Pre-established Harmony, Kant's Antinomies of Pure Reason and Metaphysical Agnosticism, Hegel's Panlogism and the notion of the Absolute, Hume's denial of Causality and even Bergson's Creative Evolutionism and the Logical Positivists' Logicism and Positivism.

In the Notes the students will find suggestions for further reading. The titles in the Bibliography are under the main or more familiar names of the authors arranged alphabetically. With a few exceptions only such original works in Arabic or Persian have been mentioned as can be found also in their English and/or Urdu translations. Many important titles in Arabic have thus been left out. Titles in French and German and other European languages, even of the most indispensable works, have also been omitted, for few students in our country could benefit from them.

I wish to express my deepest gratitude to Professor M.M. Sharif but for whose continuous encouragement and interest the book might still have not seen the light of the day.

Lahore M.S.S.
23 March 1962

Chapter One

MU'TAZILISM

Though the school of Mu'tazilism, like other schools and sects in Islam, came into being in the later times of the Companions of the holy Prophet, its origin can be traced back to an earlier date. During the Prophet's own lifetime Islam consisted of simple and broad principles. This simplicity of the creed continued for some time after him. The Prophet's death was closely followed by wars with the Romans and the Persians. These wars completely absorbed the mental and physical energies of the Arabs. Further, the Muslims in the beginning were so much occupied with the propagation of their faith that they had little time to indulge in abstract discussions about its dogmas. Even then there was a group of Companions who did not have much to do with military campaigns, and thus had leisure enough to be busy with theological studies and other academic pursuits; reference here is to those of the Companions in particular who were known as 'The People of the Bench'. Though this group generally did not allow reason free traffic into matters religious, yet, where needed, they did try to work out the practical ramifications of religious doctrines in the light of reason. It may not be out of place to mention the names of 'Ali, Ibn Mas'ūd, 'Ā'ishah, Mu'ādh ibn Jabal along with them. These were the people who prepared the ground for the school of Mu'tazilism.

It was only natural that, with the advance of Islamic culture in the expanding empire, various new issues should have cropped up and new schools of thought come into existence. It is important to note, however, that only those schools and sects came into prominence which had some marked political origin. The origin of the Khārijites is an example and so is that of the Shī'ites. Later, the school of the Qadarites, the real founders of Mu'tazilism, also had its foundation in the political development of the day.

The first man who dared proclaim the doctrines of the Qadarites was Ma'bad al-Juhani. He lived in the early days of the Umayyads. These were very cruel times: there were relentless persecutions and ruthless bloodshedding in the country for the Umayyad hegemony. In consequence there was a general feeling of resentment and bitterness amongst the people. The freedom-loving Arabs could not easily brook all this; they would demand answers from the State officials to queries such as the following:

Why do you practise such barbarities?

Is not all this against the spirit of Islam?

Are you not Muslims?

With whatever innocence they could pretend, the officials would reply: We are not responsible for what we do. It is God Who does everything. His is the power for good and evil.

Historians report that Ma'bad al-Juhani with 'Aṭā' ibn Yassar, one of his companions, came one day to the celebrated Muslim divine Ḥasan al-Baṣri and said: 'O Abu Sa'īd, these rulers shed the blood of the Muslims and do grievous things and say that their works are by the decree of Allah.'

To this Ḥasan replied: 'The enemies of God, they are liars.'

Thus the first doctrine laid down by the early Mu'tazilites was: 'Man is accountable for his own evil doings; these should not be ascribed to God.' This was known as the doctrine of *qadar*; hence the designation *Qadarites* given to the early Mu'tazilites. For the same reason they were also called the *'Adalites*, that is, the holders of the justice of God, for justice of God can be vouchsafed only by holding man responsible for his actions. Ma'bad al-Juhani preached these doctrines publicly and was therefore put to death by Ḥajjāj in 80/699 by order of Caliph 'Abdul Malik.

After Ma'bad al-Juhani it was a Copt named Ghaylān al-Dimashqi who promulgated similar views. He further added that it was incumbent on every Muslim to urge people to perform right actions and to check them from doing wrong. This addition by Ghaylān overtly interfered with and threatened the maintenance of the Umayyad rule. As a consequence, he met his death at the hands of Hishām ibn Mālik soon after his accession to the caliphal seat in 105/723.

The deaths of Maʿbad and Ghaylān put life into their cause. Their teachings gained currency and exerted an ever-growing influence. Thousands of people came to subscribe to the Muʿtazilite views and outlook. At this time two great personages born in the same year 80/699 appeared like two stars on the horizon of Muʿtazilism. These two were Wāṣil ibn ʿAṭāʾ and ʿAmr ibn ʿUbayd. Both of them were the pupils of Ḥasan al-Baṣri who used to give his lectures in the great mosque of Basra. One day when Ḥasan was busy discussing some problems with his pupils, someone came to him with a question regarding the conflicting standpoints of the Murjiʾites and the Waʿidites. The first held that the perpetrator of a grave sin should be reckoned as a Muslim and not labelled an unbeliever, and that his case should be left to God. The second, laying more emphasis on the threats in the Qurʾān, maintained that the committer of a mortal sin, having *ipso facto* deviated from the right path, could not possibly be considered a believer. Before Ḥasan could give a reply, either Wāṣil or ʿAmr broke out with the assertion of a middle position, i.e., such a one was neither a believer nor an unbeliever. Ḥasan took it ill and said: *iʿtazala ʿanna* (i.e., he has seceded from us). So Wāṣil and ʿAmr left the circle of the master, went to another corner of the mosque and began teaching their own views. Those who gathered around them came to be known as the Muʿtazilites.[1]

Most of the progress and advancement of Muʿtazilism was due to Wāsil ibn ʿAṭāʾ and ʿAmr ibn ʿUbayd who carried an impressive aura of scholarship and learning around them.

[1] This explanation for the origin of the name *Muʿtazilah*, current with the *Ahl al-Ḥadīth*, is not without historical foundation, yet its underlying idea is to expel the Muʿtazilites from the orthodox circle of al-Ḥasan al-Baṣri and thus brand them as heretics. One must note, however, that the Muʿtazilites were proud of their name which they would not have been if it had been merely a nickname suggestive of heresy. Al-Masʿūdi (d. *circa* 346/957), himself a Muʿtazilite, makes it clear in his historico-geographical encyclopaedia, *Murūj al-Dhahab*, that the Muʿtazilites were named so essentially because of their doctrine of *manzilah bayn al-manzilatayn*, i.e., the state intermediate between belief and unbelief (see below, pp. 12–13), according to which they separated themselves from the standpoints of the Murjiʾites and Wāʿidites with regard to the position of a Muslim perpetrator of a grave sin. Cf. al-Masʿūdi, *Murūj al-Dhahab*, edited by Barbier de Meynard, Paris, 1861–77, Vol. VI, p. 22.

Besides the doctrines of *qadar* and *'adl*, they added many other important and subtle formulations to their creed. The prestige of the school was raised and it gained strength, so much so that it attracted the attention of the court. Yazīd ibn Walīd publicly supported Mu'tazilism and, during his reign, shortlived though it was, this group gained ascendancy over other schools of thought. After the fall of the Umayyad caliphate in 132/749, Mu'tazilism received quite hospitable treatment at the hands of the Abbasids. The second Abbasid Caliph Manṣūr and 'Amr ibn 'Ubayd were friends from early childhood and had been schoolfellows. Manṣūr appreciated the piety, devoutness and scholarship of 'Amr ibn 'Ubayd. Manṣūr even wrote an elegy on 'Amr's death, which is probably the only instance in Islamic history of a royal elegy composed on the death of a great scholar. During his reign Mu'tazilism was released from all barriers to its free development. Wāṣil ibn 'Aṭā' sent a number of missionaries to propagate the creed of Mu'tazilism in various parts of the country. 'Abdullah ibn Ḥārith was sent to Egypt, Ḥafṣ ibn Salīm to Khurasan, Ayyūb to Jazirah, Ḥasan ibn Zakwān to Kufa and 'Uthmān Tāwīl to Armenia. Mu'tazilism received a cordial welcome wherever it went.[2] Meanwhile, other important developments took place which gave Mu'tazilism supremacy and a significant position in the Islamic world. His empire well established and secure, Manṣūr now applied himself to the propagation of the arts and sciences. Whatever books on philosophy and science were available in Sanskrit, Persian, Syriac or Greek, he had them translated into Arabic. These translations, made under royal patronage, greatly encouraged the study of philosophy and science. The Jews, the Christians, the Parsees and others, gave particular attention to raising philosophical issues with regard to religious dogmas and even took the liberty of criticising Islam. Manṣūr was too tolerant and liberal to permit the suppression of these incursions on Islam with the sword. He allowed complete freedom of argument and discussion. Orthodox theologians and traditionists came forward to have intellectual bouts with non-Muslims; but the weapons of dogma were ineffective

[2] Cf. Shibli Nu'māni, *Maqālāt-i-Shibli*, Maṭba' Ma'ārif, Azamgarh, 1375/1955, Vol. V, p. 12.

in these contests, and they had to retreat honourably. At this critical juncture the Muʿtazilites came to the rescue of Islam. Fully equipped with the weapons of reason and dialectics, they smashed the arguments of non-Muslims and silenced them. This added to the prestige of the Muʿtazilites and some of the most distinguished scholars came to subscribe to their views.

Later, the Muʿtazilites received great honours at the court of al-Māmūn. The two great Muʿtazilites Abu al-Ḥudhayl Allāf and al-Naẓẓām were al-Māmūn's own teachers, and he held them in high esteeem. With regard to Abu al-Ḥudhayl, al-Māmūn used to say: 'He spreads over the art of dialectics as a cloud spreads over the people.'[3]

Al-Māmūn was very fond of listening to the debates between people belonging to different religions, and he used to allow them complete liberty of thought and speech. From all such debates and religious contests it was the Muʿtazilites who would come out victorious; they thus proved themselves to be the protectors of Islam.

The two Abbasids after al-Māmūn, namely al-Muʿtaṣim and al-Wāthiq, lent their wholehearted support to the Muʿtazilites. A great personality, Qāḍi Aḥmad ibn Dāwūd, who was an enthusiastic champion of the school of Muʿtazilism, was all in all in the courts of al-Muʿtaṣim and al-Wāthiq. Muʿtazilism held unprecedented sway under the patronage of this great man. The last name to be mentioned is that of al-Jubba'i, who presented an epilogue to this splendid drama of the movement of rationalism in medieval Islam.

Muʿtazilism was essentially a movement to interpret the dogmas of religion in terms of reason. The Muʿtazilites were mostly independent thinkers and had quite individualistic views with regard to various religious and philosophical problems. We shall consider here some of their fundamental doctrines, overlooking individual differences and minor details.

In the opinion of Abu al-Ḥusayn al-Khayyāṭ, a great Muʿtazilite authority, there are five fundamental principles of Muʿtazilism which one claiming to be a Muʿtazilite must subscribe to in their entirety. These five fundamental principles

[3] Cf. ibid., p. 13.

are:

(1) Divine unity (*al-tawḥīd*).
(2) Divine justice (*al-'adl*).
(3) The promise of reward and the threat of punishment (*al-wa'd wa'l-wa'īd*).
(4) The state between states of belief and unbelief (*al-manzilah bayn al-manzilatayn*).
(5) To order the doing of right and to prohibit the doing of wrong (*amr bi'l-m'rūf wa'l naḥy 'an al-munkar*).

The first two doctrines may be said to be more central than the rest of them for the Mu'tazilites called themselves 'the people of unity and justice'.

(1) *Divine Unity*. Although the Muslims are distinguished for their strict belief in the unity of God, the Mu'tazilites were called unitarians *par excellence* in so far as they idealised the conception of divine unity almost to a philosophical abstraction.

The Mu'tazilites raised specifically the following four issues, each of which has an important bearing on the problem of divine unity:

(*a*) the relation of the attributes of God with His essence.
(*b*) the createdness or uncreatedness of the holy Qur'ān.
(*c*) the possibility of the beatific vision of God.
(*d*) the interpretation of the anthropomorphic verses of the Qur'ān.

(*a*) *Relation of the Attributes of God with His Essence*. The Qur'ān has described God as the Knower (*'Alīm*), the Powerful (*Qādir*), the Living (*Ḥayy*). The orthodox (*Ṣifātiyah*, in particular) hold that such expressions obviously mean that God possesses the qualities of knowledge, power, life, etc. To this the Mu'tazilites objected: God is one, and describing His qualities in this way ascribes plurality to Him. The lurking fear with them was that these qualities might even come to be hypostatised; should the qualities be considered as entities apart from the Divine Being, that certainly would amount to polytheism. The Mu'tazilites explained divine attributes such as the knowing, the powerful, the living, etc., by saying that God knows, is powerful, is living, and so on and so forth, as to His being and not that He possesses the qualities of knowledge, power, life, etc., apart from His essence.

Al-Naẓẓām, the teacher of al-Māmūn, emphasised that qualities are not *in* the essence of God but *are* His essence. Thus God is omnipotent by His omnipotence, and it is His essence and not in His essence. He is omniscient by His omniscience and it is His essence and not in His essence. This appears to be mainly a distinction in the mode of expression.

Some of the Muʿtazilites maintained that these qualities must be considered in a negative way; nothing positive could be asserted of God for that would jeopardise His absolute unity. This would mean that there is in God the complexity of subject and predicate, whereas God is a unity in the purest and most absolute sense. Like the Hegelians, the Muʿtazilites reduced God finally to an absolute unity shorn of all qualities. This cold and bleak concept of unity could not satisfy the orthodox, who look for nothing less than a personal God.

The whole problem of the relation of God's attributes with His essence is a self-created difficulty of the Muʿtazilites. By its very nature it is an impossible problem, entirely above the comprehension of human reason: revelation alone has the claim to guide us here.

(*b*) *Createdness and Uncreatedness of the Qur'ān.* The Muslims feel an unbounded reverence and awe in regard to the holy Qur'ān. In it God speaks to the holy Prophet; the words are verily the words of God. That is why the Qur'ān is also called the divine speech or the speech of God (i.e., *Kalām Allah*), but Muslim piety goes further and holds that the Qur'ān is uncreated and has existed from all eternity with God; its revelation to the Prophet, of course, is an event of time. The orthodox bring their evidence, indeed, from the holy Qur'ān itself, to support this thesis. God created everything through the word *kun*, i.e., 'Be,' but this word itself could not have been created, otherwise a created word would be a creator. Therefore, God's word or God's speech, i.e., *Kalām Allah* or the Qur'an, is uncreated. Again, it is pointed out that the Qur'ān, in one of its verses, says: 'Are not the creation and the command His?' (vii. 54). The command here is evidently different from the creation; i.e., it is uncreated. But God's command surely is in His word. Hence God's word, i.e., the Qur'ān, is uncreated. But the Muʿtazilites very strongly denied the eternity of the Qur'ān on the plea that God alone is eternal. According to them, those who believe in the uncreatedness of the Qur'ān and make it co-eternal with God take to themselves two gods and hence are polytheists.

(*c*) *Possibility of the Beatific Vision of God.* All the Muslim scholastic philosophers, Muʿtazilites and orthodox alike, have maintained that the beatific vision is the *summum bonum* of human life. They differ, however, with regard to the nature of that vision. The Muʿtazilites are unanimous in holding that God cannot be seen with physical eyes either in this world or in the next as, in their opinion, He is above space and time. Abu al-Ḥudhayl and the majority of other Muʿtazilites maintained: 'We would see God only with our mind's eye; i.e., we would know Him only through the heart.' The proofs that they adduced in support of their view may be summed up under the following heads:

(*A*) *Proof from the Qur'ān*

(*i*) Vision comprehendeth Him not but He comprehendeth all vision (vi. 103).

This verse, according to them, is of general application and means that the physical eye sees God neither in this world nor in the next.

(*ii*) 'Thou wilt not see Me,' said God with an emphatic negation in reply to Moses' supplication: 'My Lord, show me Thyself so that I may gaze upon Thee' (vii. 143).

(*iii*) They asked a greater thing of Moses than that; for they said: 'Show us Allah manifestly'; a storm of lightning seized them for their wrongdoing (iv. 153).

Had the people of Moses asked for a possible thing from God, they would not have been called wrongdoers and would not have been consequently overtaken by the storm of lightning.

(B) Proof from the Optical Sciences

The Mu'tazilites maintained that the following conditions were necessary in order to see a thing:
(*i*) One must possess sound sight.
(*ii*) The object of vision must be in front of or opposite to the eye just as a thing to be reflected in a mirror must needs be opposite to it.
(*iii*) It must not be too distant from the eye.
(*iv*) It must not be too near the eye.
(*v*) It must not be too fine to be looked at; i.e., it must be a coloured object or one sufficiently coarse.
In the opinion of the Mu'tazilites, since God as an object of vision does not satisfy the relevant conditions mentioned above, He cannot be seen with bodily eyes.

(C) Proof from the Ḥadīth

As for the saying ascribed to the holy Prophet: 'You will see your Lord as you see the full moon while you will not disagree amongst yourselves in regard to His vision' (Tirmidhi), the Mu'tazilites hold that the tradition in question is of the category of *aḥad* and not that of *mutawātir*, that is, it comes only through a single channel of transmitters and as such is not acceptable when in conflict with an explicit verse of the Qur'ān such as: 'Vision comprehendeth Him not but He comprehendeth all vision' (vi. 103). They, on the other hand, alluded to a saying of The Lady 'Ā'ishah according to which she questioned even the Prophet's having seen God here in this world: 'He who says that the Prophet saw God in person tells a lie' (Bukhāri).

(*d*) *Interpretation of the Anthropomorphic Verses of the Qur'ān.* In the holy Qur'ān we find many anthropomorphic expressions about God such as the following:

(*i*) So glory be to Him in Whose hand is the kingdom of all things (xxxvi. 83).
(*ii*) That which I have created with My hands (xxxviii. 75).
(*iii*) Which swims forth under Our eye (liv. 14).
(*iv*) And the countenance of thy Lord would abide full of

majesty and glory (lv. 27).

(*v*) The Merciful (God) has seated Himself on His throne (xx. 5).

(*vi*) Thou shalt see the angels circling the throne uttering the praises of their Lord (xxxix. 75).

As may be gathered easily from their view of the beatific vision, the Mu'tazilites naturally interpreted all the anthropomorphic statements in the Qur'ān such as the face, the hands, and the eyes of God or His sitting upon the throne as merely *metaphorical expressions*. They repudiated literalism of all types in order to maintain the pure unity of God. The Mu'tazilites perforce made an allowance for the principle of interpretation (*tāwīl*) of the verses of the holy Qur'ān. The Mu'tazilites also denied the Prophet's ascension to the heavens in the physical sense. They denied physical punishment in the grave, and so also 'the Balance,' 'the Bridge' and other eschatological representations. They recognized, however, the possibility of the resurrection of the body, as well as paradise and its sensuous pleasures, and hell and its bodily torments.

(2) *Divine Justice*. The orthodox maintain that there can be no necessity for God even to do justice. He is absolutely free in what He does. Good and evil have their nature by God's will and man can know them only through God's injunctions and commands. Thus, except through revelation, there can neither be theology nor ethics. The Mu'tazilites vehemently opposed this view by holding that good and evil can be apprehended by, and distinguished through, the activity of reasoning. Like the Kantians, they made morality independent of theology and emphasised the objective validity of good and evil.

Al-Naẓẓām, in particular, taught in an absolute way that God can do nothing to a creature either in this world or in the next that would not be for the creature's own good and in accordance with strict justice. It is not that God would not do this but that He does not have the power to do this. It seems as if the personality of God, in the Mu'tazilites' view, was steadily vanishing behind the absolute law of righteousness.

Anyhow, it would be wrong to allege, as MacDonald does, that the Mu'tazilites were so much overawed by the Greek conception of law or fixed principles subsisting in the universe, that with them this conception superseded Muḥammad's conception of God as an Absolute Will, as the Sovereign Power over all.[4] It is important to observe that, according to the holy Qur'ān, God is essentially just and righteous. The Muʿtazilites based their doctrine of divine justice not on borrowings from Greek thought but on the teachings of the holy Qur'ān. Attention may be called to such verses of the Qur'ān as the following:

(*i*) God is not unjust to His servants (xii. 10; xl. 31).
(*ii*) Lo, Allah wrongeth not mankind in aught (x. 44).
(*iii*) God truly will not wrong anybody the weight of an atom and if there be any need He will repay it (xxi. 47).

The Muʿtazilites deemed some degree of human freedom a necessary postulate to vouchsafe man's moral responsibility and God's justice. They further maintained that God does not burden human beings with tasks beyond their power. The holy Qur'ān says: 'God does not impose (any task) on the soul but to the extent of its capacity' (ii. 286). This reminds one of Kant's dictum: 'I can; therefore I ought.'

Since they were followers of the Qadarites, the Muʿtazilites were strong upholders of the freedom of man. Man's freedom and God's justice must both go together. Man should be considered responsible for his actions, otherwise God would not be justified in punishing the sinners in life after death.

Some of Muʿtazilites argued that infants in no case would be condemned to the punishments of hell because, having never exercised free will, no responsibility devolves upon them.

(3) *The Promise of Reward and the Threat of Punishment.* This doctrine is intimately related to that of divine justice. Since God is just, He should punish the sinners and reward the virtuous in the life after death. Has not God Himself given the promise of reward and the threat of punishment in the holy Qur'ān?

(*i*) Allah has promised to the believers, men and women,

[4] Cf. D.B. MacDonald, *Development of Muslim Theology, Jurisprudence and Constitutional Theory*, London, 1903, pp. 144, 145.

Gardens (ix. 72).

(*ii*) And lo, the wicked verily will be in hell (lxxxii. 14).

(*iii*) Whosoever doth good an atom's weight will see it and whosoever doth evil an atom's weight will see it (xcix. 7–8).

The Muʿtazilites maintain that it is *obligatory on God to reward the virtuous and punish the wicked* and that He cannot do otherwise. Contrary to this, the orthodox and particularly the Ashʿarites believe that *reward and punishment are entirely God's gifts*. He can reward whom He wills and punish whom He wills. It is certain, however, that He will favour the righteous and punish the wicked as He has promised to do so; but no consideration can bind His discretion and compel Him to do this or that. To impose compulsion on Him is to reduce Him to a dependent being or even to a machine which must move and act without any choice of its own. What would be the difference between God if He is compelled to reward the virtuous and punish the wicked, and a magistrate or a judge whose decisions are guided by a penal code?

On the other hand, according to the Muʿtazilites, the Qur'ānic promise of reward and threats of punishment cannot go unfulfilled, otherwise God's truthfulness becomes doubtful. God never changes His words and so it is given in the holy Qur'ān: "There is no changing in the words of Allah" (x. 64).

The orthodox agree with the Muʿtazilites that the virtuous will go to paradise and the wicked to hell. But, according to the Muʿtazilites, the conclusion is necessary and irresistible. According to the orthodox, it is only contingent and probable. God is absolutely free to do what He wills. The orthodox insists that, should He so will, the virtuous might go to hell or, at least, the wicked to paradise. According to the Muʿtazilites, God's freedom would in that case be reduced to mere capriciousness and His justice would lose all meaning and significance. The Muʿtazilites, like the Kantians, put morality before theology, whereas the orthodox put theology before morality.

(4) *The State between the States of Belief and Unbelief.* This doctrine, whose acceptance gave the very name to the Muʿtazilites, was more political than theological in nature. The Muʿtazilites submitted that as soon as a man commits a mortal

sin he neither remains a believer nor becomes an unbeliever, but occupies a middle position. Should he die without repentance, he would be condemned to hell-fire, with the only difference that the punishment inflicted upon him would be less severe than that inflicted on an unbeliever. They based this doctrine also on the authority of the Qur'ān and the Ḥadīth. 'Is he who is a believer like unto him who is an evil-doer? They are not alike" (xxxii. 18). Again, the holy Prophet is reported to have said: "He who is not secure against a mortal sin has no faith, nor is he an unbeliever."

(5) *To Order the Doing of Right and Forbid the Doing of Wrong*. This doctrine belongs to the practical theology of the Muʿtazilites. The orthodox also admit the need to urge people to do good and check them from doing wrong. But the Muʿtazilites considered this incumbent upon every Muslim: a *farḍ-al-ʿayn,* i.e., the duty of perfect obligation. According to the orthodox, on the other hand, it is only a *farḍ al-kifāyah*, i.e., it would suffice if someone carried out this injunction on behalf of the group.

Because of this doctrine the Muʿtazilites deemed it necessary to spread their creed not only by word of mouth but also—though this was quite contrary to the spirit of Islam—by force of State authority. Under the glorious patronage of al-Māmūn, this doctrine of the Muʿtazilites led to the institution of inquisition or *miḥnah* against all those who did not subscribe to their religious views, particularly that of the createdness of the Qur'ān.

Al-Māmūn issued a letter of authority to all the Qādis (judges) of the State to test the beliefs of officials with regard to the createdness of the Qur'ān. The Caliph commanded that the penalty of death should be inflicted upon those who even refused to take the test. This naturally led to very strong feelings against Muʿtazilism and was consequntly one of the reasons for its downfall.

Chapter Two

ASHʿARISM

Ashʿarism is a protest against the religious rationalism of the Muʿtazilites who held that the mysteries of the universe and profundities of religious dogmas could be expressed and met in terms of human reason. It is a reaction from the impossible task of building a system of purely rationalistic theology in reliance upon the word of God (Qur'ān), the tradition (*Ḥadīth*) and the usage (*Sunnah*) of the holy Prophet and the pattern of the early community (*salaf*).

Its beginnings are shrouded in obscurity. At first, it was only a gradual and scarcely conscious shifting of attitude, and people did not recognize its existence. Afterwards, when they looked back upon it, the tendency of the human mind to ascribe broad movements to single men asserted itself and the whole was attributed to Abu al-Ḥasan ʿAli ibn Ismāʿil al-Ashʿarī (d. *c.* 330/945). It is true that with him the change suddenly leaped into self-consciousness, but it had already been long in progress.[1] As a matter of fact, many schools of theology, similar to that of al-Ashʿarī's, arose simultaneously in different countries, e.g., the Zāhirites' school in Spain, al-Ṭaḥāwī's school in Egypt, and Māturīdī's school in Samarqand.

Al-Ashʿarī's school superseded them all and flourished because it had amongst its adherents and exponents such able thinkers as Bāqilānī, Imām al-Haramayn, al-Ghazāli, and Fakhr al-Dīn Rāzi.

The main doctrines of Ashʿarism which were bitterly controverted by the Muʿtazilites may be summed up as follows:

(1) Attributes of God and their relation with His essence.

[1] Cf. D.B. MacDonald, *Development of Muslim Theology, Jurisprudence and Constitutional Theory*, London, 1903, pp. 186, 187; cf. also his article, 'An Outline of the History of Scholastic Theology in Islam,' in *The Moslem World*, Vol. XV, 1925, pp. 140–8.

(2) Createdness or uncreatedness of the holy Qur'ān.
(3) Possibility of beatific vision.
(4) God's seating Himself on the throne.
(5) Freedom of will.

(1) *Attributes of God and Their Relation with His Essence.* (*i*) The Ash'arites admitted that God has qualities but with the qualifications of *mukhālafah lilḥawādith* and *bila kayfa wala tashbihah;* i.e., the qualities and the attributes ascribed to God must be understood to be inapplicable to human beings and so we should not 'ask *how* and draw comparisons'. Terms used for human beings must have quite different meanings when applied to God. God's attributes do not differ from those of mankind in degree only, as He is wiser and more powerful than human beings; they differ in their whole nature. Expressions or ideas regarding God should be divested of all human element, according to the Ash'arite principle of *tanzīh.*

(*ii*) Al-Ash'ari is reported to have rebutted Abu al-Hudhayl Allāf's identification of God's attributes with His essence in the following manner: 'Abu al-Hudhayl Allāf says that God's knowledge is God, and so he makes God knowledge. He must be asked to invoke knowledge instead of God, both being identical, and say in his prayers: "O knowledge, forgive me."' This was not merely a witticism on the part of al-Ash'ari; he probably made these remarks in all seriousness. With Abu al-Hudhayl and others the concept of God's unity which emphasized the complete coalescence of divine attributes and essence had developed into deism and even into stark scepticism. With Abu Hāshim, for instance, the conception of God's unity became merely an abstract possibility about which nothing could be predicated positively. With Ibn Ashras and al-Jāḥiẓ (the goggle-eyed) this conception developed into deistic naturalism. Al-Jāḥiẓ, in fact, began to favour a thoroughgoing scepticism.

But, on the other hand, though al-Ash'arī's formulas of *bila kayfa* and *mukhalafah,* may satisfy an orthodox believer, they do not bring any comfort to a philosophic mind or to the inquiring spirit who would refuse to succumb to the childlike helplessness of religious *naiveté.*

(2) *Createdness or Uncreatedness of the Holy Qur'ān.* (*i*) The Ash'arites very strongly upheld the eternity and the uncreated-

ness of the Qur'ān. They based their view, not as some of the Orientalists and even the Mu'tazilites have alleged, on the Jewish or Christian concept of the Logos, but on verses of the holy Qur'ān such as: (*b*) 'The command is God's first and last' (xxx. 4), that is, the command which indeed is through God's word (*Kalām Allah*) is eternal and uncreated. (*b*) 'Are not the creation and the command His?' (vii. 54). Here God speaks of the command as something other than the act of creation which, according to the Ash'arites, implies that God's command does not belong to the category of created things. Further, God's command, by its very nature, is through His word or His speech; hence *Kalām Allah* (the Qur'ān) is uncreated. (*c*) God says: 'Our word to a thing when We intend it is only that We say to it, "Be," and it is (*kun fa yakūn*)' (ii. 117). Al-Ash'arī argued, if the Qur'ān were supposed to be 'created,' the word 'Be' must have been uttered to it before it could have come into existence. If God should say 'Be' to the Qur'ān which is itself the 'word of God,' a word would be said to another word. From the very logic of this position it would become necessary that a word should be uttered to another word for the latter to come into being. Thus one word would depend upon another and the other upon the next and so on and so forth to an infinite regression which, according to the Ash'arites, is unthinkable and impossible. Thus, by reducing a supposition to an absurdity, they claimed to have proved that the Qur'ān is uncreated.

(*ii*) The Mu'tazilites made the allegation that the Ash'arites, by preaching the doctrine of the uncreatedness of the Qur'ān, were advocating the Christian idea of the Logos and tripping into *shirk,* i.e., polytheism. They argued that, should the Ash'arites insist upon the uncreatedness of the Qur'ān, they would make it co-eternal with God and thus teach that God had His partner co-existent with Him from eternity. Interestingly enough, the Ash'arites made a similar charge against the Mu'tazilites and called them polytheists of the first order. They argued that whosoever insists on the createdness of the Qur'ān comes very close to favouring the view of the infidels that the Qur'ān was a product of the Prophet's own mind. The Ash'arites alluded to a verse of the holy Qur'ān in which God has spoken of the polytheists' belief about the Qur'ān that 'it is merely the word of a mortal' (lxxiv. 25).

(3) *Possibility of Beatific Vision.* The Ash'arites advanced the following proofs in support of their view about the possibility of beatific vision even in the physical sense:

(*A*) *Proof from the Qur'ān.* Reference was made to the following verses of the Qur'ān in support of their position:

(*i*) That day will the faces be resplendent, looking towards their Lord (lxxv. 22, 23).

The possibility of beatific vision is clearly indicated herein, according to the Ash'arites, as a gift which would be granted by God to the people of paradise on the Day of Resurrection.

(*ii*) He (Moses) said: My Lord, show me Thyself so that I may gaze upon Thee (vii. 143).

Al-Ash'ari contended that had the vision of God been impossible of realization, Moses would not have asked for it. Moses was an apostle of God and thus free from sin or gross error. How could he ask for an absurd and impossible thing?

(*B*) *Proof from the Hadīth* (Tradition of the Prophet). The Ash'arites called the attention of the Mu'tazilites to the following saying of the holy Prophet in which, in reply to a question about the possibility of seeing God on the Day of Resurrection, he is reported to have said: 'You will see your Lord as you see the full moon while you will not disagree amongst yourselves.'

(*C*) *Proof from Logic.* The so-called logical arguments in favour of beatific vision are listed below; they are representative of the peculiar dialectics of the Ash'arites:

(*i*) God can show us everything that exists.
He exists.
Therefore He can show Himself to us.

(*ii*) He who sees things sees himself.
God sees things.
Therefore God sees Himself.
He who sees himself can make himself seen.
God sees Himself.
Therefore He can make Himself seen.

(*iii*) The highest good is realizable in the highest world.
The beatific vision is the highest good.
Therefore beatific vision is realizable in the highest world.

Al-Ashʿarī alleged that those who denied the beatific vision of God reduced God to a mere philosophic abstraction and even to a nonentity.

(4) *God's Seating Himself upon the Throne.* From the following verses of the Qur'ān it was quite clear to the Ashʿarites that God is seated on His throne high up in the heavens:

(*i*) The Merciful is seated on the throne (xx. 4).
(*ii*) The good word riseth up to Him (xxxv. 11).
(*iii*) God took him (Jesus) up to Himself (iv. 156).
(*iv*) Hereafter shall they come up to Him (xcii. 4).
(*v*) What! Are you sure that He who is in the heaven will not cleave the earth beneath you? (lxvii. 16).
(*vi*) And thou shalt see the angels circling around the throne, uttering the praises of their Lord (xxxix. 74–75).

These verses of the Qur'ān were further corroborated by a tradition of the Prophet in which he is reported to have said that God descends every night to the lower heavens and asks: 'Is there anyone who is to make a request? I am here to grant it to him. Is there anyone who asks for forgiveness? I am here to forgive him.' This goes on until dawn.

In addition to the above evidence from the Qur'ān and the Ḥadīth for God's seating Himself upon the throne, al-Ashʿari advanced the following arguments typical of his dialectical temperament: If God is at all places as the Muʿtazilites have maintained, this would compel one to admit that God is under the depths and created things are below Him. If this is true, He must be under that above which He is and above that under which He is. Since this is a complete absurdity, one cannot say that God is at all places.

Al-Ashʿari attacked the Muʿtazilites and others who made use of allegorical interpretations and asserted that God is at all places, by saying that if this interpretation were true then it might be logically concluded that God is also in the womb of

Mary, in the latrines and in the waste.

(5) *Freedom of Will.* Al-Ash'arī's exposition with regard to the problem of free will has been very well presented by MacDonald in his book *Development of Muslim Theology.*[2] According to MacDonald, the old orthodox position was absolutely fatalistic; the Mu'tazilites, following the principle of divine justice, made out a case for man's free will. Al-Ash'arī struck a middle path. 'Man cannot create a thing; God is the only creator; nor does man's power produce any effect on his actions at all. God creates in His creature power (*qudrah*) and choice (*ikhtiyār*). Then He creates in him his actions corresponding to the power and choice thus created.' According to al-Ash'arī, though the action of the creature is created by God, both as to its initiative and as to its production, yet it is acquired by the creature. Acquisition (*kasb*)[3] corresponds to the creature's power and choice previously created in him; he is only the locus (*maḥall*) or subject of his action. In this way al-Ash'arī is supposed to have accounted for free will and made man responsible for his actions. For example, he says, a man writes with a pen on a piece of paper. God creates in his mind the will to write and at the same time He grants him the power to write, thus bringing about the apparent motion of the hand and the pen and the appearance of the words on the paper. It becomes doubtful whether the theory of acquisition is any better than the mere cloaking of pure determinism. Neverthe-

[2] Cf. pp. 191, 192; also Majid Fakhry, 'Some Paradoxical Implications of the Mutazilite View of Free-will,' *The Muslim World,* Vol. XLIII, 1953, pp. 95–109.

[3] Cf. al-Ash'arī's *Maqālāt al-Islamiyyen,* edited by H. Ritter, Istanbul, 1929, p. 542, and also *al-Ībānah 'an Usūl al-Diyānah,* English translation by Walter C. Klein, New Haven, 1940, pp. 103 ff. Al-Ash'ari uses two terms for his doctrine of acquisition: *kasb* and *iktisāb,* both of which occur in a verse of the Qur'ān: 'Allah does not impose on a soul responsibility beyond its capacity. It has that which it has acquired (*mā kasabat*) and it owes what it has acquired (*mak-tasabat*)', (ii. 286). The commentators have sometimes made a distinction between the two terms by saying that while *kasb* refers to good actions both for one's own self and for others, *iktisāb* refers to bad actions and to actions which pertain to one's own self only. For a further discussion of al-Ash'arī's doctrine of aquisition, cf. Hammouda Ghoraba, 'Al-Ashari's Theory of Acquisition (*al-Kasb*)', *Islamic Quarterly,* Vol. II, 1955, pp. 3–8 and also M. Badruddin Alavi, 'Fatalism, Free-will and Acquisition as Held by Muslim Sects,' *Islamic Culture,* Vol. XXVIII, 1954, pp. 319–29.

less, it has been claimed that al-Ash'arī, with regard to this new-fangled theory of man's freedom, came very close to propounding Leibnitz's doctrine of pre-established harmony; MacDonald, for one, ranks al-Ash'arī, in this respect, as an original thinker of a very high order. The whole theory of acquisition, as fathered upon al-Ash'arī, amounts to saying that the significance of man's freedom lies in his consciousness of freedom in himself. Man gives assent to the works which are accomplished in him by God and claims these as his own.[4]

[4] It is important to note that W. Montgomery Watt has cast serious doubt on al-Ash'arī's being the father of the doctrine of acquisition. The real originator of the doctrine according to him was either Imām Abu Hanīfah or some one of his immediate followers. Cf. his 'The Origin of the Islamic Doctrine of Acquisition,' *The Journal of the Royal Asiatic Society,* 1943, pp. 234–47, and also *Free Will and Predestination in Early Īslam,* Luzac & Co., London, 1948, p. 168. Cf. also A.J. Wensinck, *The Muslim Creed,* Cambridge, 1932, p. 93.

Chapter Three

HISTORICAL ORIGIN AND SOURCES OF SUFISM

Von Kremer and Dozy trace Sufism from Indian Vedantism; Merx and Nicholson ascribe it to Neoplatonism and Christianity; Browne regards it as an Aryan reaction against an unemotional Semitic religion.[1]

All these theories are based on a very superficial view of historical causation. As historical causation deals with highly complex phenomena, its validity remains extremely doubtful. It will be readily admitted that historical causation can never be the same as physical causation, mainly because of the freedom or creativeness of the human ego as one of the forces working in the historical process. Tracing the chain of historical causes presupposes a very deep insight into the working of many cultural forces. Even then, this insight may not attain that degree of certainty that can be attained in the study of sciences such as physics or chemistry.

Sweeping generalisations of the Orientalists such as those recorded above, even when partially true, ignore the principle that, in order to establish an historical connection between two historical phenomena, A and B, it is not enough to bring out their similarities to each other without showing at the same time:

(1) that the actual relation of A to B is such as renders the assumed connection possible;

(2) that the possible hypothesis is very well borne out by all the

[1] Cf. Shaikh Muhammad Iqbal, *The Development of Metaphysics in Persia*, Luzac & Co., London, 1908, p. 97. The chapter on Sufism in this work is one of the most valuable contributions on the subject; the first section: 'The Origin and Quranic Justification of Sufism' is the principal source of the ideas presented below though we are also greatly indebted to R.A. Nicholson's 'Introduction' to his *Mystics of Islam*, London, 1914, and his article, 'A Historical Enquiry concerning the Origin and Development of Sufism . . .' in *The Journal of the Royal Asiatic Society*, 1906, pp. 303–48.

relevant historically ascertained facts; and

(3) that the possibility of A and B both being the effects of a common cause has been fully analysed and eliminated.

It should be borne in mind that in historical determinism cause is not ascertained merely by its temporal priority to effect. The fundamental fact cannot be ignored that the human mind, acting on its own initiative, can gradually evolve out of itself truths which have been anticipated by others ages ago.[2]

Further, in tracing the origin of Sufism and, for that matter, of any idea in the history of Muslim philosophy, the cultural principle is not to be overlooked that no idea can seize a people's mind unless in some sense it is that people's own.[3] The cultural ideas can never be injected into the minds of others, merely from without; they have always to grow from within. External influences might at best wake them up from their unconscious slumber.

While considering the historical evolution of ideas or cultural phenomena, it is necessary to keep in mind that their value or significance is not to be determined by their origins. This is necessary to avoid the fallacy of historicism, also called the genetic fallacy. It is interesting to note that the Orientalists are more liable to trip over this fallacy than the Muslim scholars.

We shall now consider the various theories regarding the origin of Sufism in the light of these general observations.

(1) *Christianity*. It is not easy to deny the influence of Christianity on Islamic mysticism. We may, following Von Kremer, point to the Christian influence even on the pre-Islamic culture and thought. Christian monasticism was familiar to the Arabs in the country fringing the Syrian desert and in the desert of Sinai. Of this we have evidence in the pre-Islamic poetry. For example, Imrā' al-Qays, in one of his poems, refers to a Christian monastery in the desert as follows:

Friend, see the lightning, it flashed and is gone, like the flashing of two hands on a crowned pillar;

Did its blaze flash forth? Or was it the lamp of a monk who poured oil on the twisted wick?

[2] Iqbal, op. cit., pp. 97–8.

[3] Ibid.

(*a*) The woollen dress in fashion among the early Sūfīs, from which, according to one interpretation, the very name *ṣūfī* has been derived, was surely of Christian origin. The early Muslim ascetics who clothed themselves in wool probably borrowed this practice from Christian monks. Farqad Sabakhi (168/784) who used to dress in woollen garb was reproached by Himād ibn Salm thus: 'Put off this emblem of Christianity'.

(*b*) In some of the older Ṣūfi *Tadhkirahs* (Collections of Biographies) the Christian monk or anchorite often appears in the role of a teacher giving instruction and advice to the wandering Muslim saints. Many Gospel-texts and apocryphal sayings of Jesus Christ are also cited in the biographies of great Ṣūfīs.

(*c*) Vows of silence and the practice of *dhikr* or litanies were also introduced into Sufism from Christian quarters. The ascetic and quietistic tendencies in the early Muslim Ṣūfīs were to some extent derived from the Christian temperament of thought. The doctrine of divine love which emerged in the early stages of Sufism undoubtedly was reinforced by the Christian influence.

(*d*) The doctrine of *tawakkul*, (complete trust in God) amounting to self-abnegation and an attitude of resignation in the practical affairs of life, can also be traced back to the dissemination of Christian ideas.

It was but natural that the early Muslim ascetics and Ṣūfīs should have been highly susceptible to Christian influence because they considered Christianity the sister religion of Islam. The holy Prophet himself made it clear that he had not brought a new revelation to mankind but one which was in continuation of the revelations received by Jesus, Moses, and other prophets.[4] It was principally the actual life of Christian hermits rather than their religious ideas or ideals that mostly fasci-

[4] The Qur'ān says: 'Naught is said unto thee (Muhammad) save what was said unto the messengers before thee...' (xli. 43). Yet after speaking of the Gospel (v. 44–47), it also says: 'And We have revealed to thee the Book with truth, verifying that which is before it of the book and a guardian over it' (v. 48). Thus the Qur'ān, though in continuity with the previous revelations, is the judge and guardian over them all. For the relation between Sufism and Christianity, cf. D.B. MacDonald, 'The Unity of the Mystical Experience in Islam and

nated the minds of early Muslim saints. All along they had a keen realisation that the complete unworldliness of the Christian monks, though extremely fascinating in itself, was quite contrary to the spirit of Islam and the practice of the holy Prophet.

(2) *Neoplatonism.* Oriental Christian mysticism had long ago accepted the ideas, and even adopted the language, of the Neoplatonists. Thus Christianity, already saturated in Neoplatonism, brought a large share of its mystical moods and ideas to Islamic mysticism. The doctrine of emanation and the language of illumination, ecstasy and gnosis came to flourish with the Ṣūfīs much in the same way as Muslim philosophy came under the grip of Neoplatonism. There is no gainsaying the fact that the Arabs obtained their first knowledge of Aristotle through his Neoplatonic commentators. The system with which Arab philosophers became imbued was that of Porphyry and Plotinus. The most eagerly read 'Theology' of Aristotle, the Arabic version of which appeared in the ninth century of the Christian era, was really a paraphrase of the last three books of *The Enneads* by Plotinus.

There is no doubt that Plotinus (205–70 A.D.) and Porphyry (232–304 A.D.) were well known to Muslim thinkers. Plotinus is explicitly mentioned by name in the remarkable encyclopedic work, *al-Fihrist*, by Nadīm (385/995). Shahrastāni (469–548/1076–1153), while referring to Plotinus a number of times in his book *Kitāb al-Milal wa'l-Niḥal*, however, calls him Shaykh Yūnāni—the Greek teacher. Porphyry was much better known to the Muslims. Seven or eight of his writings are listed in *al-Fihrist*.

Although the connection between Neoplatonism and Sufism is plain, there are yet certain unanswered questions:

(*i*) What elements of their philosophy did the Neoplatonists originally borrow from the East and especially from Persia which country Plotinus had visited expressly to study the system of philosophy taught there? We cannot exclude the possibility that the main doctrines of Neoplatonic philosophy might have been derived from the Persian system of thought.

Christianity,' *The Moslem World*, Vol. XXV, 1935, pp. 325–35, and also J.W. Sweetman. 'Sufism and Christian Teaching,' ibid., pp. 156–60.

(*ii*) It is true that a group of seven Neoplatonist philosophers, who were driven from their homeland by the intolerance of Justinian, took refuge in Persia at the court of Nūshīrwān in 532 A.D. But how far was it possible for this small group of Neoplatonist refugees to found, during their short stay, a school of Neoplatonism in Persia, or to propagate their ideas in that country?

Here we see that, instead of A being the cause of B, there is a possibility of B being the cause of A. Anyhow, it requires further research to establish this possible reversal of the relation between A and B.

(3) *Buddhism.* Before the Muslim conquest of India in the eleventh century A.D. the teachings of Buddha exerted considerable influence in Eastern Persia and Transoxania. We hear of Buddhist monasteries flourishing in Balkh, the metropolis of ancient Bactria, a city famous for the number of Ṣūfīs who hailed from there. Goldziher has called attention to the significant fact 'that the Ṣūfi ascetic Ibrāhīm bin Adham appears in Muslim legends as a prince of Balkh who abandoned his throne and became a wandering dervish'. He considers this to be the story of Buddha all over again. Nicholson is of opinion that the Ṣūfīs learned the use of rosaries and the practice of holding the breath from Buddhist monks.[5] Further, the doctrine of *fanā'* which is said to be a form of *nirvāna* and the system of stations (*maqāmāt*) on the mystic path (*ṭarīqah*) also are supposed to be Buddhistic in origin. Sufism, so far as it involves an ethical self-culture, ascetic discipline and mental abstraction, might be said to have something in common with Buddhism. But the features which the two systems have in common cannot cover the fundamental differences between them. The Buddhist moralises himself; the Ṣūfi becomes moral only through knowing and loving God. Further, it would be wrong to identify *fanā'* with *nirvāna*; both terms imply the passing away of individuality, but while *nirvāna* is purely negative, *fanā'* is to be accompanied by *baqā'*, i.e., 'everlasting life with God'. As a matter of fact, the principles of *fanā'* and *baqā'*, i.e., self-negation and self-affirmation, might work as

[5] Cf. his article 'Sufism' in *Encyclopaedia Britannica*, 14th edition, and also *Mystics of Islam*, London, 1914, p. 17.

two aspects of the same experience in the sufistic communion with Divine Reality.[6] Maybe much is attributed to Buddhism which in reality is Vedantic or even Indian in origin, rather than specifically Buddhistic, e.g., this very theory of *fanā'* as mentioned above.

No real influence can be shown to have been exerted over the Muslim countries by Indian religions before the Muslims began to take an active interest in the language and the culture of the Indians. Al-Bīrūni is reported to have been the first to study the Sanskrit language, and the geography, history, literature and thought of the Indians; but that was long after the development of the Ṣūfi system had completed itself. So far as the common Muslim was concerned, he would rather despise a Hindu idolater than accept his ideas. Hindu and Buddhistic mysticism involves the ideas of incarnation, transmigration of the soul, etc. Such ideas were entirely foreign to Islam.[7]

(4) *The Aryan Reaction Theory*. This theory regards Sufism as essentially a Persian product. 'But how would one explain that some of the most notable and most influential mystics such as Muḥyi al-Dīn ibn al-'Arabi and Ibn al-Farīd were men of Arabic speech in whose veins there was not a drop of Persian blood?' The whole theory is based upon a doubtful ethnological hypothesis.

The external influences, by and large, could at best evoke certain appropriate tendencies already inherent in Islam. Even if Islam had been miraculously shut off from contact with foreign religions and philosophies, some form of mysticism would perforce have arisen within it, for the seeds were already there.[8] Instead of searching in vain for a single cause, we should

[6] Cf. Mir Valiuddin, 'The Conception of Fana (Passing away) in Islamic Mysticism,' *Proceedings of the Indian Philosophical Congress*, 19th Session, 1944, pp. 149–52.

[7] One cannot, however, ignore the more widespread and penetrating influence of Sufism on Indian religious and philosophical thought. Cf. M.M. Sharif, *Muslim Thought: Its Origin and Achievements*, Sh. Muhammad Ashraf, Lahore, 1951, pp. 85–7; Tara Chand, *Influence of Islam on Indian Culture*; Emanul Haq, 'The Sufi Movement in India,' *Indian Culture*, Vol. I, 1934–5, pp. 295–8, 333–432 and 573–7; Vol. II, 1935–6, pp. 17–22 and 435–46.

[8] Cf. R.A. Nicholson's article 'Sufism' in *Encyclopaedia of Religion and Ethics*.

endeavour to study the working of various influences which constituted the environment in which the mystic doctrine developed. Among them are to be reckoned all political, social and intellectual conditions which favoured the growth of Sufism.[9]

As we study the history of the period when the Ṣūfi ideal of life came into existence, we find it to be a time of more or less political unrest. The latter half of the eighth century presents, besides the political revolution which resulted in the overthrow of the Umayyads, certain movements, e.g. those of the Ismā'īlites, Bāṭinites and Qārmaṭians, which, by exploiting the credulity of the people, 'cloaked political projects under the guise of religious ideas'.

In the beginning of the ninth century of the Christian era we find Māmūn and his brother Amīn engaged in a terrible struggle for political power. 'The early years of Mamun's reign present another social phenomenon of great political significance, viz. the Shu'ubiyah controversy,' which progressed with the rise and establishment of independent Persian families: the Ṭāhirids, the Saffarids, the Sāmānids and others. 'It was, therefore, the combined force of these and other conditions of similar nature that drove men of devotional character away from the scene of continual unrest to the blissful peace of an ever-deepening contemplative life.'[10]

Some of the Mu'tazilites had developed the sceptical tendencies in their systems, and these found an earlier expression in the poems of Bashshār ibn Burd and Abu al-'Alā' al-Ma'arri. Bashshār was a stone-blind sceptic poet of Zoroastrian leanings; he deified fire and scoffed at all non-Persian modes of thought. 'The germs of scepticism latent in rationalism ultimately necessitated an appeal to a supra-intellectual source of knowledge which asserted itself in the works of such eminent Sufis as al-Qushayri', al-Hujwīri and others.

Religious discussions among the representatives of various creeds encouraged by al-Māmūn and especially the bitter theological controversies between the Ash'arites and the Mu'tazilites tended to confine religion within the narrow limits

[9] In what follows we have heavily drawn on Iqbal's *Development of Metaphysics in Persia*, London, 1908, pp. 98–101.

[10] Ibid., p. 99.

of sects and schools. This stirred up the more genuinely religious-minded people to rise above the fanatical sectarian wranglings and dialectical logomachies and take refuge in the spiritual haven of mysticism.

The gradual softening of the religious fervour brought about by the rationalistic tendencies of the early Abbasid period and 'the rapid growth of wealth which tended to produce moral laxity and indifference towards religious life,' at least in the upper circles of the Muslim society, were some of the predisposing causes for the development of Sufism in Islam.

Above all, it can easily be shown that in the Qur'ān as well as in the traditions of the holy Prophet there are the germinal ideas of sufistic doctrines. It would, however, be going too far to claim that the holy Prophet actually communicated certain esoteric doctrines to ʿAli or Abu Bakr. There is no evidence, historical or otherwise, to authenticate this view.[11]

Some of the verses of the holy Qur'ān[12] and sayings of the holy Prophet bearing on the Ṣūfi doctrines and mode of life may be referred to as follows:

(*i*) Whithersoever ye turn, there is the face of Allah (ii. 115).

(*ii*) He is the first and the last, and the outward and the inward (lvii. 3).

(*iii*) There is no god but He, everything is perishing except His face (xxviii. 88).

(*iv*) We are nearer to him (man) than his neck artery (l. 16).

Surely, the seeds of mysticism are embedded in such verses as these. The support for the naturalistic pantheism[13] of the scientists can be derived from verses of the following kind:

[11] Ibid., p. 107.

[12] For a fairly comprehensive treatment of the Sūfi doctrine from the point of view of the teachings of the Qur'ān, cf. Dr. Mir Valiuddin, *The Quranic Sufism*, Motilal Banarsidas, Delhi, 1959.

[13] Cf. C.E. Wilson, 'Remarks on Sufism and Its Relation to Pantheism and Islam,' *Islamic Culture*, Vol. V, 1931, pp. 142–65; also Mir Valiuddin, 'The Problem of the One and Many in Islamic Mysticism,' *Hyderabad Academy Studies*, Vol. II, 1940, pp. 35–67, etc.

(*i*) Do they not look upon the camel, how she is created? (lxxxviii. 17).

(*ii*) Have they never looked up at the birds subjected to Him in heaven's vault? (xvi. 79).

(*iii*) The bee too furnishes a sign for those who consider (xvi. 68).

Verses of this kind can be quoted at length. They urge us to study Nature, for the phenomena of Nature are verily the signs of God and the laws of Nature are the habits of God. The Qur'ānic teaching is very clear on this. A mystico-poetic spirit, however, finds a superb expression of felicity in verses of another description.

Hast thou not seen how all those who are in the heavens and the earth utter the praise of God, and the birds when they spread their wings? Every creature knoweth its prayer: and God knoweth what they do. And God's is the kingdom of the heavens and the earth and to God is the final goal (xxiv. 41–42).

The mystic's mode or style of life is given clearly in such Qur'ānic lines as:

In the places of worship which God hath allowed to be raised, that His name may therein be remembered, do men praise Him in the morning and in the evening; men whom neither merchandise nor traffic diverts from the remembrance of God and the keeping up of prayer ... (xxiv. 36–37).

Muslim saints took to the practice of wandering and roaming about in the world because the Qur'ān says:

Journey through the earth, and see how He hath brought forth created beings (xxix. 20).

The Qur'ān describes the blessed saints in paradise in the following terms: 'He loveth them and they love Him' (v. 54).

Herein lies the support for the Ṣūfi doctrine of love, the founder of which is reported to be the great woman saint,

Rābi'ah al-Baṣri.[14]

There is a significant passage in the holy Qur'ān relating to the victorious battle of Badr:

So it was not ye who slew them but God slew them; thou didst not cast (arrows) when thou didst cast, but God cast (viii. 17).

From this verse some of the pantheistic mystics unfortunately took support for their fatalistic outlook on life. A school of Sufism known as *Ishrāqi Taṣawwuf*, i.e. 'Sufism of Illumination,'[15] ascribed to Shihāb al-Dīn al-Suhrawardi Maqtūl, based itself on the verses of the following kind:

God is the light of heavens and of earth. His light is like a niche wherein is a lamp—the lamp encased in a glass, the glasses as it were a glistening star (xxiv. 35).

The Prophet has been reported to have said:

God said: My servant continues to draw near to Me through works of supererogation until I love him. And when I love him I am his ear, so that he hears by Me, and his eyes so that he sees by Me, and his hands so that he takes by Me.

This clearly bears out the Ṣūfi doctrine of the identity of man with God through unitive experience.

The Prophet has also reported God as saying:

My earth and My heaven contain Me not, but the heart of My faithful servant containeth Me.

Again, according to the Prophet, God said:

I was a hidden treasure and I desired to be known, I created the creation in order that I might be known.

[14] Cf. Margaret Smith, *Rabi'ah: The Mystic*, Luzac & Co., London, 1944.

[15] Cf. E.J. Jurji, *Illumination in Islamic Mysticism,* Princeton University Press, Princeton, 1938, especially Introduction, pp. 1–24.

From such sayings as these the Ṣūfīs derived their belief that *Insān-i-Kāmil*[16] or the ideal man is the mirror of God's attributes.

The Prophet is reported to have said to one of his followers:

Consult thy heart and thou wilt hear the secret ordinances of God proclaimed by the heart's inward knowledge which is real faith and divinity.

Further: 'Whosoever knows himself knows his Lord.'

Such sayings of the Prophet allude to a deep kinship between man's inmost nature and the nature of the Divine Reality. Further, they point to a kind of knowledge which comes from the depths of the heart and is different from one that comes through senses and reasoning. The Prophet is also supposed by the mystics to have warned the ordinary folk of the supernatural knowledge of a great Ṣūfi for he sees by the light of God. It is possible for him to see the past of a man or the inmost secrets of his heart or to communicate with another person at a distance without the physical media (telepathy), and also to know events before they happen (clairvoyance).

By loving God and knowing God, the faithful can even attain to miraculous powers, for the Prophet said:

If ye know God as He ought to be known, ye would walk on the seas and the mountains would move at your call.

[16] For the doctrine of *Insān-i-Kāmil* in Islamic mysticism, cf. article 'Al-Insān al-Kāmil,' *Shorter Encyclopaedia of the Islam*, Leiden, 1953. For 'Abd al-Karīm al-Jīlī's famous conception of *Insān-i-Kāmil*, see R.A. Nicholson, *Studies in Islamic Mysticism*, Cambridge, 1921, pp. 77–142, and Iqbal, op. cit., pp. 150–74.

Chapter Four

PHILOSOPHY OF THE IKHWĀN AL-ṢAFĀ'

Ikhwān al-Ṣafā' was a secret association of scientists and philosophers established at Basra in about 373/983 with a branch in Baghdad. It used to hold meetings at which the members would read out treatises on subjects scientific, philosophical and religious.

The Arabic phrase *Ikwān al-Ṣafā'* has been rendered into English variously as *The Brethren of Purity*, *The Brethren of Sincerity, The Faithful Brethren* or *The Faithful Friends.* The full name of the association was *Ikhwān al-ṣafā' wa khullān al-wafā wa ahl al-'adl wa abnā' al-ḥamd*, i.e., The Brethren of Purity, the Faithful Friends, the Men of Justice and the Sons of Praiseworthy Conduct. Different explanations have been offered for the appellation *Ikhwān al-Ṣafā'*. According to Goldziher, it refers to a fable in *Kalīlah wa Dimnah* (The Fables of Bidpai) in which it is narrated how a group of animals, by acting as faithful friends (*ikhwān al-ṣafā'*), escaped the snares of the hunter. The chief aim of the Brethren, it is said, was to further the salvation of their immortal souls by mutual assistance and by remaining faithful to one another. Another explanation is that they were called the Brethren of Purity because, after Plato, they believed first and foremost in the purifying effect of the study of philosophy on the soul. Nicholson and Levy have given a more definite explanation based on the authority of Ibn al-Qifṭi's *Tārīkh al-Ḥukamā'*, a collection of the lives of the Muslim philosophers and scientists.[1] According to this explantion, the Brethren derived the title from their declaration that the religious law (*Sharīah*) in their time had become defiled with ignorance and adulterated by errors, and the only way to purify it was by means of philosophy. This in

[1] Cf. Ibn al-Qifṭi, *Tārīkh al-Ḥukāmā'*, Urdu translation by Ghalām Jīlāni Barq, Anjuman-i-Taraqqi-i-Urdu, Delhi, 1945.

particular indicates their aspiration for the moral and spiritual renovation of Islam through philosophy.

In religion the Brethren had leanings towards Muʿtazilism and Shīʿism, and in philosophy towards a very extensive eclecticism. But it has been alleged that the underlying motives of the association were essentially of a political nature. It is said that the Brethren were in some way connected with the Ismāʿīlite propaganda against the Abbasids and that their eclectic idealism represented the religio-political teaching of the Fāṭimids, the Qārmaṭians and the Assassins, all of whom wanted to overthrow the Abbasid caliphate. Strong evidence in support of this view has been offered by a manuscript discovered by P. Casanova in 1898.[2] This manuscript contains, with fragments of the *Rasā'il Ikhwān al-Ṣafā'* (Treatises of the Brethren of Purity), a hitherto unknown treatise, *Jāmiʿah* (Summary). This tract, which is said to be the very essence of the *Rasā'il*, manifestly preaches the Ismāʿīlite views. Treatises of the Brethren of Purity, fifty-two in all (sometimes numbered as fifty or fifty-one), form a sort of Arabic encyclopedia of science, religion and philosophy, possibly the first of its kind in the world of literature.[3] The authors of this work concealed their names, but sent the treatises to booksellers of the day to be made available to the public. The following names have come down to us through later references as members of the association and collaborators in compiling the Encylopedia: (1) Abu Sulaymān Muḥammad ibn Mushīr al-Busṭī al-Muqadassi, (2) Abu al-Ḥasan ʿAli ibn Hārūn al-Zanjāni, (3) Muḥammad ibn Ahmad al-Nahrajūri, (4) al-ʿAwfi, (5) Zayd ibn Rifāʿah.[4]

[2] Cf. R.A. Nicholson, *A Literary History of the Arabs*, Cambridge, 1930, p. 371.

[3] Cf. M.M. Sharif, *Muslim Thought: Its Origin and Achievements*, Lahore, 1951, p. 57, n. 1; cf. also A.L. Tibawi, 'Ikhwan as-Ṣafa' and Their Rasail: A Critical Review of a Century and a Half of Research,' *Islamic Quarterly*, Vol. II, 1955, pp. 28 46.

[4] Cf. George Sarton, *Introduction to the History of Science*, Baltimore, 1927, Vol. I, p. 661. There is some variation in the spellings of these names, for example the list given by Nicholson, op.cit., p. 370, mentions first as Abū Sulaymān Muḥammad ibn Maʿshar al-Bayusti or al-Muqaddasī (Maqdisī) and third as Abū Aḥmad al-Mihrajānī. Cf. M. Stern, 'The Authorship of the Epistles of the Ikhwan-as-Ṣafa', *Islamic Culture*, Vol. XX, 1946, pp. 367–72, and Vol. XXI, 1947, pp. 303–4.

The style of the treatises is rather long-winded and repetitive. They are full of devout phraseology, religious parables, metaphorical expressions, and figurative turns of speech. As a matter of fact, the treatises were not intended for professed savants but for a more popular audience. They nevertheless cover a wide field and illustrate what the Brethren regarded as the capacity for scientific and philosophical knowledge possessed by the educated class of Muslims in the tenth century. Almost every branch of knowledge has been dealt with in these treatises. Fourteen treatises deal with mathematics and logic, ten with metaphysics, eleven with mysticism, astrology and magic and seventeen with natural sciences such as astronomy, meteorology, geography, botany, zoology, physiology, embryology, physics, chemistry, anthropology, etc. The Encyclopedia includes a classification of sciences, essentially an Aristotelian one, as it was earlier transmitted by al-Fārābi (d. 339/950). The nature and organisation of the association are explained in an essay in the fourth part of the Encyclopedia (treatise No. 45).

The Encyclopedia is of special interest to the natural scientist. We find in it an attempt to explain many natural phenomena such as, for instance, tides, earthquakes, eclipses, sound-waves, meteors, thunder, lightning, rain, dew, snow, hail, rainbow, climate, seasons, flora, biological evolution, formation of minerals, etc., etc. It would not be fair to judge the value of these explanations from the point of view of modern developments in science. The Brethren, like the Pythagoreans, had a great fascination for numbers. In the treatises we find much number mysticism: magical squares, amicable numbers[5] and numerical classifications. The spiritual significance of the

[5] Amicable numbers are two such numbers as have the sum of the divisors of one equal to the other. For example, 220 is equal to the sum of 1, 2, 71, 142 which are the divisors of 284 which itself is equal to the sum of the divisors of 220, i.e. 1, 2, 4, 5, 10, 11, 20, 22, 44, 55, 110. The first to mention explicitly 220 and 284 as a pair of amicable numbers was Iamblichus, the Neoplatonist who died in about 327 A.D., though they might well have been known earlier as the Pythagoreans were deeply interested in the properties of numbers. The medieval thinkers believed in the erotic power of amicable numbers, hence the name. It is interesting to note that the second pair of amicable numbers was discovered only in 1639 by the famous French mathematician Fermat and they are as large as 17,296 and 18,416,

number four, for example, has been suggested by enumerating things that go by four: four elements, four bodily humours, four temperaments, four seasons, four directions, etc.

These treatises were later introduced into Spain, but we are not quite sure whether it was Maslamah ibn Aḥmad al-Majrīṭi, the Muslim astronomer and mathematician, who flourished in the tenth century, or his disciple al-Karmāni (367–459/977–1066), himself a mathematician and surgeon, who introduced it.[6] If it was Maslamah, the transmission must have taken place soon after the original publication. This transmission was effected in spite of the fact that the *Rasā'il* were considered heretical in the East and eventually burnt in Baghdad in 545/1150 by the order of the Abbasid Mustanjid. Right after publication, the treatises were submitted to an authority on religious matters, Abu Sulaymān al-Manṭiqi al-Sijistāni. He returned them with very unfavourable comments, declaring that the authors had attempted to conceal philosophical heresies under the cloak of the *Sharī'ah* and had failed.[7] In spite of this charge, the treatises continued to circulate and exercised an influence both on Muslim and Jewish philosophy—equally on al-Ghazāli and Ibn Rushd, and on Ibn Gabirol and Jehuda Halevi.[8]

The philosophy of the Ikhwān al-Ṣafā' was highly eclectic including such diverse elements as Zoroastrian, Christian, Hebraic, Syriac, Hindu, Arabic and Greek. The Brethren seem to have some knowledge of Aristotle's system, particularly of his logic and psychology. But the apocryphal works, viz. 'The Theology' of Aristotle and 'The Book of Apple,' were considered by them, as by other Muslim philosophers of their time, the Greek master's genuine works. The former was really the abridgement of the last three books of *The Enneads* written by Plotinus and the latter was the work of an unknown author written in imitation of Plato's *Phaedo*. The Brethren were, however, more at home in the Pythogorean, the Platonic and the Neoplatonic doctrines. Their knowledge of Greek philosophy was, however, inferior to that already exhibited by

[6] Cf. Sarton, op. cit., pp. 668, 715.

[7] Cf. al-Qifṭī, op. cit., pp. 131–7.

[8] For the influence of the treatises of the Brethren on Jewish thinkers, see I. Husik, *History of Medieval Jewish Philosophy*, New York, 1930, p. xxxix.

philosophers such as al-Kindi (188-*c.* 260/803–873) and al-Fārābi (*c.* 257–339/870–950). A general conception that prevailed among them was that science, philosophy and religion must in the end be compatible with one another; hence they gave free rein to their intellectual curiosity and deliberately cultivated a breadth of vision. The treatises offer ample evidence of the fact that the writers were honest in their eclecticism and that they were, therefore, receptive to the ideas they derived from surveys of Greek philosophy, from Indian and Persian wisdom literature and from Jewish and Christian books of religion. A clear indication of this fact may be found in the sixth section of the fourth treatise, which Stanley Lane-Poole in his book *Studies in a Mosque* has described as containing 'the worthiest record of the life of Jesus that can be met with in Arabian literature'.[9]

As one goes through the contents of the Encyclopedia, one finds many separate treatises dealing with problems of great philosophical and religious interest. Titles of some of the treatises with their serial numbers are as follows: The *Isagoge* of Porphyry (10); the Aristotelian Categories (11); The Prior Analytics (13); The Posterior Analytics (14); Development of the Individual Souls (27); The Contemplation of Death and Life (29); Spiritual Principles according to Pythagoras (32); Spiritual Principles according to *Ikhwān al-Ṣafā'* (33); The World as a Man on a Large Scale (34); Thought and Its Object (35); Theory of the Spheres and the Genesis and Dissolution of the World (36); The Soul's Love and Longing for God (37); Resurrection (38); The Way to God (43); Immortality of the Soul (44); Prophetic Revelation (47); etc.

It is rather difficult to give a clear and systematic account of the philosophical views of the Brethren because of their avowed eclecticism; an eclectic philosophy by its very nature is liable to be incoherent. In order to reconcile the half-baked science and

[9] Stanley Lane-Poole, *Studies in a Mosque*, London, 1883, p. 95. It appears in treatise 44, section 6; see *Rasā'il Ikhwān al-Ṣafā'* edited by Khayr al-Din al-Zirikli, Cairo, 1347/1928, Vol. IV, pp. 94–7; cf. L. Levonian, 'The Ikhwan al-Safa and Christ,' *The Muslim World*, Vol. XXXV, 1945, pp. 27–31, and also J. Windrow Sweetman, *Islam and Christian Theology*, Lutterworth Library, London, 1945, Part I, Vol. I, pp. 37–9.

philosophy of their age with religion they were driven to give the one a gnostic and the other an allegorical interpretation, thus displeasing both the philosopher and the theologian. The figurative turns of style, frequent use of metaphors and parables add to our difficulty. Some of the important doctrines of their philosophical teaching may, however, be summed up under the following three heads: Theory of Knowledge, Cosmology and Ethics.

Theory of Knowledge. The theory of knowledge of the Brethren was worked out more or less on Platonic lines. It was based fundamentally on the notion of the dualism of soul and body; by soul they meant the rational and spiritual element in man. The ultimate purpose of knowledge, according to them, is to purify the soul by conducting it from the sensible to the spiritual, from the concrete to the abstract. The sense-experience of material objects comes through the bodily sense-organs, but the knowledge of the abstract laws of logic and the axioms of mathematics come to the soul intuitively without the intermediation of body. This shows the independence of the soul from the body and alludes to its real source and sojourn, i.e., the realm of the rational and the supersensible. Liberally interpreted, the Brethren seem to hold that this is the realm where the universals of Plato, laws of logic, axioms of mathematics, absolute values and religious verities all subsist. The soul, before coming to the world of matter, the Brethren believed, lived in this realm of spirit and reason. This is why it has the reminiscence or recollection of the laws of pure reason and an inherent craving or yearning for spiritual verities and absolute values of truth, beauty and goodness. Like Socrates, the Brethren maintained that all real knowledge is potentially present in the soul of the individual. The position of the teacher is similar to that of a midwife. Teaching is not the act of putting something in the soul from without but helping it give birth to the truths that already lie embedded in it.

For the purification of the soul it is very necessary that an individual should undergo a hard discipline in abstract sciences such as logic and mathematics. But the movement of the soul from the particular to the universal, from the concrete to the abstract, or from the sensible to the supersensible, is a gradual process. One has first to discipline oneself in the sciences that are less abstract and slowly and gradually move towards those that are more abstract. For example, the study of solid geometry, which is comparatively less abstract, should precede the study of plane geometry, and all this should come before the study of pure mathematics. It is interesting to note here that, according to the Brethren, though logic and mathematics are cognate sciences, logic is inferior to pure mathematics. Mathematics is removed further than logic from what is sensible. Logic takes an intermediate position between physics and metaphysics. In physics we have to deal with bodies; in metaphysics, with pure spirits or thought. Logic—and here they include in it the inductive method as well—deals with the ideas of the latter as well as the representations of the former in our soul. This preference for mathematics over logic by the Brethren, though quite in line with the modern development in logic, only indicates their devotion to Pythagoras.

Here arises an interesting question. If the purification of the soul depends on a strict discipline in logic and pure mathematics, how about the souls of those individuals who by nature lack the ability to study these abstract sciences? Should they forgo every hope for the purification and salvation of their souls? No, the Brethren do not teach any such pessimism. They have laid equal, if not greater, emphasis on righteous conduct and religious life as measures for the purification of the soul. Knowing the limitations of the multitude, the prophets, according to them, had been very wise in recommending these measures of more universal application.

Cosmology. In the metaphysical views of the Brethren we find very clear traces of Neoplatonic doctrines. Like Plotinus they believed that God is above all knowledge and above all the categories of human thought. The ordinary man cannot conceive of God as an abstract unity, for he cannot easily dispense with sensuous imagery in his conception of God. The philosopher, at the higher reaches of his spiritual development, dispenses with sensuous conceptions and ordinary usages prevalent among the common people with regard to the idea of God.

From God, the highest being, who is exalted above all distinctions and oppositions both of the material and the mental kind, the world is derived by way of emanations. This is certainly a Neoplatonic doctrine to explain the origin of the world. The material world emanates from God not directly but through successive, intermediary agencies; and there is a spiritual hierarchy of these agencies. The various grades of emanation have been catalogued by the Brethren as follows: (1) The First Intelligence, (2) The World-Soul, (3) The Primitive Matter, (4) Nature, (5) The Spatial Matter, (6) The World of Spheres, (7) The Elements of the Sublunary World, (8) Minerals, Plants and Animals (composed of these elements). These, then, are called by them the eight essences which together with God, the absolute one, complete the series of original essences corresponding to the cardinal numbers, i.e., nine in all. All this looks more like a piece of mythology rather than philosophy to the modern reader. But the whole theory is more of a borrowed one from Neoplatonic and other sources than the original product of the Brethren.[10]

The central point in this doctrine is the heavenly origin and the return of the soul to God. Individual souls are only part of 'the world-soul' to which they return purified after the death of the body just as the world-soul will return to God on the Day of Judgement. Death is called the minor resurrection and the return of the world-soul to God the major resurrection.

The human soul has emanated from the world-soul, and the souls of all the individuals taken together constitute a substance which may be called 'The Absolute Man' or 'The Spirit of Humanity'.

Every individual soul, however, is involved in matter and must gradually purify itself from it. To that end it possesses many faculties or powers, of which the speculative and religious are the highest. It is due to these that we have philosophy and religion. The object of all philosophy as well as of every religion is to make the soul become like God so far as it is humanly possible.

Ethics. The whole system of the Brethren converges in their ethics, for ethics is the art of purifying the soul *par excellence*.

[10] See below, chapter on Ibn Sīna.

Their ethical system is of a spiritualistic and ascetic character and their eclecticism finds its expression as much here as anywhere else.

As already stated, the spiritual for the Brethren is identical with the rational. The essence and proper nature of man's soul lies in his reason. Those actions are right that are performed according to man's proper nature, i.e., according to his reason. 'Those actions are really praiseworthy,' they say, 'which proceed from purely rational considerations.' It is not difficult to recognise the Kantian strain in their ethical pronouncements. Further, they say that the spiritual in man is aroused when he loves God and craves union with Him. This love is the highest virtue, for one who acquires it shows a form of religious patience and forbearance with all the created beings. This love for the divine brings serenity of soul, freedom of heart and peace with the whole world.

Their ethical asceticism proceeds as follows. Body is made up of matter to which at death it will return. But the soul comes from Allah; though it is here associated with the body, its return is to Allah. Since man's soul comes from an eternal source, its concern is mostly for the eternal and the spiritual life hereafter, and since the body will die out, its interests are all for seeking ephemeral pleasures. According to the Brethren, all virtues such as knowledge, reason, continence and bravery are due to the soul and all vices such as ignorance, folly, lewdness and cowardice are due to the body. But though at times the Brethren go to the length of saying that the death of the body is the life of the soul, they never teach full-fledged asceticism of a desperate type. They add, 'Nevertheless the body must be properly treated and looked after so that the soul may have time to attain its full development.'[11]

The Brethren had their own idea of *Insān-i-Kāmil*, i.e., the ideal or the perfect man. The specific requirements for the ideal man of the Brethren are interesting to note, for they evidence their eclecticism at its best. 'The ideal man should be of East Persian origin, Arabian in faith, Babylonian in education, Hebrew in astuteness, a disciple of Christ in conduct, as pious

[11] Cf. D.M. Donaldson, *Studies in Muslim Ethics,* London, 1953, p. 105.

as a Syrian monk, a Greek in natural sciences, an Indian in the interpretation of mysteries, but above all a Ṣūfi or a mystic in his whole spiritual outlook.'[12]

[12] Cf. T.J. de Boer, *The History of Philosophy in Islam*, London, 1933, p. 95.

Chapter Five

AL-KINDI

Abu Yūsuf Ya'qūb ibn Isḥāq al-Kindi (188-*c.* 260/803–873), the first Arab philosopher and the only great philosopher of the Arab race, was, like most other Muslim philosophers, a polymath: he had an encyclopedic scholarship in the scientific knowledge of his day including such a variety of subjects as arithmetic, geometry, astronomy, theory of music, physics (particularly optics), meteorology, geography, medicine, pharmacy, politics, etc. He was well acquainted with the philosophical views of Socrates, Plato, Aristotle and his commentators, particularly Alexander of Aphrodisias. He was also a student of comparative religion. In philosophy, he had leanings towards Neoplatonism and Neopythagoreanism, and in Muslim theology towards the then flourishing school of Mu'tazilism. He wrote on all subjects; the number of his treatises amounts to 265, though, unfortunately, very few of them are extant now.

His was essentially an effort to bring about reconciliation between science and philosophy, on the one hand, and of both with religion, on the other. This led to the development of syncretic philosophy or syncretism which is indeed the characteristic feature of the systems of almost all the Muslim philosophers.

Science and Philosophy. Al-Kindi brought science and philosophy close together by strongly emphasising, after the Pythagoreans and Plato, that nobody could be a philosopher without being thoroughly disciplined in mathematics. This was confirmed by his own mathematical applications of quantitative methods in the fields of medicine, optics, music, etc. There may be some justification for making the claim that he forestalled, at least in some rudimentary form, the most modern developments in scientific methodology. One is reminded of the observation made by Briffault in his work, *The Making of*

Humanity, that Muslim thinkers were the first in the history of scientific thought to realize the importance of quantitative methods.[1]

It is interesting to note that al-Kindī's application of quantitative methods to medicine brought him very close to propounding the Weber-Fechner Law. If a particular ingredient in a medical compound, he suggests, is to have its efficacious value in arithmetical progression, its quantity in that compound should be increased in geometrical progression. In physiological optics, the application of mathematical methods duly won him a word of praise from Roger Bacon who, along with Witelo and others in the thirteenth century, was influenced by him in the development of his own related views.[2] Al-Kindi further applied mathematics to the theory of music, on which subject he wrote seven books; four of these have come down to us. This mathematical advance in the theory of music gave al-Kindi a prominent place in the history of Arabian music. According to H.G. Farmer, al-Kindī's treatises on music had a fairly considerable influence on later writers for two centuries.[3] No less a musician himself, the great al-Fārābi was also indebted to him.

Religion and Philosophy. His tendency towards syncretism urged al-Kindi to attempt a reconciliation between philosophy and religion or, as he put it, between reason and prophecy. Reason and prophecy are both equally important and valuable avenues for the knowledge of ultimate reality; it would be unfortunate to hold only one of them to be the sole avenue. As he studied the subjects of comparative religion and philosophy, it became clear to al-Kindi that both religion and philosophy refer ultimately to the same reality; the first cause, the one and the eternal of the philosophers, is verily God Himself of the prophets. A true philosopher bears witness to the prophetic revelations by readily recognizing the profound truths dispensed by them.

Cosmology. The universe, according to al-Kindi, is an archi-

[1] R. Briffault, *The Making of Humanity*, London, 1928, pp. 191–4.

[2] Cf. G. Sarton, *Introduction to the History of Science*, Baltimore, 1927, Vol. I, p. 559.

[3] H.G. Farmer, *History of Arabian Music*, London, 1929, pp. 127–8.

tectonic whole. There runs a causal connection throughout all its events. But there are grades of causation as there are grades of beings. Causes may be of higher or lower order. This conception of graded causation, indeed, goes back to the Neoplatonic theory of emanation. Lower causes are the effects of higher causes. All higher existence affects the lower, but that which is lower has no influence upon the higher. The nexus of causality in the events of the universe and their hierarchical organisation enable us to predict future events, e.g. the position of planets in astronomy. Further, it is possible to understand the whole scheme of things in the universe from a single existent thing if it is thoroughly known. Thus every object is a mirror of the universe; one is the microcosm, if the other is the macrocosm.

Five Essences. The fundamental principles governing the physical universe are named ʿessences' by al-Kindi. They are matter, form, movement, time and space, and are presented in a treatise, *On the Five Essences.* This scheme of essences is based upon his knowledge of Aristotle's *Physics* and *Metaphysics.* O'Leary represents al-Kindī's essences in the following manner.[4]

(1) *Matter.* Matter is that which receives the other essences but it cannot be received as an attribute; so if matter is taken away, the other four essences are also, necessarily, removed.

(2) *Form.* Form is of two kinds. First, that which is essential to a thing and is inseparable from the matter; it serves to describe the thing in terms of Aristotelian categories of quality, quantity, place, time, etc. Secondly, form is the faculty whereby a thing is produced from formless matter; without form matter remains an abstract idea which becomes a thing only when it takes form.

(3) *Movement.* Movement is of six kinds. Two are variations in substances as either generation or corruption. Two are variations in quantity by increase or decrease. One is variation in quality and one is change in position.[5]

[4] De Lacy O'Leary, *Arabic Thought and Its Place in History*, London, 1922, pp. 141–3.

[5] For an authoritative account of Aristotle's notion of movement, see W.D. Ross, *Aristotle*, London, 1923, pp. 81–3.

(4) *Time.* Time is very much akin to movement. Whereas movement shows diversities in direction, time proceeds always and only in one direction. Time is known only in relation of *before* and *after* like a movement in a straight line and at a uniform rate. Thus it can be expressed only in a series of continuous numbers.

(5) *Space.* Space is supposed by some to be a body, but it is rather the surface which surrounds the body. When the body is taken away, the space does not cease to exist; the vacant space is instantly filled up by some other body, e.g. air, water, etc., which has the same surrounding surface.

Neoplatonism. Though the basic concepts as presented in the treatise *On the Five Essences* are of Aristotelian origin and though al-Kindi is known as one of the Pĕripatetics because of his translations of and commentaries on Aristotle's works, his Aristotelianism undoubtedly takes the form of Neoplatonism. Most important is the crucial fact that al-Kindi mistook the apocryphal 'Theology of Aristotle' to be a genuine work of Aristotle; it was, in fact, the paraphrase of the last three books of *Enneads* by Plotinus.

Neoplatonism was readily accepted by al-Kindi, for it gratified his syncretic tendencies to synthesise Pythagoreanism, Platonism and Aristotelianism and reconciled all this with religion. It came as a welcome relief to him that Aristotle himself had made this possible by producing such a magnificent work at his 'Theology'. Al-Kindī's various doctrines, such as the theory of emanation, relation of soul with body, on the one hand, and with God, on the other, its salvation and immortality, the fourfold division of intellect, are all based on the philosophy of Neoplatonism.

The Theory of Emanation. To explain the relation of God with the world is one of the most difficult problems in the philosophy of religion. It is well-nigh an impossible task, and philosophers of all times have stumbled over it. Al-Kindi readily accepted the Neoplatonic doctrine of emanation ascribing it to Aristotle, for so it was given in the 'Theology of Aristole'. According to the Neoplatonic theory, God did not create the world through an act of volition, for creation thus understood implies consciousness and will, both of which are limitations with regard to the

Absolute. Knowing implies an object which confronts the knower as something alien to him. God being infinite and absolute has nothing outside His being; hence nothing can confront Him as something other than He. Willing implies some desire or want which had not been fulfilled or some purpose which is yet to be realized. But God is above all such deficiencies; hence willing cannot be ascribed to Him either.

The universe, al-Kindi believed, is an emanation from God, an inevitable overflow of His infinite being or a necessary result of His creativity. The world emanates from God as light emanates from the sun or the properties of a triangle from a triangle.

The world, however, does not emanate from God directly but through intermediary spiritual agencies which, considered from the point of view of theology, may be conceived as angels. These intermediary agencies are of various grades; the lower agency emanates from the agency of a higher order and from it emanates another of the lower order. Between the last item of this graded series of spiritual agencies and the material world stands the world-soul as the final connecting link.[6]

Human Soul. In this highly speculative scheme of 'emanationism' human souls are supposed to have originated from the world-soul. In its actual operations the human soul is no doubt bound up with its body, yet in its spiritual essence it is independent of the body and belongs to the supersensible sphere of the world-soul. Al-Kindi finds no difficulty in explaining the immortality of the human soul. Having descended from the world-soul, and being independent of body, it is an uncompounded, simple, imperishable substance.

The salvation of the human soul is explained more or less on Platonic lines. Like Plato, al-Kindi believes that a man's soul continuously suffers from the reminiscences or recollections of the conditions of its earlier existence in the supersensible realm. The human soul does not feel at home in this world, nor does its true happiness consist in the gratification of bodily desires. Bodily desires are myriad and endless; their gratification is followed by an awareness of those which have not yet

[6] See below, chapter on Ibn Sīna. For a criticism of the theory of emanation, see below, chapters on al-Ghazāli and Ibn Khaldūn.

been gratified. Further, the human soul cannot be satisfied with that which is ever-changing. It always longs and yearns for the eternal and the permanent, but the eternal and the permanent is to be found only in the realm of reason and spirit. The real happiness and salvation of the human soul, therefore, lies in the life of reason and in the spiritual life, that is, in philosophical and scientific pursuits and religious and moral activities.

Theory of Intellect. Al-Kindī's theory of intellect, as expounded in his treatise *On the Intellect,* heavily draws upon Alexander of Aphrodisias's commentary on Aristotle's *De Anima* (The Soul).[7] It is closely connected with his theory of

[7] The problem of intellect so keenly discussed by almost all the Muslim Peripatetics originated primarily from somewhat obscure and ambiguous statements of Aristotle in the last book of his treatise on the soul (*De Anima*) in which he makes the distinction between the active or creative intellect on the one hand and the passive intellect on the other. Active intellect, according to Aristotle, is the third between the object and the passive intellect, as light is the third besides the eye and the object. Thus active intellect is said to create the truths that we know just as light may be said to make colours which we perceive by its aid. We see here Aristotle's general principle that 'what is potentially comes to be actually by the agency of something that already is actually' (*Metaphysica*, 1049*b*24). In passive intellect all concepts are merely potential, they are made real or actual by active intellect; actualised intellect thus may be called intellect in action. The active intellect is clearly stated to be 'separable from matter and impassive and unmixed. being in its essential nature an activity... There is no intermission in its thinking; it is only in separation from matter that it is fully itself and it alone is immortal and everlasting, while the passive intelligence is perishable and there is no thinking at all apart from this' (*De Anima*, 430). Aristotle has left unexplained the precise relation between the active and passive intellects and the unity and individuality of human personality and it seems vain to look in his doctrine for the possibility of personal immortality. The true interpretation of Aristotle on these points was disputed even among his own immediate personal disciples. A really serious attempt to clarify some of the disputed issues was made some five hundred years later by Alexander of Aphrodisias, the head of the Lyceum from 198 to 211 A.D. and the greatest commentator on Aristotle, so much so that he was called the 'exegete'. He concluded that active intellect is numerically one and the same in all individuals and is identical with God. Now this was really not being true to the *ipsissima verba* of Aristotle. Hence the Muslim philosophers, though they were certainly influenced by Alexander of Aphrodisias's commentary on Aristotle's *De Anima*, started new ventures into the problem of the intellect, incorporating in their final formulations and refinements elements of Neoplatonic and Stoic philosophies and those derived from the eclectic Helle-

knowledge which is indeed based on the metaphyiscal dualism of the sensible and spiritual.[8] Our knowledge is acquired either through body or through spirit, either through senses or through reason. Senses apprehend the particular or the material, and reason conceives of the universal or the spiritual since the senses belong to the bodily realm and reason to that of the spiritual.[9]

Al-Kindi describes the degrees of reason or intellect to be four, of which three are innate in the human soul but one comes from without and is independent of it. This fourfold division of intellect runs as follows:

(1) Active intellect or agent intellect: *'aql fa'āl.*

(2) Latent or potential intellect: *'aql hayyulāni.*

(3) Acquired intellect: *'aql mustafād.*

(4) Manifest intellect or intellect in action: *'aql ẓāhir* or *'aql bil-fi'l.*

Active Intellect is the over-mind of the universe; the same as the *Nous* of Plotinus, the *Logos* of Philo or the *world of the universals* of Plato. It is the source of fundamental laws of thought, mathematical axioms, eternal truths and spiritual verities. From thence comes, it is believed, the mystic's illumination, the prophet's revelation, the poet's inspiration and also that of the scientist and the philosopher.

Since the principle of active intellect or *'aql fa'āl* could explain the pure reason of the philosophers, the revelations of the prophets and the visions of the saints, it is no wonder that it had such a fascinating appeal for a syncretic philosopher like al-Kindi.

Latent or Potential Intellect. We all have the latent capacity to acquire the eternal truths subsisting in the realm of active

nism of the early centuries of Christian era such as suited the requirements of their own religious needs. The result was a theory of intellect much more complicated and subtle than Aristotle or his commentators could possibly conceive.

[8] This shows that al-Kindī's agreement with Plato is of a very fundamental nature, though he is more generally known 'as the first Peripatetic of Islam'.

[9] According to Professor M.M. Sharif, al-Kindi, long before Kant, held imagination to be a mediating faculty between sense-perception and reason: the senses give knowledge of the particular and reason of the universal and imagination of the universal-particular. See his *Muslim Thought: Its Origin and Achievements*, Lahore, 1951, p. 90.

intellect, but very few of us actually come to acquire them. The acquisition of these truths, in the case of the selected few, transforms their latent intellect into acquired intellect. To give a clear enunciation and explicit formulation of the truths so acquired or to put them into practice is the function of the intellect in action.

The acquisition of eternal truths is really the gift of God, but to put the acquired intellect into activity and thus to have actual intellect or intellect in action is the act of man himself. This somewhat complicated scheme of intellects, of which it is not easy to give an interpretation is modern terms, may be illustrated by taking the example of poetic experience. The poet's experience comes to him from active intellect as an inspiration to his latent intellect transforming it into acquired intellect. To give expression to this inspiration in words and thus to put acquired intellect into activity, i.e., to give it the status of intellect in action, is the poet's own work.

Of all the philosophical doctrines of al-Kindi his theory of intellect and its fourfold division was cherished by subsequent philosophers, viz. al-Fārābi, Ibn Sīna,[10] Ibn Rushd and the rest, as the most treasured piece of inheritance. Indeed, most of the philosophical problems selected by al-Kindi gave starting points to the subsequent developments in Arabic philosophy. Thus it may justifiably be claimed that as Descartes was the father of modern philosophy, al-Kindi was the father of Arabic philosophy.

[10] For a scholarly account of al-Fārābi's and Ibn Sīnā's subtle and rather sophisticated treatment of the problem of intellect, see F. Rahman, *Prophecy in Islam*, London, 1950, pp. 11–20 *et seq.*

Chapter Six

ABU BAKR AL-RĀZI

Abu Bakr Muḥammad ibn Zakarīya al-Rāzi (250?-*c.* 312/864?–*c.* 924) is the celebrated Muslim physician, physicist, alchemist, psychologist and philosopher. He is, however, better known as a physician than as a philosopher. As a physician, he is sometimes ranked even higher than Ibn Sīna. According to Max Meyerhof, he is 'undoubtedly the greatest physician of the Islamic world and one of the great physicians of all times.'[1] He is called al-Rāzi because of his birthplace Rayy, a town near modern Tehran.

The chronology of his life is quite uncertain: the exact dates of his birth and death are unknown; as a matter of fact, little that is authentic is known of the details of his life. As a physician, al-Rāzī's empiricism or positivism goes without any shadow of doubt. A modern reader cannot fail to admire the keen observations, acute analyses, and scientific explanations in his medical works, for instance those found in his treatise, *On Smallpox and Measles*, which is considered to be a masterpiece on the subject even now.[2] But it would be difficult, though not altogether impossible, to say that his philosophical doctrines are also as well-grounded in empiricism as his medical

[1] *The Legacy of Islam*, London, 1952, chapter: 'Science and Medicine,' p. 323; cf. also G. Sarton, *Introduction to the History of Science*, Baltimore, 1927, Vol. I, p. 609, and E.G. Browne, *Arabian Medicine*, Cambridge, 1921, p. 44.

[2] *Kitāb al-Judari w-al-Ḥasbah*, edited by Cornelius Van Dyck, London, 1866, and Beirut, 1872, English translation by W.A. Greenhill under the title: *A Treatise on the Smallpox and Measles*, Sydenham Society, London, 1847. The work gives the first clinical account of smallpox clearly distinguishing its symptoms from those of measles and is rightly considered 'an ornament to the medical literature of the Arabs'. It was first translated into Latin by G. Valla in 1498 (Venice) and later into various other languages, and was printed some forty times between 1498 and 1866.

views.[3] Unlike most of the Muslim philosophers, al-Rāzi denies the possibility of reconciling philosophy with religion. According to him, religions—most of them—are hostile to philosophical speculation and in a way also to scientific research. In some of his books such as *Mukhāriq al-Anbiyā'* and *Hiyal al-Mutanabbiyīn* he has presented views which are evidently heretical. In these works he seems to maintain that reason is superior to revelation. It would, however, be wrong to condemn all his works as heretical.

Metaphysics. As a philosopher al-Rāzi is an original and independent thinker. He does not follow the trodden path of Aristotelian physics and metaphysics. As far as the few completely preserved books and the many fragments of al-Rāzī's philosophical works which have come down to us allow of judgement, he seems to have a strong affinity to Plato's doctrines with some inflow of pre-Socratic philosophy. A metaphysical treatise of al-Rāzī's entitled *Maqālah fi ma' ba'd al-Ṭabī'ah* (Discourse on Metaphysics) was recently discovered and published by the late Dr Paul Kraus.[4] This treatise contains a good many references to ancient philosophers such as Alexander of Aphrodisias, Democritus, Plotinus, Porphyry, Proclus, Plutarch, John Philoponos, and others. In his other philosophical works, e.g. *Kalām-i-Ilāhi*, we find mention of Pythagoras, Empedocles Anaxagoras, and other pre-Socratic thinkers. In all this al-Rāzī's knowledge of ancient philosophy is simply amazing. According to Holmyard, al-Rāzī was the most noteworthy intellectual follower of Greek philosophers of the seventh to fourth century B.C. that mankind has produced for the nineteen hundred years since the death of Aristotle. The fundamental concepts in the metaphysics of al-Rāzi are the five eternal principles which he names as follows: (1) Creator; (2) Universal Soul; (3) Primeval Matter; (4) Absolute Time; (5) Absolute Space.

These principles he has expounded in an independent work entitled: 'Discourse on the Five Eternal Elements'. An attempt

[3] See below, and note 5.

[4] Paul Kraus, a promising Orientalist and an able scholar of al-Rāzī's philosophical works, committed suicide at Cairo during the Second World War, being a victim of Nazi persecution.

has been made by de Boer to give an empirical explanation of these principles.[5] The individual sense-perceptions, according to this explanation, presuppose a material substratum beneath the perceived qualities just as the grouping of differently perceived objects postulates space. Perception of change further constrains us to assume the condition of time. The existence of living beings leads us to recognize a soul. And the fact that some living beings are endowed with reason necessitates our belief in a wise Creator whose reason has ordained everything for the best. Some Muslim thinkers, on the other hand, such as Fakhr al-Dīn al-Rāzi and al-Shahrastāni, have ascribed al-Rāzī's doctrine of five eternal principles to the Sabian thinkers of Harran. They have held that al-Rāzi, while expounding his philosophy, uses almost the same terms which were current with the Sabians. It must be noted that several earlier Muslim philosophers were also affected by Harranian literature, e.g. Abu Sahl Balkhi, Abu Ṭayyab al-Sarakhsi (a follower of al-Kindi) and the renowned Ibn Waḥshīyah. Al-Rāzi seems to belong to this group. He himself in his work *Kalām-i-Ilāhi* explicitly acknowledges the fact that his metaphysical principles were derived from the Harranians, but in other works he has ascribed his metaphysical doctrines to the pre-Socratics, such as Pythagoras, Empedocles, Anaxagoras, Democritus, and others. All these authorities, however, are also cited in Harranian literature. Paul Kraus alleges that al-Rāzi did not consistently ascribe his views to the Harranians of the ninth century but rather to the ancient Greek philosophers only as a device to conceal the heretical nature of his doctrines.[6] There is no doubt, however, that al-Rāzi is one of the main promoters of the Harranian literature and culture.

The Harranian influence on al-Rāzi is clearly indicated by the fact that al-Rāzī's explanation of the origin and destiny of the world is essentially in the form of a myth, very much in conformity with the Harranian cult. While giving an account of the origin of the world he proceeds as follows. The soul, the second

[5] T.J. de Boer, *The History of Philosophy in Islam*, London, 1933, p. 79.

[6] Article 'al-Razi,' *Encyclopaedia of Islam*. Cf. also Max Meyerhof, 'The Philosophy of the Physician al-Razi,' *Islamic Culture*, 1941, pp. 45–58, and 'Abd al-Salām Nadvi, *Ḥukamā'-i-Islām*, Maṭba' Ma'ārif, Azamgarh, 1953, pp. 189–3.

eternal principle possessing life but no knowledge, was possessed by its desire to unite with matter, and to produce within itself forms capable of procuring sensuous pleasures. But matter was recalcitrant. The Creator took pity and created this world with its durable forms in order to enable the soul to enjoy its terrestrial sojourn. This was how man was created.[7] But the Creator also sent intelligence partaking the substance of His own divinity to awaken the soul sleeping in its bodily abode, and inform it that this created world was not its true home and that its true happiness and peace lay somewhere else. According to al-Rāzi there is only one way to escape the bonds of matter, and that is the way of philosophy. When all human souls come to attain liberation from the bonds of body the world will dissolve and matter deprived of all spiritual forms will return to its primeval state.

In his physics al-Rāzi challenges the Aristotelian doctrine and bases his views, as he affirms himself, on the authority of Plato and the pre-Socratics. His atomism is different from that of the many Muslim atomists and is related more closely to the system of Democritus. In Rāzī's view matter in the primeval state, i.e., before the creation of the world, was composed of scattered atoms. Admixed in various proportions with the particles of void for which al-Rāzi, against the Aristotelians, affirms a positive existence, these atoms produced the elements. The elements are five in number: earth, air, fire, water and the celestial element or the modern ether.

The properties of elements, such as lightness and heaviness, opaqueness and transparency, are explained with reference to the proportions of matter and void entering into their composition. Earth and water being heavier elements tend towards the centre of the earth, while air and fire which are lighter because of the dominance of the particles of the void tend to rise above. The celestial element is a balanced mixture of matter and void, and circular motion is peculiar to it. This explains the

[7] It is curious to note that a closely similar mythical explanation about the creation of man had already been offered by Plato: cf. Frank Thilly, *A History of Philosophy*, New York, 1953, p. 89. One may add that al-Rāzi was quite familiar with many of Plato's Dialogues having himself written a commentary on his *Timaeus*: No. 107 in al-Bīrūnī's list of al-Rāzī's works.

rotatory movements of the heavenly bodies. Fire results from the striking of iron on stone because iron, through its impact, cleaves the air and makes it so thin that it is changed into fire.

Al-Rāzi makes a clear distinction between universal or absolute space and partial and relative space. Absolute space which was denied by the Aristotelians is explained by al-Rāzi as pure extent independent of the determinate body which it contains. It goes beyond the limits of the world; in other words, it is unlimited or infinite. The relative or partial space is that which pertains to the size or the extent of an individual determinate body. In his view of time, which, according to him, is of Platonic origin, al-Rāzi makes a similar distinction between limited time and absolute time. The Aristotelian definition of time, considered as a movement in space according to al-Rāzi, is applicable only to limited time; it is generated with the movement of the celestial spheres. Like Newton, al-Rāzi considers absolute time as an independent substance which in itself and from its own nature flows with a uniform speed. It existed before the creation of the world and will exist even after its dissolution. Al-Rāzi thus identifies absolute time with eternity and everlastingness.

Science, Philosophy and Religion. Unlike the Muslim Aristotelians, al-Rāzi denies the possibility of reconciling philosophy with religion. In a number of books such as *Mukhāriq al-Anbiyā'* and *Hiyal al-Mutanabbiyīn*, his views against religion are the most violent that appeared in the course of the Middle Ages. It is alleged that in these works al-Rāzi took up to some extent the arguments of the contemporary Manichaeans against positive religions. The principal views to be found in them are somewhat as follows. All men being equal by nature, the prophets' claim for an intellectual or spiritual supremacy is gratuitous self-glorification. The alleged miracles of the prophets are no more than pious legends and fanciful myths. The teachings of religion are contrary to one truth and the proof of this is that they contradict one another. It is blind tradition and largely custom which keep men tied to their own particular religion. Fanatical adherence to the various sets of religious beliefs is one of the major causes of wars which ravage humanity. It certainly is not easy to overlook the fact in the history of ideas that religions have been hostile to philosophical speculation and to scientific research. The so-called Holy Scriptures are the works of prophets themselves, but the writings of Plato, Aristotle, Hippocrates and Euclid have been of much greater service to humanity. Orthodox and unorthodox alike were shocked by al-Rāzī's denunciations of prophecy and religion. This led to a wholesale condemnation of all his philosophical works; hence the reason that they are hard to find anywhere now. Even the liberal-minded al-Bīrūni, a keen student of Indian philosophy and religions, joined in the general chorus of disapproval. We are, however, indebted to al-Bīrūni for a catalogue of al-Rāzī's works available during his time, which gives a list of 184 titles. Al-Bīrūni himself has confessed that in his youth he was carried away by his enthusiasm for the study of al-Rāzī's works to the extent of reading closely his metaphysical works. All the same he too was shocked by al-Rāzī's free-thinking and irreligious pronouncements. Ibn Ḥazm in his work on 'Religions and Sects' entitled *Kitāb al-Milal wal-Niḥal*, singled out al-Rāzi in particular for the denunciation of his views. Even the Ismā'īlites disowned his philosophical teaching. The poet Nāṣir Khusraw in his work *Zād al-Musāfirīn* and the theologian Ḥamīd-ud-Dīn Kirmāni in his *Aqwāl al-Dhahbīyah* subjected al-Rāzī's philosophico-religious views to severe criticism and final rejection.

Ethics. So far as his ethical views are concerned, in spite of his alleged pessimism, al-Rāzi is against all forms of asceticism. Socrates, whom he takes to be a model for moral life, was no ascetic or cynic: he keenly and actively participated in the life of others. Al-Rāzi accepts the Aristotelian dictum that no blame rests with human passions as such but only with their excessive indulgence. Al-Rāzī's general ethical position may be summed up as that of intellectual hedonism; it reflects very characteristically the outlook of a cultured Persian gentleman. Our Lord and Ruler, he says, is kind and compassionate towards us and regards us with loving care. It follows from this that He hates that anyone should experience pain. It also follows that what happens to us, not of our own earning and choosing but due to some inadvertency of chance or necessity of nature, is to be regarded as inevitable. Al-Rāzi condemns outright the Indian ways of self-mortification such as scorching the body in the sun or casting it down upon sharp spikes. Similarly he disapproves of monasticism and the hermit-life taken to by many Christians and the practice followed by some Muslims. He denounced the Muslim ascetics' practice of spending their whole time in mosques, declining to earn their living and remaining content with little and unappetising food and rough uncomfortable clothings.

In spite of his heretical tendencies, in his book entitled 'Life of the Philosophers'[8] (*al-Sīrat al-Falsafīyah*), al-Rāzi very curiously maintains that man should make himself like God in the greatest degree possible.[9] Hence the creature nearest to God is the wisest, the most just, the most merciful and compassionate. Philosophy for al-Rāzi is not a mere learning but a way of life: a knowing and acting accordingly.

[8] English translation of sections from his works, see A.J. Arberry, *The Spiritual Physick of Rhases*, London, 1950, Wisdom of the East Series.

[9] Cf. Plato, *Theaetetus*, 176b.

Chapter Seven

AL-FĀRĀBI

The full name of al-Fārābi (*c.* 257–339/870–950), Alpharabius of Latin scholastics, was Muḥammad ibn Muḥammad ibn Tarkhān ibn Uzlagh Abu Naṣr al-Fārābi. He was born at Wasij, a village near Farab, in 257/870, studied mainly in Baghdad, and flourished as a Ṣūfi, chiefly at Aleppo in the brilliant court of Sayf al-Dawlah al-Hamdāni (rule 333–57/944–67). He was the first Turkish philosopher to make his name. Being a great expositor of Aristotle's logic, he was called *al-muʿallim al-thāni* (the second teacher), i.e., the second Aristotle.

MacDonald rightly maintains that al-Fārābi was the very base of the pyramid of Muslim philosophy.[1] According to Ibn Khallikān, no Muslim thinker ever reached the same position as al-Fārābi in philosophical knowledge.[2] His system was a creative synthesis of Platonism, Aristotelianism and Sufism.

Al-Fārābi, the Turk, continued the harmonisation of Greek philosophy with Islam, which was begun by al-Kindi the Arab (188–*c.* 260/803–73), preparing the way of Ibn Sīna the Persian (370–428/980–1037). It was by the study of al-Fārābi's writings and the imitation of his philosophical systematisation that Ibn Sīna achieved such eminence in philosophy as he did. It must, however, be added that Ibn Sīna clarified and simplified what was pithy and abstruse in al-Fārābi. Ibn Sīna's contemporary Ibn Miskawayh (334–422/945–1030), a historian and philosopher of no mean repute, in his small work: *al-Fauz al-Aṣghar* ('The Smaller Salvation') more or less repeated the arguments of al-Fārābi, particularly those pertaining to the existence and

[1] D.B. MacDonald, *Development of Muslim Theology, Jurisprudence and Constitutional Theory,* London, 1903, p. 250.

[2] Cf. Ibn Khallikān, *Kitāb Wafayūt al-Aʿyān* edited by F. Wustenfeld, Göttingen, 1835–50, Vol. II, p. 499; English translation by M. de Slane, Vol. III, p. 307.

the attributes of God.[3] Later, the great Christian scholastics, Albert the Great and St Thomas Aquinas, acknowledged their indebtedness to al-Fārābi in the development of their own systems; sometimes they would quote him *ad verbum.*[4] In al-Fārābī's political theory we find some indications of the views of Spencer and Rousseau. Al-Fārābī's method, like that of Spinoza, is deductive and his system, like his, is a form of idealism.

Al-Fārābi laid down several rules for teachers honestly striving to train young students in philosophy. No scholar should start the study of philosophy until he gets very well acquainted with natural sciences. Human nature rises only gradually from the sensuous to the abstract, from the imperfect to the perfect. Mathematics in particular is very important in training the mind of a young philosopher; it helps him pass from the sensuous to the intelligible, and further it informs his mind with exact demonstrations. Similarly, the study of logic as an instrument for distinguishing the true from the false should precede the study of philosophy proper.

Above all, proper discipline of one's own character must come before entering into philosophy. Without refined self-culture the chances are that the student would fail to grasp fully the higher truths as his mind would remain clouded with crude sensibilities.

Al-Fārābī's main philosophical views may be summed up under the following five heads: (1) Ontology; (2) Metaphysical Theology; (3) Cosmology; (4) Rational Psychology; and (5) Political Philosophy.

(1) *Ontology. (a) Being.* The most ultimate and universal concept is *being. Being* cannot be defined for it precedes all other concepts and is the simplest of them all. To define a concept is to analyse its content, but *being,* having the least content, resists all efforts to resolve it into simpler thought-elements. To try to define it in words serves only to make our

[3] Cf. *al-Fauz al-Aṣghar,* English translation by Khwaja Abdul Hamid under the title *Ibn Maskawaih,* Shaikh Muhammad Ashraf, Lahore, 1946, pp. 7–32.

[4] Cf. Robert Hammond, *The Philosophy of Alfarabi and Its Influence on Medical Thought,* New York, 1947, p. 55, and also D. Salmon, 'The Medieval Latin Translation of Alfarabi's Work,' *New Scholasticism,* 1939, pp. 245–61.

minds attentive and directed towards it and does not explain the concept which is clearer than the words in which it may be defined. At times al-Fārābi identifies *being* with reality in a manner strongly reminiscent of Parmenides.

(b) Division of Being into Necessary and Contingent. Necessary being is that which exists in itself or that which cannot but exist; non-existence of it is unthinkable, e.g. God. *Contingent being* is that which receives its existence from another and the non-existence of which is thinkable or possible, e.g. this world of ours.

(c) Potentiality and Actuality. Potentiality is the capability to exist. Every created being, before it actually came into existence, had only a possibility to exist, i.e., it was in potentiality. *Actuality* is that which exists in fact. According to al-Fārābi, that which is in actuality is perfect and that which is in potentiality is imperfect. Nature as such is both in actuality and potentiality and thus *being* in *becoming*. God alone is pure actuality or act.

(d) Substance and Accident. Substance is that which exists in itself and not in another. *Accident* is that which needs a substance in which and by which it may exist.

(e) Essence and Existence. Essence is the reason why a thing is and what it is; *existence* is the actuality of essence. Thus existence is one thing and essence quite another. If essence and existence were one thing we should be unable to conceive the one without the other. In the case of created beings, we find that essence does not necessarily imply the existence of a thing, for it is possible to think of its essence without knowing whether it exists of not.[5] There is one Being alone whose essence is His very existence and that is God.

The logical separation between essence and existence with regard to all created beings was insisted upon by al-Fārābi to distinguish them from God Who is self-existent and a necessary being and Who is pure actuality and thus perfect. Since there is no dualism in Him of essence and existence, it is proved that He

[5] Separation between essence and existence of things may be more easily explained with reference to mathematical entities such as a triangle, the essence of which is easy to conceive even though it is nowhere fully exemplified in any one of its physical representations.

exists and is an absolute unity.

(f) Matter and Form. Created things are composed of two other principles, viz. matter and form. *Matter* or *hayula* is nothing but a substratum which is indeterminate. It has only the aptitude to become, by virtue of form, this or that body. *Form* is the principle that determines the matter to be actually such and such a body. Matter cannot exist without form, nor form without matter. If either were taken away, there would be no concrete thing at all.

(g) The First Principles. Closely related to the concept of being are the laws of thought called the *first principles.* If the concept of *being* is true, the first principles, likewise, are true. If the concept of *being* is based on reality, so are the first principles which are the laws not only of thought but also of reality. In fact, every first principle implies the fundamental idea of *being*. These principles, according to al-Fārābi, are: (*i*) the principle of contradiction, (*ii*) the principle of excluded middle, and (*iii*) the principle of causality.

With Aristotle, logic is primarily a method to arrive at the truth but with al-Fārābi it is method as well as the truth itself. Al-Fāṛābi presupposes an inseparability between logic and ontology. What is true of thought is true of reality. Thus, unlike Aristotle, al-Fārābi is a thoroughgoing idealist.

(2) *Metaphysical Theology. (a) Can God be Known?* One of the preliminary questions in metaphysical theology which confronted al-Fārābi was whether or not God is knowable.

On this question he could not make up his mind and hesitated to give a definite answer. 'God is knowable and unknowable, evident and hidden, and the best knowledge of Him is to know that He is something that mind cannot thoroughly know' (*Fuṣūṣ al-Ḥikam*).

It is difficult to know what God is, because of the limitations of our intellect. Light is the principle by which colours become visible. It would seem logical to conclude that perfect light produces perfect vision. Instead, the very opposite is the case. A perfect light dazzles the vision. The same is true of God. God is infinitely perfect, and His infinite perfection bewilders our mind. How can the infinitely perfect be comprehended by one who is finite and imperfect?

In spite of his hesitancy with regard to the knowability of God, al-Fārābi insisted that knowledge of God is the object of all philosophy and that it is the duty of man to rise so far as is humanly possible to the likeness of God.

(b) Proofs for the Existence of God. The arguments brought forth by al-Fārābi to prove that there is God are of various forms; three of them are briefly as follows.

(i) The Proof from Motion. In this world there are things which move. Now, every object which is moved receives its motion from a mover. As motion is to be presupposed in the mover itself before it comes to move others there must be another mover to move it and beyond that still another and so on and so forth. It is impossible to go back infinitely in the series of movers and the things moved. Therefore there must be an immovable mover and this is God.

(ii) The Proof from Efficient Causation. In the series of efficient causes it is impossible to conceive an infinite regress of causes. What is not conceivable is not possible; therefore, outside the series of efficient causes, there must be an uncaused efficient cause and this is God.

(iii) The Proof from Contingency. This argument is based on a distinction drawn earlier between necessary beings and contingent beings. A necessary being is that which exists in itself or that which cannot but exist; non-existence of it is unthinkable. Contingent being is that which receives its being from another and whose non-existence is possible. It is, for instance, possible that this world may not have existed or may come not to exist. But as a matter of actuality the world does exist; its existence, therefore, must be due to another being, and cannot be due to its own self. That other being which may be the cause of the existence of this world either is or is not itself contingent. If it is contingent, then it presupposes another being as the cause of its existence. This other cause again may in turn be contingent or not. Now, a series of contingent beings which would produce one another cannot proceed to infinity. Therefore the series of causes and effects must end in a cause that owes its existence to itself. Thus, finally, we come to the necessary being, the non-existence of which is unthinkable and the existence of which is necessarily implied in its very idea. This is

God, the self-existent.[6]

The different arguments as outlined above are in fact so many statements of the same a.gument, i.e., the cosmological argument. (The last of al-Fārābī's arguments, however, is suggestive of being also an ontological one.) In each of his three proofs he starts from a fact, applies a principle and arrives at a conclusion. The facts are respectively motion, caused being and contingency. The principle accordingly is: that which is moved is moved by another; the effect implies a cause; the contingent being implies a necessary being. The conclusion in each case is that God does exist.

(c) Attributes of God. As to the attributes of God, al-Fārābi suggests, like some of the most modern theistic philosophers, that we can have whatever knowledge possible with regard to the nature of God by means of a twofold process.

First, the process of 'exclusion,' by which we remove from the idea of God whatever implies defect or limitation.

Secondly, the process of 'pre-eminence,' by which we attribute to God in an infinite degree all such perfections as we can possibly think of.

With these considerations in mind, al-Fārābi proceeds in a purely logical way to prove that God is one, simple, infinite, immutable, intelligent, living, etc., etc.

Some of these arguments were later reproduced *mutatis mutandis* by Christian scholastics such as Albert the Great and St Thomas Aquinas.

(d) Simplicity of God. God is simple because He is free from every kind of composition, physical or metaphysical. Physical composition may be either substantial or accidental. It is substantial if the composite substance consists of two bodies. Now an infinite being cannot be a substantial composite because this would mean that God the infinite results from the union of finite parts; further that these parts would exist before Him in time and thus be the cause of His being. Nor can an accidental composition be attributed to the infinite because this would imply a capacity for an increase in perfection which the very

[6] For a further account of the distinction between the necessary being and contingent beings and its far-reaching metaphysical implications, see below, chapter on Ibn Sīna.

notion of the infinite excludes. Therefore, there cannot be, and is no, physical composition in God.

Metaphysical composition results from the union of two different concepts so referred to the same real thing that neither one by itself signifies the whole reality as meant by their union. Thus every contingent being is a metaphysical composite of essence and existence. But the composition of essence and existence cannot be applied to the self-existent or infinite being in whom essence and existence are one. Therefore, there is no composition of essence and existence in God. Nor can the composition of genus and differentia be attributed to Him. There is no genus under which it should be possible to subsume Him; He is above all such distinctions and is the ultimate source and ground of all things.

(e) Unity of God. God is only one. If there were two Gods they would have to be partly alike and partly different in which case the simplicity of each would be logically impossible.

If there were anything equal to God, then He would cease to possess the fullness of being for fullness implies impossibility of there being anything besides itself. If God possesses the fullness of being, i.e., is infinite and absolute, then it is impossible to conceive of anything besides Him as other than He. Therefore, there is only one infinite being, only one God.

God is one because He is free from all quantitative divisions. One, in the case of God, means the indivisible; that which is indivisible in substance is one in essence. Hence there is only one God.

(f) Infinity of God. The uncaused being is infinite, for if it were not so, it would be limited and therefore caused, since the cause of a thing is its limit. But God is uncaused; hence it follows that God is unlimited, i.e., is infinite.

(g) Immutability of God. God is the first cause such as is pure actuality without the admixture of potentiality. Everything which is in any way changed is in some way in potentiality. But in God there is no potentiality, for He is pure actuality. Hence there is no change in God. So God is immutable.

(3) *Cosmology.* That God exists is an established truth; that the world exists is a factual truth. The most difficult question which man tries to solve is: What relation is there between God

and the world, between the one and the many? In order to explain the relation of the one with the many, of the unity with the multiplicity, keeping the unity of the one securely intact, al-Fārābi, like al-Kindi, resorted to the principle of emanation of the Neoplatonists. World emanates from God not directly but through a number of intermediary agencies. Between God and the world al-Fārābi places the intellects and the souls of the heavenly spheres of the various planets as enunciated in the Ptolemaic system.[7]

The theory of the intellects and the souls of the spheres as taught by al-Fārābi and some other Muslim philosophers seems very much like a myth to a modern student of philosophy.[8] But Muslim philosophers, one should not forget, were inspired to elaborate this cosmological scheme mainly because of Aristotle's belief that the heavenly spheres possess soul and that they are perfect.

(4) *Rational Psychology.*[9] Man is composed of two principles: body and soul. Body is composed of parts, is limited by space and is measurable and divisible, while soul is beyond such bodily qualities. The former is a product of the created world, while the latter belongs to the last separate intellect of the supersensible world.

The spirituality of the soul is demonstrated by its specific functions which are intellection and volition (moral). The operation of a being is according to the nature of that being. Now, intellect and will at the higher levels feel at home only in the abstract and the spiritual; therefore, the soul itself must also be spiritual and independent of matter.

Immortality of the Soul. Al-Fārābī's views with regard to the immortality of the human soul, like those of Aristotle, are

[7] For a fuller description of al-Fārābī's theory of emanationism, see below, the account given in the chapter on Ibn Sīna.

[8] Al-Ghazāli considers this theory of the intellects and the souls of the spheres to be a mere conjecture and wild guess-work: cf. his *Tahāfut al-Falāsifah*, English translation by S.A. Kamali, Lahore, 1958, p. 77. For al-Ghazāli's bitter criticism of the philosophers' emanationism, see below, chapter on al-Ghazāli.

[9] For an account of al-Fārābī's empirical psychology, see Mu'tazid Wali-ur-Rahman, 'The Psychology of Al-Farabi,' *Islamic Culture*, 1937, pp. 228–47.

rather doubtful.[10] In his works we find passages both for and against immortality. In one place he says: 'The only thing that survives the dissolution of the body is the active intellect.' Now, active intellect with al-Fārābi is something altogether different from the human soul; it is merely an impersonal principle. Hence at best this statement vouchsafes only the possibility of corporate immortality and leaves no scope for personal immortality. This standpoint is confirmed by another passage which reads as follows:

> Man's supreme good in this life is to attain knowledge. But to say that man after death becomes a separate form is an old wives' tale: for whatever is born and dies is incapable of becoming immortal.

Yet there is a curious passage in which al-Fārābi speaks of bliss in the next world. This passage occurs in his famous work *al-Madīnat al-Fāḍilah* (The Ideal City), where he explains that the final aim of the State on earth is to make souls happy in the next world. The souls of the citizens belonging to the ideal city would assemble generation after generation in the next world and their happiness would increase according to increase in their number.[11] This passage assumes that each soul would be endowed with individual feelings in the life hereafter. The assumption is reiterated in other similar passages such as: 'After death the human soul will be unhappy according to its merits or demerits.'[12]

(5) *Political Philosophy*. In political philosophy al-Fārābi wrote two very important books entitled 'A Treatise on the Opinions of the People of the Ideal City' and 'Political Economy.'[13] The first book opens with the Hobbesian descrip-

[10] Aristotle, *Metaphysica,* 1070*a*26; cf. also W.D. Ross, *Aristotle,* London, 1923, pp. 151 *et seq.*

[11] It is interesting to note that al-Fārābi has no doctrine of the torture (*shaqā'*) in life after death but only that of the bliss (*sa'ādah*); cf. F. Rahman, *Prophecy in Islam,* London, 1958, p. 25, note 20.

[12] For a further confirmation of al-Fārābi's belief in personal immortality, see *al-Madīnet al-Fāḍilah,* edited by al-Kurdi, Cairo 1368/1948, p. 64.

[13] That is, *Kitāb Ārā' Ahl al-Madīnat al-Fāḍilah* and *Kitāb al-Siyāsat al-Madanīyyah.* For an account of al-Fārābī's views about political philosophy, see

tion of the law of Nature as one of perpetual struggle of each organism against all the rest; 'every living thing in the last analysis sees in all other living things a means to its own ends' is the principle of the law of Nature, rather the law of the jungle as enunciated by Hobbes. In order to explain the emergence of human society from this law of the jungle al-Fārābi considers two views: one more or less like Rousseau's theory of social contract and the other resembling Nietzsche's principle of 'will to power'. He opposes the Nietzschean view with an appeal to his fellow-men to build a society not upon envy, power and strife, but on reason, devotion and love. With such a society alone there is hope of creating the ideal city of which al-Fārābi gives an elaborate account. Describing the various aspects with regard to the governance of the ideal city he compares it, like Herbert Spencer, with a 'hierarchical organism analogous to human body. The sovereign who corresponds to the heart is served by functionaries who in their turn are served by others of lower ranks'.[14] In this ideal city the object of association is the happiness of its citizens and the sovereign is to be perfect morally and intellectually. Differing from Plato, al-Fārābi regards a philosopher *qua* philosopher to be incompetent to guide the destinies of the citizens of a State until and unless he is also a man with perfect moral character, i.e., is a prophet, or very much like a prophet.[15]

E.I.J. Rosenthal, *Political Thought in Medieval Islam*, Part II, chapter VI, and his article, 'The Place of Politics in the Philosophy of al-Farabi,' *Islamic Culture*, 1955, pp. 157–78; H.K. Sherwani, 'El-Farabi's Political Philosophy,' *Proceedings: Ninth All-India Oriental Conference,* 1937, pp. 337–60, and Dr M. Saghir-ul-Hasan, 'Al-Farabi's Political Philosophy,' [Proceedings of] *Fourth Session, Pakistan Philosophical Congress* (1957), Lahore [1958], pp. 333–40.

[14] Cf. *al-Madīnat al-Fāḍilah,* Cairo, 1368/1948, pp. 53, 54.

[15] Cf. *Siyāsat al-Madanīyyah,* Hyderabad, 1346 H., p. 50.

Chapter Eight

IBN SĪNA

Abu 'Ali al-Ḥusayn ibn 'Abdullah ibn Sīna (370–428/980–1037), generally known as Ibn Sīna or Avicenna (a Latin distortion from Hebrew—Aven Sina), was an encylopedist, philosopher, physiologist, physician, mathematician, astronomer and poet. According to George Sarton, he is the most famous scientist and philosopher of Islam and one of the greatest of all races, places and times.[1] It is admitted on all hands that his thought represents the climax of Arabian philosophy; he is called by the Arabs *al-Shaykh al-Ra'īs*, i.e., 'the shaykh and prince of the learned'.

Some of the most important of his philosophical views may be summed up under the following three heads: (1) Logic, (2) Psychology, and (3) Metaphysics.

(1) *Logic*. Ibn Sīna develops his logical views more or less on the model of al-Fārābī's commentary on the logical *Organon* of Aristotle.[2] We find his logic mostly in some parts of the philosophical compendium entitled *al-Najāt* and in some important passages in another work called *al-Ishārāt*. In a small but important monograph on 'Classification of Sciences'[3] Ibn Sīna subdivides the science of logic into nine different parts which correspond practically to the eight books of Aristotle preceded by Porphyry's *Isagoge*, i.e., Introduction, one of the best known

[1] *Introduction to the History of Science*, Baltimore, 1927, Vol I, p. 709; cf. also V. Courtois, 'Avicenna, the Prince of the Learned,' *Indo-Iranica*, 1952–53, Vol. VI, No. 3, pp. 46–53.

[2] For an account of al-Fārābī's logic in English, see H. Blumberg, 'Al-Farabi's Five Chapters on Logic,' *Proceedings of the American Academy for Jewish Research*, 1934–5, pp. 115–21; also D.M. Dunlop, 'Al-Farabi's Introductory Sections on Logic,' *Islamic Quarterly*, 1955, pp. 264–82.

[3] See 'Fi Aqsām al-'Ulūm al-'Aqlīyyah' in *Tis' Rasā'il fi al-Ḥikmah w-al-Ṭab'īyyat*, Cairo, 1326/1908, pp. 104–9. A similar classification had already been given by al-Fārābi in his *Kitāb Iḥsā' al-'Ulūm* which seems now to have been lost in the original Arabic.

works of the Oriental middle ages.

The first part, corresponding to the *Isagoge*, is a kind of general philosophy of language which deals with terms of speech and their abstract elements, The second deals with simple and abstract ideas, applicable to all beings, and is called by Aristotle the *Categories*, i.e., *al-Māqūlāt*. The third deals with the combination of simple ideas in order to form the propositions named by Aristotle as *Hermeneutica* and by Muslim philosophers as *al-'Ibārah* or *al-Tafsīr*. The fourth combines the propositions in the different forms of syllogisms and is the subject-matter of Aristotle's *First Analytics*, i.e., *al-Qiyās*. The fifth discusses the conditions to be fulfilled by the premisses from which the subsequent chain of reasoning proceeds and is called the *Second Analytics*, i.e., *al-Burhān*. The sixth considers the nature and limitations of probable reasoning which corresponds to Aristotle's *Topics*, i.e., *al-Jaḍl*. The seventh brings out the fallacies of logical reasoning, intentional or otherwise, and is the *Sophisticii* or *al-Maghālīṭ*. The eighth describes the art of persuasion through oratorical devices and is the *Rhetoric* or *al-Khaṭābah*. The ninth and the last part explains the fine art of stirring the soul and the imagination of the audience through the magic of words. It is the *Al-Shi'r* or the *Poetics* of Aristotle considered by Muslim philosophers to be a part of his logical *Organon*.

Logic is taken by Ibn Sīna in a very broad sense; syllogistic logic is considered by him only a part of it. Although Ibn Sīna gives logic a very important place among the sciences, he does at the same time recognize its limitations. Its function, he explains very clearly, is in greater measure only negative. 'The aim of logic,' he says in his book *al-Ishārāt*, 'is to provide us with some rules the observance of which would be a safeguard against falling into errors in our reasoning.'[4] Thus logic, strictly speaking, does not discover new truths but helps us make the best use of those we already possess and prevents us from making wrong use of them.

Reasoning, according to Ibn Sīna, starts from certain terms which have to be accepted at the outset. These are the first data of experience or the first principles of understanding. The chain

[4] See *Kitāb Ishārāt w-al-Tanbīhat*, edited by J. Forget, Leiden, 1892. p. 2.

of deductions proceeding by the known, deduced from the previously known, is not unlimited; it must have its starting point which would be the base of the whole fabric of logical structure. This starting point is to be found not in logic itself but outside it.

This clearly indicates that logic as such is merely a formal system, neither true nor false; the truth-content of that system comes not from within but from without, i.e., from the first data of experience.

Descriptions or definitions are formed first from direct experiences or ideas and then arranged by means of these arguments. Interestingly enough, Ibn Sīna suggests a pragmatic justification of both definitions and arguments: by definition a man is enabled to represent objects and by arguments he is enabled to persuade.

Ibn Sīna gives both experience and reason a share in the formation and growth of the data of the scientist. With regard to our knowledge in general there develop certain primary beliefs which all people hold because of common feelings, or because of the opinion of the learned which the uneducated dare not contradict. Others again arise from habits formed in childhood and still others are based on the experiences of life. All these primary beliefs join with the first principles of reasoning which are produced in man by his intellectual faculty without requiring the slightest conscious effort to persuade him of their truth. So far as these first principles are concerned, the mind feels itself convinced of their validity and is not even aware of how the conviction has arisen. This is true, for example, of the mathematical axioms such as, for instance, the whole is greater than the part, or of the laws of thought, such as A cannot be both B and not-B at the same time. The eminent French Orientalist Carra de Vaux holds that Ibn Sīnā's logic is open and sincere, at many places recalling the analysis of Leibnitz.[5]

While discussing the form and matter of definitions and arguments, Ibn Sīna distinguishes between definition and description and sums up, in the manner of the Peripatetics, the different kinds of questions that arise in science; first of all, what a thing is, and if it is, how it is; next, where it is, and,

[5] Article, 'Avicenna,' in *Encylopaedia of Religion and Ethics*, Vol. II, p. 274.

lastly, why it is. This is the application of the Aristotelian categories to the knowledge of the phenomenal world. It is interesting to note that for Ibn Sīna, as for Kant in modern times, the categories of thought are primarily subjective in nature.

Ibn Sīna, following Aristotle, recognizes four causes, —material, formal, efficient and final. He shows that they may all appear together in a definition. Thus a knife may be defined as an iron implement of such and such a shape made by the ironsmith for cutting things. Ibn Sīna also explains the various predicables, viz. genus, species, difference, property and common accidents, with the help of which we have another method for the formulation of definitions.

The sciences are based on experiences and reasonings; they have objects, questions and premisses. There are universal premisses but in addition each science has its own peculiar premisses. Different sciences establish a hierarchy according to the dignity of their subject-matter, the more abstract being on the top. Logic has a certain likeness to mathematics in so far as the subject of mathematics may also be abstractions from matter, yet, according to Ibn Sīna, the mathematical sciences are capable of being represented by the senses and constructed by imagination, while the logical sciences have their existence only in pure intellection. Hence the logical sciences are more formal than those of mathematics and thus higher than the latter.

(2) *Psychology*. Ibn Sīnā's psychology gives a carefully systematised account of the various kinds of minds and their faculties. These have been classified methodically according to a hierarchic arrangement. The general plan of this grand construction is as follows.[6]

According to Ibn Sīna, there are three kinds of minds: (*a*) the vegetable mind, (*b*) the animal mind, and (*c*) the reasonable or the human mind.

(*a*) The vegetable mind possesses three faculties: (*i*) nutritive power; (*ii*) power of growth; (*iii*) power of reproduction.

[6] For a full account of Ibn Sīnā's psychology in English, see F. Rahman, *Avicenna's Psychology*, London, 1952; cf. also Mutazid Wali-ur-Rahman, 'The Psychology of Ibn Sina,' *Islamic Culture*, 1935, pp. 335–58.

(*i*) Nutritive power which when resident in a body changes another body into the form of the first.

(*ii*) The power of growth by which the body itself continues to increase without changing its form till it attains full maturity.

(*iii*) The power of reproduction which draws from the body a part similar to itself in potentiality, capable of producing other bodies similar to it in actuality.

(*b*) The animal mind possesses two kinds of faculties: (*i*) motive faculties and (*ii*) perceptive or cognitive faculties.

(*i*) The motive faculties include appetitive powers and efficient powers. The appetitive power is itself either attractive or repulsive. If attractive, it is simply desire, and if repulsive it is irascibility. The efficient powers which are the producers of bodily movements reside in the motor-nerves and the muscles.

(*ii*) The perceptive or cognitive faculties of the animal mind are classified as external and internal. The former include the five senses: sight, hearing, smell, taste and touch. The latter have their beginning in common sense, a sort of centre in which all the perceptions assemble before being elaborated by the higher faculties. The common sense is situated in the front part of the brain. The first faculty to act on the perception is the formative faculty or imagination situated in the middle part of the brain. Imagination frees the sensible percepts from the conditions of place, time and magnitude, and enables the mind to have images of objects even after they cease to make impressions on the senses.

The formative faculty is followed by the cogitative faculty which abstracts the common elements from the percept and images and forms conceptual notions out of these.

The estimative faculty next on the list groups these notions into what might be called judgements. These judgements are characterised by Ibn Sīna as instinctive rather than intellectual. It is the estimative faculty which constitutes animal intelligence, e.g. the sheep knows by this faculty to flee from the wolf. The last of the faculties in the animal mind is memory which is situated in the hind part of the brain.

(*c*) The human mind alone possesses reason. Reason or 'intelligence' is considered by Ibn Sīna to be of two kinds more or less on the Kantian lines, namely, the practical reason and the theoretical reason. The practical reason or the active intelligence is that on which morality depends. The theoretical reason or speculative intelligence is that which enables us to have abstract thinking.

Ibn Sīnā's entire psychological construction may be represented by the following map.

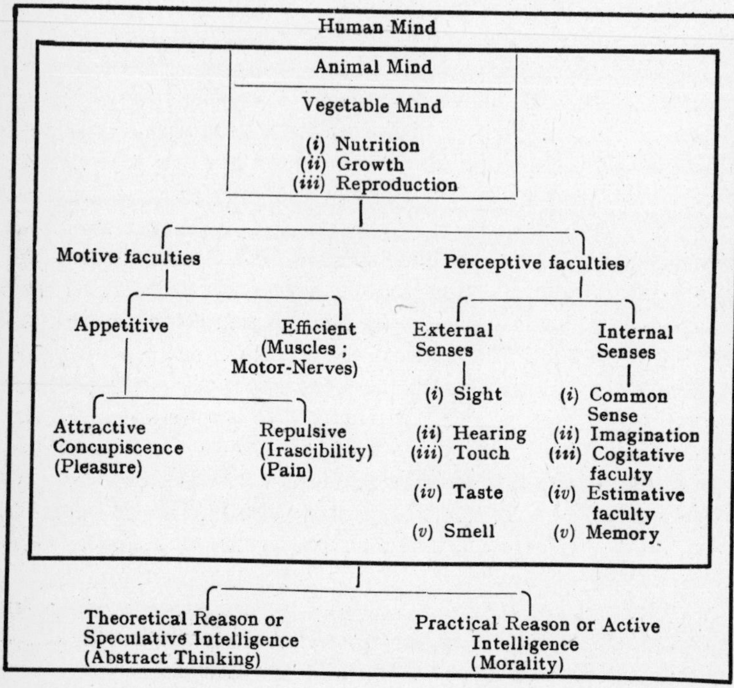

(3) *Metaphysics.* There is a part of Ibn Sīnā's metaphysics which seems quite old-fashioned now. In it he talks of a number of intelligences and the souls of planetary spheres emanating from God in a hierarchical order. It is unfortunate that de Boer and O'Leary give a larger place to this outmoded part of the philosophies of Ibn Sīna and al-Fārābi[7] than they give to that

[7] Cf. T.J. de Boer, *The History of Philosophy in Islam*, London, 1933, pp. 115–8, 136–43; De Lacy O'Leary, *Arabic Thought and Its Place in History*, London, 1922, pp. 152–6, 178–9.

part which may be interpreted in modern terms.

The theory of emanationism, as conceived by Muslim philosophers in general, works under two governing principles. First, from God Who is a pure unity it is not thinkable that anything should proceed from Him except that which is itself a unity; from one only one can follow. Secondly, being has two aspects—it is either necessary or possible, it is either essence or existence. In the case of God alone essence and existence are found together; in all other beings essence is separate from existence. From this it follows that all real beings are possible by their essence, and they become necessary by the existence given to them by God.

The first emanation from the Necessary Being is numerically one; it is the first intelligence. In one aspect its existence is possible in itself and in another necessary through the First Being; it knows its own essence as well as the essence of the First Being. It has a twofold existence, possible and necessary, and is the spring of multiplicity, for it has three kinds of 'knowledge': of the First Being, of its own essence in so far as it is necessary, and of its being as possible. Thus from the first intelligence emanate three beings: the second intelligence, the first soul, and the first sphere of the fixed stars. From the second intelligence emanates another intelligence, a second heavenly sphere and its soul. Now, according to the Ptolemaic system, besides the sphere of the fixed stars, there are only eight planetary spheres which rotate in concentric circles with earth in the centre. So, starting from the First Being the emanations proceed till the last or the tenth intelligence appears and with it the ninth sphere of the moon and its soul.[8] This tenth intelligence, also called the active intelligence, which is in the lowest sphere, acts in our world. It produces the first matter (*hayula*) which is passive and formless, but which is the basis of the four

[8] The nine spheres in the graded order are: (1) the sphere of the *primum mobile*; (2) the sphere of the fixed stars; (3) the sphere of Saturn; (4) the sphere of Jupiter; (5) the sphere of Mars; (6) the sphere of the Sun; (7) the sphere of Venus; (8) the sphere of Mercury and (9) the sphere of the Moon. It may be noted that, according to modern astronomy with its heliocentric view, the order of the planets, nine in all, according to their increasing distances from the Sun is: Mercury, Venus, Earth, Mars, Jupiter, Saturn, Uranus, Neptune and Pluto; the Moon is not a separate planet but is merely a satellite of the Earth.

elements from which all creatures are made. The composition and decomposition of the elements is the cause of the generation and dissolution of all bodies. The tenth intelligence, as it is the producer of matter, is the dispenser of forms (*wāhib al-suwar*). It gives to each matter its proper form and it also gives each body a soul, which in fact is its form, when that body is ready to receive it. Thus the last intelligence is also the cause of the existence of the human soul. But the human soul does not feel at home in its present abode and yearns for nothing less than the First Being itself. Hence it starts its spiritual journey back to the original source traversing the various stages of intelligences of the spheres.

This cosmological scheme comprising the intelligences and souls of the heavenly spheres has got its own historical justification at that stage of the development of thought at which we find Ibn Sīna, al-Fārābi and other Muslim philosophers struggling to build up their philosophical world-views. It cannot be overemphasised that the whole theory is more a borrowed one than an original product of the Muslim mind. Some of the reasons for making this kind of cosmological standpoint current in Muslim philosophy may be given as follows.

(*i*) The view which explains the origin of the world as a creation of God through an act of volition is full of difficulties of its own. The notion of creation necessarily implies change in the being of God and leads us to the problem of reconciling the change in God with His perfection and absoluteness. Secondly, will implies deficiency in the Divine being; for it means that He desires or wants to have that which He lacks. Thirdly, this world is a multiplicity, i.e., full of diverse elements; how can multiplicity originate from God Who is pure unity?

(*ii*) The theory of emanation of the Neoplatonists which explains the origin of the world as a necessary outflow from the being of God like the rays of light from the sun or, better, the properties of a triangle from a triangle[9] is apparently not open

[9] This is how Spinoza later conceived of emanation as an eternal process: 'From the infinite nature of God all things . . . follow by the necessity, and in the same way, as it follows from the nature of a triangle, from eternity to eternity that its three angles are equal to two right angles' (*Ethics*, Part I, Section 17, note). The influence of Arabic philosophy on Spinoza through the Jewish

to the aforementioned objections.

(*iii*) The world, however, is not to be conceived as a direct outflow from the being of God; that would be too crude a notion philosophically and even more so religiously. Could this mundane world of ours with all its sordidness be a direct emanation from God Who is pure spirit, nay, something unwordable and unspeakable? This is not at all the teaching of the theory of emanation as stated above. Between God on the one hand and the world on the other the theory contrives to interpolate a finely-graded series of intermediate spiritual agencies: the one next to God is more like God and the one immediately before the world more like the world. The elaborate scheming of a number of intelligences and souls greatly adds to the plausibility of this grand construction. It is quite easy and even fascinating to conceive of the various intelligences and souls in terms of angels as described by the theologians. The Muslim version of emanationism further brings comfort to the so-called logical demand that from God, Who is one, only one can follow: an axiom supposedly made current by Ibn Sīna.

(*iv*) The reason for a definite number of celestial spheres and their souls lies in the astronomical system of Ptolemy then current. According to Ptolemaic cosmogony, the earth is surrounded by nine concentric spheres like the peels of an onion; eight of these are the planetary spheres and the ninth is the sphere of the fixed stars.

(*v*) The view that the celestial spheres, i.e., stars and the planets, are perfect and have souls or intelligences superior to those of men had the overwhelming authority of Aristotle.[10] Belief in the perfection of the celestial bodies continued to remain unquestioned till the time of Galileo when the spots in

sources is now more or less an established fact; cf. article 'Spinoza' in the *Encyclopaedia Britannica*, 14th edition. For the influence of the Ibn Sīna on Jewish thinkers in particular including Spinoza, see E.I.J. Rosenthal, 'Avicenna's Influence on Jewish Thought,' in *Avicenna: Scientist and Philosopher*, edited by G.M. Wickens, London, 1952, chapter IV.

[10] Cf. Aristotle, *De Caelo*, 285 ^{a}29, ^{b}292 ^{a}20, ^{b}1, and *Metaphysica*, 1073 ^{a}26-^{b}1. For the Aristotelian ingredients in the theory of emanationism, cf. W.D. Ross, *Aristotle*, London, 1923, pp. 161 *et seq.*; A.E. Taylor, *Aristotle*, London, 1943, pp. 98 *et seq.*, and A.H. Armstrong, *The Architecture of the Intelligible Universe in the Philosophy of Plotinus*, Cambridge, 1940, by index.

the moon were discovered for the first time.

Criticism. In spite of so many reasons advanced above for the justification of emanationism, the theory in the final analysis remains untenable. It is perhaps no more than a philosophical myth. Ibn Sīna, al-Fārābi and other Muslim and Neoplatonic philosophers start with the proposition 'from one only one can emanate,' but when, descending from the planetary spheres, the last of which is the sphere of the moon, they come to what is variously called the soul of the world, the active intelligence, or the active intellect, they completely disregard the principle with which they started, viz. from one only one can follow. The active intelligence, according to them, leads not to the emanation of one but of a whole multiplicity, for all the human souls and the four elements are supposed to have emanated from the active intelligence. Further, at this stage of the series the process of descending is suddenly changed into that of ascending for reasons known only to the exponents of the theory. It is from the four elements that the whole world is supposed to have been evolved. The human souls in particular have an overwhelming yearning to go back to the original source, i.e., to the active intelligence, and thence to God.

As a matter of fact, the principle that from one only one can follow breaks down at the very outset. The first intelligence which emanates from God, according to this theory, is not pure unity; this intelligence knows itself and knows God at the same time. From this double knowledge arises a duality. This duality changes into triplicity and so on and so forth. Still, the Muslim Peripatetic philosophers and the Neoplatonists both do readily grant that the first intelligence which is the first emanation from God is not God Himself; its being is different from the being of God. One may argue that if after all it has to be different from God, then the principle—from one only one can follow—becomes nonsensical. If from one can follow another one which is different from its author, the emanationistic principle that only one follows from one, so glibly repeated, cannot be logically different from the principle of creation. One wishes that such a critical view of the theory could have been taken by the Muslim philosophers right from the outset. In that case the very grounds for the importation of the Neoplatonic series of emanation and the intelligences of the heavenly spheres would have ceased to exist. Unfortunately we find the tedious repetition of the theory in the philosphical systems of almost all the Muslim philosophers.[11]

Ibn Sīna and Modern Philosophy. Contemporary research in the philosophical thought of Ibn Sīna has brought to light some very significant aspects of his metaphysics. Professor J.L. Teicher of Cambridge University, for one, is of the opinion that in Ibn Sīnā's speculative system we come across clear anticipations of some of the foremost views of Descartes, Kant and even those of Bergson[12], only Ibn Sīnā's philosophical terminology, according to him, is somewhat foreign to a modern student of philosophy. Descartes is certainly forestalled by Ibn Sīna in his (1) methodological doubt, (2) the certitude of 'I think; therefore I am', and (3) the ontological and cosmological arguments for the existence of God. So far as the views of Kant are concerned, we meet in Ibn Sīna not only a well-marked distinction between theoretical and practical reason as mentioned above (see last section: Psychology), but also a clear-cut statement of the Antinomies of Pure Reason. Though certainly we are given in Ibn Sīna glimpses of the Bergsonian doctrines of intuition and creative evolution, yet to establish much closer parallels between the two philosophers more research is needed than has perhaps been done so far.

Ibn Sīna and Descartes. In Ibn Sīna we meet at the outset a pivotal distinction which is very important in the history of religio-philosophical thought and which is claimed to have originated with him, certainly in the form in which he expounded it. It is the distinction between the necessary being and the possible being. The necessary being is that the non-existence of which it is impossible to think, whereas the possible being may or may not exist or the existence of which may be otherwise than what it is. Ibn Sīna observes that without violating any principle of logic we can think that all beings in the world taken collectively or individually may not have existed. The exper-

[11] Al-Ghazāli and Ibn Khaldūn are the notable exceptions; for their bitter criticism of emanationism, see below, pp. 135–6, 192–3.

[12] Cf. G.M. Wickens, (Ed.), op. cit., chapter II, 'Avicenna's Place in Arabic Philosophy.'

iment of thought that abolishes in mind the existence of one or all beings in the world involves no logical contradiction whatsoever. Hence it is evident that all beings in the world or the world as a whole, when considered by itself, have the status merely of the possible. The possibility or the contingency of the existence of the world necessarily presupposes the existence of the necessary being.

What Ibn Sīna insists is that we possess an intuitive apprehension of the reality of the necessary being. It dawns upon us with such a sense of immediacy and directness as makes it impossible for us not to have a keen realization of the fact of its objective existence. To think concretely of the non-existence of the necessary being is as impossible as to think concretely of the existence of square circles or married bachelors. (The examples are not those of Ibn Sīna but this is exactly what he means to say.) It is most important to note that Ibn Sīna does not affirm the existence of the necessary being merely as the terminus of the usual cosmological argument. He does not merely argue that the existence of the necessary being must needs be postulated in order to avoid the infinite regress or circularity of causes and effects. Many subsequent philosophers including some modern European rationalists have expounded the notion of the necessary being merely as the end-product of an abstract process of reasoning which exposes their argument to the fallacy of ontologism. But such is not the case with Ibn Sīna; the main thrust of his argument is that the necessary being is the object of our direct intuition. He emphasises that the existence of the necessary being cannot be proved or argued about. It can only be intuited in our own person; to others, it can only be referred to or expressed indirectly.

If we should now forget Ibn Sīnā's philosophical terminology and mode of exposition and try to recapture in our mind the actual process of thought underlying his statement in its existential actuality, we may find to our surprise that we are performing a thought-experiment claimed to have been first performed in modern times by Descartes through his famous methodological doubt. Does not Descartes' methodological doubt really amount to an attempt at contemplating the possibility that the beings in the world may not exist, i.e., they may only be possible and not necessary? Does not Descartes, pursuing his doubt persistently, come at the end to an intuitive notion of himself as a thinking being? Does he not perceive immediately that it is impossible for him to entertain the thought that his thinking may not exist, for to think that thinking may not exist is as much thinking as any? Finally, does not Descartes, probing deeper into the notion of himself as a thinking substance, discover that his own finite existence is due ultimately to God Whose disdaining to deceive us is the only guarantee of the truth of our belief in the existence of the external world?

Ibn Sīnā's conception of the necessary being and the being possible, which latter becomes necessarily existent only through its association with the former, anticipates all the three important notions of Descartes' philosophy, namely, the methodological doubt, the intuitive certitude of *cogito ergo sum*, and the idea of God as a necessary ground of the reality of all beings.

The Cartesian form of the ontological argument for the existence of God briefly runs as follows. To say that an attribute is contained in the concept of a thing is the same as to say that the attribute is true of that thing. Now since necessary existence is contained in the very concept of God it may be truly affirmed of Him: in other words, God exists. Descartes, like Ibn Sīna, supplements his ontological argument with the cosmological one, though the language of the two is different. According to Descartes, nothing can come out of nothing; whatever exists must have a cause for its existence. Moreover, there must be as much reality in cause as there is in effect. Now, in our thoughts we certainly have a constant reference to the idea of a perfect and infinite being. We cannot be the cause of this idea, for we are finite and imperfect. Nor can Nature be the cause of it, for Nature exhibits nothing but change, and is thus imperfect and relative. Corresponding to the idea of the perfect, therefore, there must be a cause which must have as much perfection in it as there is in the effect and this is God, the Perfect and the Absolute. In Ibn Sīna too we find a cosmological argument which is based mainly, like Descartes', on the unthinkability of something coming out of nothing as well as like Aristotle's, on the impossibility of the infinite regression of causes. The cosmological and the ontological arguments of Descartes are open to very serious objections; every student of philosophy is familiar with the treatment meted out to them by Kant. Though Ibn Sīnā's cosmological argument is similarly not defensible, his ontological argument is not exposed to Kantian criticism. It is because Ibn Sīnā's ontological argument in its innermost intention is not a rational argument like Descartes'. It is essentially rooted in an intuitive, almost mystical, encounter with the ultimate reality.

It may be added that Ibn Sīna comes very close to propounding Descartes' dictum: *Cogito ergo sum,* not only in his metaphysics proper but also in his psychology. It is where he makes clear the distinction between body and mind and emphasises the complete independence of the latter from the former. He invites our attention to an experimental situation: 'Imagine a man full-grown and in perfect bodily state created all at once. His eyes however have been so screened that he is unable to see any external thing. Imagine further that this man is lifted in the air in some such special manner that he does not have any sensation at all, not even of the touch and friction of the air. Imagine, in short, a man without any sensations whatsoever, even of his own body.' Such a man, Ibn Sīna maintains, would nevertheless be able 'to reflect upon himself and assert with absolute certainty that he himself exists, although he is unable to prove the existence of his own body or of any other external object'.

Ibn Sīna and Kant. Taking Ibn Sīnā's metaphysics and physics together we find the following problems to be the very nuclei of his thought-system. In fact they are the central problems of the speculative systems of the majority of Muslim philosophers and scholastics:

(1) Eternity (*qidām*) and createdness (*ḥuduth*) of the world or infinity and finitude of time and thereby also of space.
(2) Indivisibility and the possibility of infinite divisibility of the material particles.
(3) Infinite regress of causes and the first causeless cause.
(4) Contingency or possibility and necessity of the existence of the phenomenal world.

It does not require much of an effort to jump from the above-mentioned problems to what Kant has described as the Antinomies of Pure Reason. A comparison between the four antinomies of pure reason as formulated by Kant and the four problems as stated above certainly makes a very stimulating and refreshing study.

The first antinomy as expressed by Kant runs as follows: Universe must be conceived either as infinite or finite, both with regard to time and space. In case we consider time to be infinite, then an infinite past has been brought to an end at the present moment. But a past that has been brought to an end has to be regarded as finite. Yet it remains true that it is hard to think of a definite beginning of time at a specific moment in the past which should not have been preceded by another moment before it. The universe thus has to be conceived as having a past which is both finite and infinite.

As to the spatial infinity of the universe, we must admit that for the universe to be spatially infinite it is necessary for it to be temporally infinite as well, for an infinite space is a space that takes infinite time to traverse. The conception of an infinite space is thus involved in the conception of infinite time, which is contradicted by that of finite time.

The second antinomy of Kant confronts us with Zeno's dilemma that matter is either infinitely divisible or is composed of indivisibles, i.e., unextended parts. We cannot possibly imagine a particle of matter, however small, that would not have an upside and a downside and a right and a left, so as not to be further divisible. Therefore, all matter must be composite and infinitely divisible. But if every particle of matter were to be infinitely divisible it ultimately would have to be simple and unextended, whereas it is impossible to conceive of extended bodies composed of unextended parts even if they were infinite in number.

The third antinomy has to do with causation. On the one hand, it is impossible to conceive of any first causeless cause in the chain of causes and effects since it questions the very initial assumption of causation that every event has a cause and no event is without it. On the other hand, it is equally impossible to think of an infinite regress of causes which starts nowhere.

The fourth antimony shows that there must be some necessity for the existence and the particular nature of the phenomenal world. For the presence rather than the absence of this kind of world there must be some compelling reason. This reason, since there can be no reason for its being otherwise, must be what it is. On the other hand, it can be maintained that any particular event in the world taken singly is contingent in the sense that it is possible to think of its having been otherwise than what it is. Now, just as any particular event need not logically be what it is, for it might be otherwise, so the totality of events, which indeed the world is, might logically be different from what it is, i.e., is possible. Thus for equally good reasons the world must have both a reason and no reason for existence, and for being what it is; so it is both necessary and possible.

The antinomies of pure reason with their theses and antitheses thus present various dilemmas which are difficult to escape from. They pose certain impossible problems the solutions of which require all the sophisticated ingenuity of a philospher. Ibn Sīnā's various positions with regard to these antinomies may be briefly summed up as follows.

(1) The world is both eternal and created. This is how Ibn Sīna tries to meet the claims both of Aristotelian philosophy and religious dogma.

(2) As to the second antimony, whether bodies are infinitely divisible or otherwise, he takes the side of thesis rather than antithesis and admits that bodies are divisible *in potentia* to infinity. This standpoint of Ibn Sīna was taken mostly in opposition to the atomism of the Ash'arites and others.

(3) The chain of causation, according to Ibn Sīna, cannot be traced back indefinitely. It must have its start in the First Causeless Cause, i.e., God Who is a Necessary Being.

(4) As to the fourth antinomy, he holds that the world is both possible and necessary.

Apparently the above views of Ibn Sīna are vulnerable and precarious. His positions with regard to the second and third antinomies are definitive and dogmatic and hence indefensible from the point of view of the opposite camp; those with regard to the first and fourth antinomies are ambiguous and self-contradictory. It is interesting to note that Ibn Sīnā's ambiguous and self-contradictory statements when explicated carefully and with understanding lead to very significant philosophical disclosures.

The world is both created and eternal. Ibn Sīnā's notion of 'createdness' here is intimately bound up with his notions of the possible being and the being necessary of itself. The world is created just because it is both possible and necessary: it is possible by itself, but becomes necessary through its connection with the necessary being. Between the two apparently disparate entities, viz. what is necessary by itself and what is possible by itself becoming necessary through its association with the necessary being, there is an intervening process commonly called creation. The notion of the beings 'possible-in-themselves' certainly conveys the clear idea that they are not mechanically and necessarily determined by antecedent causes, otherwise there would be no meaning in calling them possible. The possible beings cannot be regarded as fixed or predetermined possibilities and must be conceived as open and real possibilities with an element of 'contingency at the heart of things' in the sense in which James Ward has used this phrase. Yet, curiously enough, these possible beings are nevertheless considered by Ibn Sīna to be determined since their existence indeed is the effect of the necessary being. They are creations brought into existence through a process and for a reason that was absolutely necessary. We must recall that the two seemingly contradictory predicates, possible and necessary, are present in every temporal process, more precisely in every process of creative evolution in the Bergsonian sense. In such a process new events emerge which are possible in themselves, i.e., are contingent in the diction of Ibn Sīna or Ward, and yet necessitated by the whole process of evolution itself.

A very crucial question arises here. Is this process of creation conscious and voluntary and, thus, direct, i.e., does it involve a sudden jump of something from nothing? In short, is *creatio ex nihilo* as understood by the theologians and scholastics possible? There is no uncertainty about Ibn Sīnā's answer to this most vexing question. His philosophical intuition envisages the necessary being and the beings possible in themselves through a single indivisible act in which reality reveals itself as undergoing a process of 'evolution' of the possible beings from the necessary being. This process of 'evolution' takes place necessarily (not consciously or voluntarily) and continuously and successively (not suddenly and directly) through finely-graded stages of emanation proceeding from the supremely necessary being, i.e., God Who is the First Causeless Cause.

Since creation means here the necessary emanation of the possible being from the being necessary by itself, it is with Ibn Sīna a process beyond time in the sense that the category of time does not apply to it. Hence the world is eternal. Both God and the world are eternal: there arises no question of the temporal priority of the one over the other in the super-celestial realm of the divine, for time yet was not. The divine time indeed is that in which the entire sweep of emanations regarded as an ordered string of specific events is contained in a single super-eternal now. Time from the human point of view, according to Ibn Sīna, much like Leibnitz, later appears only as a phenomenon related to the external aspects of events.

God has, however, the logical priority over the world, for He is the ground and the necessary reason for the existence of the world and is the underlying cause of its becoming what it is, has been, and will be. Though the world is thus lower in essence and rank, yet as it is now in its determinate form and nature, it is necessary to God. To ask the question whether another world with a different nature would not have been possible is to ask something from the present point of view for which we have no justification, since our notion of the possible emerges from our knowledge of the actual which is actually prior. Thus Ibn Sīna maintains, much like Pringle-Pattison and Whitehead in our own times, that whereas God is certainly necessary to the being of the universe, the universe too, despite its being just one possibility out of God's infinite possibilities, is necessary to the being of God.

Chapter Nine

AL-GHAZĀLI

With Abu Hāmid ibn Muḥammad al-Ghazāli (450-505/1058-1111) we come to one of the greatest and most original thinkers, not only in the history of Muslim philosophy, but also in the history of human thought. He is called 'Islam's convincing proof,' 'the ornament of faith,' considered a *mujaddid* and reckoned equal in rank with the four Imāms. There have been many philosophers and scholars in Islam and other religions, but the peculiarity of al-Ghazāli is that his life and work are so intimately connected that it is difficult to separate one from the other. According to MacDonald, he is the equal of Augustine in the philosophical and theological disciplines; by his side the Aristotelian philosophers of Islam seem beggarly compilers and scholiasts; only al-Fārābi—and he too by virtue of his mysticism—approaches him with some degree of closeness.[1]

We find al-Ghazāli forestalling Descartes' method of doubt, Hume's scepticism, Kant's criticism of pure reason, and the spiritual empiricism of some of the philosophers of religion of our own times.

Al-Ghazāli and Descartes. Like Descartes, al-Ghazāli was by nature inquisitive and restless from the very beginning and filled with an intense desire for truth. He himself narrates the story of his spiritual struggle as follows:

The thirst for knowledge was innate in me from an early age: it was like a second nature implanted in me by God.... No sooner had I emerged from my boyhood than I had already broken the fetters of tradition and authority and freed myself from hereditary beliefs.... The diversity in beliefs and religions and the variety of doctrines in the sects which divide men

[1] D.B. MacDonald, *Development of Muslim Theology, Jurisprudence and Constitutional Theory*, London, 1903, p. 215.

are like a vast ocean strewn with shipwrecks.... Each sect believes itself to be exclusively in possession of truth and of salvation.... From the period of adolescence I have again and again plunged myself into this vast ocean.... Struck with the contradictions which I encountered in endeavouring to disentangle the truth and falsity of these opinions, I was led to make the following reflection:

The search after truth being the aim which I propose to myself, I ought in the first place to ascertain what are the foundations of certitude. In the next place I ought to recognize that certitude is the clear and complete knowledge of things such as leaves no room for doubt nor possibility of error...[2]

Al-Ghazāli examined the sum total of the knowledge that he had acquired hitherto and found that none of it could stand the test proposed by him. He says: 'We cannot hope to find truth except in matters which carry their evidence in themselves, i.e., in sense-perception and in infallible and necessary principles of thought. We must, therefore, first of all establish these two on a firm basis.'

But he doubted the evidence of sense-perception; he could see plainly, as Descartes did later, that the senses often deceive us. 'No eye can perceive the movement of a shadow, but still the shadow moves; a gold piece would cover any star, but a star is a world larger than the earth.'

The data given by sense-experience can be contradicted and convicted of falsity in an indisputable manner by the verdict of reason. Al-Ghazāli's confidence in sense-data having been shaken, he turned towards the scrutiny of what he called the necessary principles, but he doubted even these. According to al-Ghazāli, in spite of his great respect for mathematics and formal logic, it is not possible to guarantee absolutely the truth of mathematical axioms and laws of logic. Is ten more than

[2] Cf. *al-Munqidh min al-Ḍalāl,* English translation by Claud Field, *The Confessions of al-Ghazali,* London, 1909, pp. 12–4, *ad passim.* This is precisely the first of the four rules laid down by Descartes in his *Discours de la méthode* and the second rule of his *Regulae ad Directionem Ingenii.* Cf. *The Philosophical Works of Descartes,* translated by E.S. Haldane and G.R.T. Ross, Cambridge, 1911, Vol. I, pp. 3, 92, 101.

three? Can a thing be and not-be at the same time? Perhaps he could not tell. His senses have sometimes deceived him, why should not his reason? His doubt with regard to sense-perception made him very hesitant to accept the infallibility of reason. He believed in the testimony of the senses till it was contradicted by the verdict of reason. 'Well,' says al-Ghazāli, 'perhaps there is above reason another judge who if he appeared would convict reason of falsity and if such a third arbiter is not yet apparent, it does not follow that he does not exist.'

Al-Ghazāli could not find a way out of this doubt and his experience of the phenomenon of dreaming deepened it yet the more. 'While asleep you assume your dreams to be indisputably true; once awake you recognize them for what they are, i.e., baseless chimeras. Who can assure you then of the reliability of the notions which when awake you derive from the senses and from reason? In relation to your present state they may appear real but is it not possible that you should enter upon another state which will bear the same relation to your present state as the latter does to your condition when asleep? With awakening into that new state you might recognize that the conclusions of reason are themselves no more than mere chimeras of their own brand.' Al-Ghazāli later suggests that that state may be death itself. He says that when awake in life-after-death, it would be a true though different existence.[3] Finally, he came to believe that it may be the state which the Ṣūfīs call ecstasy: when absorbed in themselves with the sense-perceptions suspended, they have visions such as are beyond the reach of intellect.

Al-Ghazāli finally owed his deliverance from this state of utter doubt and thoroughgoing scepticism not to reason but to mystic experience: to the light which God caused to enter his heart. Descartes, starting with doubt, disbelieved the senses, distrusted all the knowledge acquired by him and disowned all traditional authority and stopped at thought, finding certainty in the dictum *cogito ergo sum*—'I think; therefore I am.' Al-Ghazāli also passed through all these stages of doubt but went

[3] This refers to a tradition of the Holy Prophet: 'People are asleep, when they die they awake.' Cf. *Kīmiyā'-i Sa'ādat*, Urdu translation by M. 'Ināyat Allah, Lahore, n.d., pp. 738, 740.

further and doubted even thought as an organ for the knowledge of reality. While Descartes held that reason was competent to explain the ultimate reality, al-Ghazāli like Kant disbelieved in the absolute powers of reason also and found it incompetent to answer the metaphysical questions raised by it. Thus al-Ghazāli was happily saved from the fallacies of ontologism committed by rationalists like Descartes. With one lucky stroke he made a jump from Descartes to Kant and proved the impossibility of building up metaphysics on reason alone in his book entitled *Tahāfut al-Falāsifah* ('Destruction of the Philosophers'). In this work, as MacDonald puts it, he smote the philosophers hip and thigh; he turned the philosophers' own weapon against them as was done by al-Ash'ari earlier and proved that with their premisses and methods no certainty could be reached.[4]

Dispute between al-Ghazāli and the Philosophers. Al-Ghazāli challenges in his *Tahāfut* (under twenty Disputations) almost all the doctrines of Aristotle and Plotinus and their Muslim representatives such as al-Fārābi and Ibn Sīna. He argues, with a dialectical and analytical skill comparable to any in the history of philosophy, that many of their doctrines were positively false and baseless, such as: the eternity and everlastingness of the world; emanation from God of intelligences and souls of the celestial spheres and these spheres' possessing the knowledge of the particulars and having a purpose in their rotatory motions; delimitation of God's knowledge merely to that of universals; denial of miracles based on a view of causation which ascribes to natural causes the power to produce the effects; the denial of bodily resurrection in the life hereafter, etc. What is more, al-Ghazāli clearly shows that even where the conclusions of the philosophers were not untrue and in fact were in alignment with religious dogma, their arguments were confused, faulty and non-conclusive such as they offered, for example, to demonstrate the existence, the unity, the simplicity, and the incorporeality of God, or to establish His being the creator and the sustainer of the world, or to prove the spirituality and immortality of the human soul, etc. Of all these it is with reference to three of the philosophers' doctrines that

[4] MacDonald, op. cit., p. 229.

al-Ghazāli becomes very bitter with them and charges them with downright infidelity, viz. (1) eternity of the world, (2) denial of God's knowledge of the particulars, and (3) denial of bodily resurrection. While many other doctrines of the philosophers were also born of religious indifference and heresy mainly under the misguided orientation given by Aristotle and others, these three in particular, according to al-Ghazāli, cut the very grounds of religion. He declared therefore that no compromise on them was possible between him and the philosophers.

(1) *Eternity of the World.* Al-Fārābi and Ibn Sīna, as true Muslims, did affirm that God is the eternal creator of the universe, but as true Peripatetics also maintained that the world though created has no beginning, i.e., is eternal. They employed all the philosophical ingenuity to reconcile the religious belief in the createdness of the world with the Aristotelian doctrine of the eternity of the Prime Matter. Apparently they advanced very convincing arguments for holding the eternity both of God and the world. For instance, they called attention to certain basic and obvious assumptions: (*i*) nothing comes out of nothing—in other words, every effect has a cause; (*ii*) when a cause comes into operation the effect is produced immediately; and (*iii*) a cause is something other than the effect, i.e., is external to it. Granted these assumptions—and they must be granted—it is not at all difficult to proceed further with the argument for the eternity of the world. To come into existence the world must have a cause. This cause cannot be a physical cause, for *ex hypothesi* none yet existed. If this cause be the will of God, as is held in religion, the divine will must have been moved into action by some cause before it. This latter cause, according to the third assumption already accepted, must be external to God, but again nothing outside God existed yet. So we are left only with two alternatives: either nothing ever came into existence from the Being of God or the world must have existed from all eternity. The first alternative is impossible, for the world does exist as a fact. Hence it is proved that the world is eternal, certainly as an eternal creation of (better, emanation from) eternal God.

Al-Ghazāli, in order to refute the above argument of the philosophers, starts from the beginning all over again and seriously questions their so-called obvious assumptions, all three of them as listed above, for none of these according to him has any *logical* necessity or coerciveness about it. By logical necessity is meant that of which it is impossible to think otherwise. Now it is not impossible to think that God's will has no cause; if it needs must have a cause it is not impossible to think that this cause is not external to it; in short, that God's will is free and self-initiated. Do not the philosophers themselves pronounce God to be the First Causeless Cause. Similarly, it is not necessary that God's will should produce its effect immediately; it is possible to think that God's will may have a 'delayed effect,' i.e., the effect should appear after some period of time. Al-Ghazāli, like St Augustine, maintains the possibility of the eternity (*qidām*) of God's will and the temporality and the originatedness (*ḥuduth*) of the world as the object of that will. It is possible to think, for example, that God has eternally willed that al-Fārābi and Ibn Sīna should be born at such and such a time and that one should be born before the other. Similarly, God eternally willed that the world should come into existence at some specific period in time. Hence there is no violation of any logic in affirming the orthodox belief that the world had its origination in time, i.e., is not eternal. On the other hand, the philosophers' thesis that though the world is created, it is yet eternal, is a logical impossibility on the very face of it, for the notion of an eternal creation is a self-contradictory notion. Does it make sense to speak of the creation of that which exists eternally?

Another exchange of arguments between the philosophers and al-Ghazāli may be noted here, for it relates to the pivotal distinctions of the former with reference to the possible, the impossible and the necessary which together make a totality of all the categories of thought and being. Before its origination, the philosophers propose, the world might have been either possible or impossible or necessary. Now it could not have been impossible, for that which is impossible never comes into existence, whereas the world does exist. Nor could it have been necessary, for non-existence of that which is necessary is impossible to think, and it is not the case so far as this world is concerned. The only alternative left is that the world must always have been possible before its origination, otherwise it would never have come into existence. But possibility is an attributive notion; it presupposes something, i.e., a substance, in the Aristotelian sense, which is in the process of becoming actual. We certainly cannot speak of possibility subsisting in itself or subsisting in nothing; nor does it make sense to speak of the possibility subsisting in God. Thus there is nothing but matter to serve as a substratum for possibility and as susceptible to it. Now this matter cannot be said to have originated, for had it been so the possibility of its existence would have preceded its existence. In this case either possibility would have existed in possibility, which is unintelligible, or again in another matter which is not originated and this is to admit finally that matter is eternal.

Al-Ghazāli is not the least overwhelmed by this sophisticated logomachic dialectic of the philosophers. He points out forthwith in the Kantian fashion that possibility like impossibility is merely a conceptual notion to which nothing needs correspond in actuality. If possibility requires a substratum to subsist in, so does impossibility; but it is impossible that impossibility should have a concrete existent to correspond to it. It may be argued perhaps that it is a little different with possibility, for it is possible in its case to conceive of or assume the substratum to which it may be attributed without any violence to logic. But, points out al-Ghazāli, there is a wide gulf between the conceptual assumption of the substratum and the actual existence of it which cannot be bridged through any pholosophical jump, however strenuous it may be. It is, as we moderns put it, to derive the actual existence of mermaids from the proposition: 'Mermaids swim,' i.e., to commit a palpable ontological fallacy.

The fact that al-Ghazāli was conscious of the ontological fallacy, though he did not quite use this Kantian diction, becomes evident from his criticism of the philosophers' grandiose theory of emanationism. It may be recalled that, according to this theory, though only one emanates from one, yet three things may emanate from the three kinds of knowledge possessed by the first intelligence, one from each kind. As the first intelligence knows God, there emanates from it the second intelligence; as it knows its own essence, there emanates from it the soul of the highest celestial sphere; and finally as it knows itself as a possible being only, there proceeds from it the body of that sphere.[5] Among many other bitter things that al-Ghazāli says about this theory he rightly asks: Through what kind of Plotinian magic can the three kinds of actual existents be juggled out of the three kinds of knowledge? Above all, how can an intelligence, i.e., the knower, jump out of mere knowing? No wonder, he exclaims: 'If someone says he saw things of this kind in a dream, it would be inferred that he was suffering from some disease.'[6]

Whereas the philosophers endowed the first intelligence—and in a similar fashion all the subsequent descendent intelligences—with three kinds of knowledge as stated above, they circumscribed God's knowledge to that of His own glorious self only. It was in keeping with the Aristotelian description of God as thought thinking itself: 'it must be itself that thought thinks, and its thinking is thinking on thinking.[7] It is a strange view, says al-Ghazāli, which makes the effect know of its cause but lets the cause remain ignorant of its effect. Further explication of this issue brings us to the next crucial dispute between al-Ghazāli and the philosophers, i.e., with regard to the range and mode of God's knowledge. Before we go into it, it is most important to note that though al-Ghazāli strongly affirms the orthodox belief in God's having created the universe out of sheer nothingness at a specific moment in time, yet he insists that it is not for us humans to have even the shadow of a comprehension of God's creative activity. To comprehend or explain the nature of God's creative activity is as difficult as to try to look at ourselves by jumping out of our own skin, for we and all our comprehensions and explanations are in a very deep sense finally the creatures of that very activity. All philosophical explanations have their ultimate terminus and the doctrine of *creatio ex nihilo* is one among them.

(2) *God's Knowledge of the Particulars.* Apparently there

[5] See above, chapter 8.

[6] S.A. Kamali (Tr.), *Tahāfut al-Falāsifah*, 1958, p, 77.

[7] Aristotle, *Metaphysica*, 1072 ^{b}20; cf. also *De anima*, 424 ^{b}18.

seems to be no justification in al-Ghazāli's allegation that the philosophers denied to God the knowledge of the particulars, i.e., restricted His knowledge merely to that of the universals or things in general. It has even been suspected, and for good reason, that there is some lack of understanding on the part of al-Ghazāli in not being able to make a true interpretation of the philosophers' real position with regard to God's knowledge. Ibn Sīna, for example, did not at all deny that God's knowledge encompasses the knowledge of all the particulars and has maintained in his major philosophical work *al-Shifā'* ('Metaphysics,' viii, 6) that 'nothing, not even as much as a particle of dust in the heavens or on the earth, remains hidden from His knowledge,' which statement indeed is in conformity with the text of the Qur'ān (x. 61; xxxiv. 3). He has, however, insisted that God's way of knowing the particulars is not itself particular but universal, i.e., is not perceptual but rational and conceptual. It is not like the way we know the particulars but the way we know the universals, i.e., things in general, their set patterns, uniformities and laws. An astronomer, for example, may know, and with great precision, the behaviour of a planet, not by actually looking at it, but through working out a certain set of mathematical formula. The real distinction to which attention is being drawn here is between the mode or character of God's knowledge and the objects of that knowledge; the former, according to the philosophers, is purely universal, while the latter may be either universals or particulars. Al-Ghazāli in his criticism of them seems to have overlooked this distinction a little.

The reason for the philosophers' insistence upon God's knowledge of the particulars being rational or conceptual and not perceptual was that perceptual knowledge implies change, not only in the perception as such, but also in the percipient, whereas God is above change—absolutely above the distinction of *is, was,* and *will.* To conceive of God as being enmeshed within the category of serial time is to challenge His perfection and absoluteness and even His unity. The Muslim philosophers as Muslims were most uncompromising where the unity of God was concerned. It was among other things this passion for Islamic monotheism that made them subscribe to the Aristotelian conception of God as thought thinking itself. But they added emphatically that God's thought or knowledge of Himself necessarily includes the knowledge of all the things in the universe, even of the particles of dust in the air and the tiniest leaves on a tree, for God is the ultimate source and ground of all that exists. This in outline is the real view of the philosophers with regard to God's knowledge of the particulars and on the face of it it is quite in alignment with the teachings of the Qur'ān. If so, one may be surprised at al-Ghazāli's branding them as infidel. Maybe he misunderstood them. Slight misunderstanding perhaps there was, but his criticism of them is not misplaced—it hits the mark and cuts deep.

It is most interesting to note that the central part of al-Ghazāli's criticism revolves round the consideration of time from the point of view of its bearing on religious experience. According to the philosophers, God knows the particular events not at the time when they occur but beforehand from all eternity. He knows human beings not as they are in their particular *heres* and particular *nows* but universally and eternally. He knows John, for example, not as he is doomed to his particularity but in a general way through His eternal omniscience that John, a character of such and such a type placed in such and such circumstances, would be either a pious believer or a sinful infidel. And God knew the prophets too in the same general way. God knew even Muḥammad's proclaiming himself a prophet eternally, and not as a particular event when it occurred.

This creates quite a gulf, and an unbridgeable one too, between God and man: more precisely a gulf between God's eternality and man's temporality. God lives transcendentally in the unchanging, immutable, inexorable realm of eternity; man is doomed to the ever-changing, ever-fleeting, ever-trembling realm of transiency. All our experiences are trembling with *time*, albeit a living time, but there is according to the philosophers no counterpart of such a time in the Being of God. If so, what relation can there be between us the humans and God the Divine, which relation indeed is the very essence and soul of religion? What meaning would there be in our religious invocations and solicitations to God, our praises and prayers if the Lord in His super-eternal transcendence remains untouched by them at the time we make them? It gives such a bleak and cold picture of the Lord that we may cry in despair: Of what use is He to us? All religious communion and fellowship with God become meaningless. Such is the tragic end of the philosophers' thesis of God's knowledge: it has cut at the very nerve-centre of religion and taken all warmth and life out of it. No wonder that al-Ghazāli charged them with infidelity on this count.

Further, God's eternal knowledge of all the particular events, (that *are, have been,* and *will be*) in one single manifestation means that these events are strung already through the thread of time like the beads of a rosary. In the mirror of God's knowledge all the events including the future events are thus passively reflected with a pattern of sequence which is fixed and unalterable, precisely like the pattern of sequence of the past events recorded in history. This evidently leads to a closed and absolutely deterministic system of reality in which no possibility is left for the exercise of free will and creative action not even for God Himself. There certainly is no scope for the happening of miracles in such a system. In the philosophers' universe, past becomes linked with present and present with future through a necessary connection so that the relation between cause and effect is such that it is impossible to have an effect without its cause, one to one. They indeed insisted that an escape from or infringement of the inexorable law of causality pervading the entire scheme of things was a logical impossibility. This apparently intellectualistic-deterministic world-view of the philosophers openly militated against the voluntaristic-occasionalistic world-view of orthodox Muslim theology, which laid special emphasis on the omnipotence and providence of God and made liberal allowance for the happening of miracles. The philosophers were blind to this, according to al-Ghazāli, because they had the blinkers of Greek philosophy on them and things had gone so far that they were emboldened to deny even the bodily resurrection in the hereafter.

(3) *Bodily Resurrection.* The dispute between al-Ghazāli and philosophers with regard to the possibility of bodily resurrec-

tion cannot be easily dismissed, as has been done by de Boer on the plea that it is merely of theological interest. It does appear theological, but essentially it is a dispute with reference to the two philosophical world-views (*Weltanschauung*) as stated above: intellectualistic-deterministic of the philosophers, voluntaristic-occasionalistic of al-Ghazāli.

The philosophers indeed were staunch believers in the spirituality, unity and immortality of the human soul and had advanced quite a number of rational arguments in support thereof of which as many as ten have been reproduced by al-Ghazāli in the *Tahāfut*, though only in order to show, like Kant later, the non-conclusive character of all such rational arguments.[8] They, however, were avowedly sceptical about the physical resurrection in the hereafter which implied primarily: (*i*) the denial of the revivification of bodies but also (*ii*) the denial of physical pains and pleasures, and (*iii*) the denial of the existence of paradise and hell in the physical sense. They insisted that life hereafter is purely spiritual and that paradise and hell are the states of one's soul and not localities. They did acknowledge that many passages of the Qur'ān do speak of the life hereafter in the physical sense, but they disclaimed all fundamentalism in such matters and did not feel constrained by the literal meanings of the scriptural text. The language of these passages, according to them, is symbolic and metaphorical; the vivid imagery drawn in them is merely to make appeal to the mind of ordinary men who cannot understand everything. It is for the philosophers to seek the deeper and purer meanings of the scripture.

All this, according to al-Ghazāli, was mere deception and duplicity on the part of the philosophers. In actual practice they selected such verses of the Qur'an as served their purpose and enabled them to put their own philosophical interpretations upon them. Their denial of bodily resurrection, in fact, was grounded primarily in the Plotinian dichotomy of soul and body. Body, according to the Plotinian philosophy, is merely a hindrance and impediment in the soul's attainment of its perfection. The abode and destination of the soul is the realm of the intelligibles and divine verities, for which it yearns and pines

[8] Kamali, op. cit., pp. 197–220.

and of which it has a glimpse and reminiscence in the abstracta and universals of philosophy. Body is a tomb of the soul, its grave and prison-house; the release from it at death is indeed the first resurrection of the soul (xxvi. 7). One must needs, therefore, purify one's soul from all bodily defilements in this life rather than look for its association with body once again in the life hereafter. The philosophers indeed called attention to the verses of the Qur'ān and the Tradition of the Prophet as evidence in support of their position. Has not the Qur'ān vouchsafed a purely spiritualistic conception of resurrection by saying '... hereafter is much superior in respect of degree and much superior in respect of excellence' (xvii. 21)? Has not the Prophet said about things in paradise: '... that which no eye has seen and no ear has heard and which the heart of man cannot conceive' (Bukhāri, 59: 8)? Again, has it not been further confirmed by the Qur'ānic verse: 'No soul knows what is hidden for them' (i.e., for the people of paradise) (xxxvii. 17)? All this by way of a positive support grounded in theology but there were perhaps stronger negative arguments against the possibility of bodily resurrection based on reason and experience. They argued for example: 'The body of man in the grave is reduced to dust or eaten by worms and birds and then changes into blood or vapours and gets inextricably mixed up with all the things in the world.' Would it be possible for this body to be resurrected in the sense that all its original parts be gathered into it once again? What has passed away is never reborn in its identity. There are similar other overwhelmingly sophisticated arguments of the philosophers but according to al-Ghazāli, howsoever strong they may be, they fail to prove the impossibility of bodily resurrection; at best they allude to its improbability which is quite a different matter.

The real difficulty of the philosophers, al-Ghazāli diagnosed, was their adherence to a through and through deterministic world-view on account of which they sought a naturalistic explanation of all things—more precisely explanation in terms of cause and effect—and did not at all admit the possibility of the occurrence of the extraordinary and the supernatural. This led al-Ghazāli to the task of making an acute and critical analysis of the philosophers' notion of causality, which, as we shall see presently, has a surprisingly close similarity to that of Hume and Mill.

Thoroughly grounded as the philosophers' view of causality was in their theory of emanation, there were two important aspects of it to be noted in particular:

(*i*) The relation between cause and effect is a relation of necessity: where there is the cause there is the effect and *vice versa*.

(*ii*) The relation between cause and effect is the relation of one to one: the same cause, the same effect and *vice versa*.

Al-Ghazāli strongly challenges both these statements. With regard to the first he proclaims that there is no compelling necessity in the relation between cause and effect.[9] Take, for example, fire and burning, or drinking and quenching of thirst, or eating and feeling of satiety; there is no necessity to be seen here between the one and the other, in all cases, of the kind which we find in the logical notions of identity, implication, disjunction or reciprocity. The mind is not *coerced* to move by any *imperative necessity* from the affirmation of one to the affirmation of the other, nor from the denial of one to the denial of the other. The existence of one does not necessarily presuppose the existence of the other. It is possible to suppose that fire is there and it does not burn, or water is there and it does not quench thirst; there is no contradiction involved in such suppositions.

The reason is not far to see. Fire and burning or drinking and quenching of thirst are the phenomena of Nature and Nature as such, according to the philosophers' own admission, does not belong to the realm of necessity but to that of possibility such as may or may not exist. Any two events in Nature considered cause and effect are merely *possible* existents and *per se* there can be no *necessary* connection between them. Hence the causal relation is a natural, i.e., a possible, relation and not a logically necessary relation. Logical relations belong to the sphere of thought and not to that of Nature. Now we certainly do get a semblance of necessity subsisting in the relation of cause and effect because it gets transferred from the order of Nature to that of thought through a repeated conjunction or association of ideas of cause and effect in our mind. Two successive events

[9] Ibid., p. 185.

which as such are external to each other in Nature, through our repeated observations of them get internally conjoined in our mind. So whatever necessity there is in the causal relation, it is a pseudo-necessity, for it is a psychological necessity and not a logical one.

There certainly is no internal relation between cause and effect as such except that which is established by our own mind, for an effect is always observed as happening along with the cause either conjoined with it or immediately succeeding it; but never has it been observed to be happening through the cause. Cause either co-exists with the effect or precedes it, but it is never the producer of it. No will and agency can be attributed to causes—in fact to none of the natural existents, not even to the celestial spheres and the planets and stars, for they, one and all, are inert and lifeless entities. The only will in the entire choir of heavens and furniture of earth is the omnipresent and omnipotent will of God. It is only when He wills, and only through His willing it so, that the celestial spheres begin to swing in their orbits and the natural course of events takes to a regular uniform causal pattern: fire burns, sun gives light, water quenches thirst, etc., etc. Not even a mote in the air, nor a leave on a tree, nor a fin of the fish in the depths of the sea moves but through the will of God. Would that the philosophers realized it.

Further, the relation between cause and effect is not that of one to one as supposed by the philosophers, which they did mainly because of their prepossession with Plotinian emanationism—and that in a double sense. Cause certainly is not a unitary event but a composite one with an indefinite number of contributory factors some of which are positive and others negative, but the knowledge of both of which is necessary to understand the effective operation of a cause. Even an apparently simple phenomenon, such as our seeing an object, is a complex affair inasmuch as it depends upon our vision, light, absence of dust or smoke in the air, the distance and direction of the object from us, its size and colour and shape, absence of an interposing object, etc., etc. More important to note, however, is that an effect is not the result of one singular cause but of a plurality of causes. The same effect may be produced individually by a number of different causes, which number indeed cannot be confined just to those causes which we ourselves have observed, for our observation is limited and circumscribed.

According to the opinion of all those who are competent to judge, the above analysis of al-Ghazāli is one of the most original contributions to the history of human thought, but it has been undertaken by him with the express purpose of proving the possibility of the extraordinary and the miraculous, i.e., among other things, the possibility of the bodily resurrection in the hereafter. As such it calls our attention to a number of important facts. Causes and effects belong to the realm of Nature which is the realm of possibility, not that of necessity, nor of course of impossibility. The relation between cause and effect is not the relation of logical implication or entailment so that by negating the one we must negate the other. Causes by themselves being inert entities cannot produce the effect through an agency and will of their own but only through the will of God which indeed is the only will operating in the entire universe. Causes are very complex phenomena, not only because of their composite character, but more especially because of there being a plurality of causes, so that it is logically impossible to negate an effect merely on the negation of one particular cause; it requires the negation of all the various—in fact, all the possible—causes. This latter possibility is also really an impossibility so far as we humans are concerned, for not even the best of encyclopedic geniuses amongst us—not even the Ibn Sīnās and Aristotles—can claim to have a complete and exhaustive knowledge of all the causes there are in the world for an effect, much less of the causes which are possible for the omnipotent will of God. The will of God, according to al-Ghazāli, being unconstrained by any external will or law, except the self-imposed law of contradiction, can bring about all kinds of logical possibilities—even more wonderful and mysterious than the bodily resurrection in the hereafter. Nothing is impossible for God except the logically impossible. Hence all the so-called rational arguments of the philosophers against bodily resurrection, in so far as they show only its improbability and fail to prove its logical impossibility, stand openly refuted in the language of the Qur'ān thus:

> And they say: When we are bones and decayed particles, shall we then be raised up as a new creation? Say: Be stones or iron, or some other creature of those which are too hard (to receive life) in your minds! But they say: Who will return us? Say: He Who created you at first... (xvii. 49–51).

And again:

> What! when we shall have become bones and decayed particles, shall we then be indeed raised up into a new creation? Do they not consider that God, Who created the heavens and the earth, is able to create their likes? (xvii. 98–99).

There are many more verses of this kind in the Qur'ān which strongly affirm the possibility of bodily resurrection. Among other things they call attention to two kinds of facts, viz. our creation here in this life, and the creation of heavens and earth. The first fact according to al-Ghazāli is so mysterious and wonderful that none of the philosophers, howsoever sharp-witted he might be, can by merely looking at a fertilised ovum of human parents deduce through all his logic of cause and effect 'the fully developed man with flesh and nerves and bones and muscles and cartilages and fat ... having eyes which will consist of seven different strata and the tongue and teeth whose softness and hardness make them so different from each other in spite of their contiguity.'[10] If the creation of our body here is so incomprehensible to the philosophical understanding, what right has it to question the possibility of the resurrection of the body in the hereafter? Similarly, the reunion of the soul with its new body would be no more wonderful than its first union with the earthly body here—indeed the association between soul and body is so deep a mystery that the philosophers have not been able to fathom it. In fact the whole of 'Nature' is so wonderful and mysterious that it is no less miraculous than the so-called miracles, for it is through and through invested with the presence of God.

The second fact on which the Qur'ān urges us to reflect is

[10] Ibid., p. 245.

God's creation of heavens and earth, i.e., the creation of them *ex nihilo*. This makes it abundantly clear to al-Ghazāli that the philosophers' denial of bodily resurrection is closely connected with their affirmation of the eternity of the world, i.e., that of the Prime Matter. The basic difficulty with regard to both these problems is the philosophers' gratuitous confidence in their theory of causation according to which the relation between cause and effect is that of a logical implication or entailment and there is always the same cause for the same effect. It is because of these unfounded notions that the philosophers think it necessary to presuppose in one case the existence of the material cause, i.e., that of the Prime Matter, in view of the existence of the material world, and in the other the impossibility of bodily resurrection in view of the impossibility in the hereafter of the existence of the same causes and conditions as obtain here in this life for the origination and growth of a body.

Had the philosophers realized the sheer baselessness of their causal theory which they adhered to in blindly following the Aristotelian tradition, they certainly would have found no logical impossibility in *creatio ex nihilo* nor in bodily resurrection in the hereafter. Nor would they have sought a naturalistic explanation of all the ways of God.

The philosophers are, however, not far wrong in their Plotinian insistence upon the greater perfection and superior excellence of the life hereafter, for it is in accordance with the teaching of the Qur'ān. They are also right in speaking of the hidden and concealed nature of things in the hereafter such as no eye has seen nor has any ear heard, for these they refer to the verses of the Qur'ān and the Tradition of the Holy Prophet. But they are certainly not justified in deducing from such positive statements of the Qur'ān and the Tradition the negative conclusion about the possibility of bodily resurrection. These statements refer to the belief that life hereafter is a life in a spatio-temporal order different from the present order: 'when the earth shall be changed into a different earth and the heaven as well' (xiv. 48). Nor are the philosophers justified in alleging that the language of the Qur'ānic passages speaking of bodily resurrection is merely metaphorical or allegorical, for these passages are very many and are in plain, direct Arabic. To label them as merely metaphorical is tantamount to charging the scripture with sophistry and fraudulence.

The real argument of al-Ghazāli against the philosophers, however, is that the philosophers' one-sided and warped interpretation of the text of the Qur'ān, on this score as well as on others, suffers heavily from misleading prepossession with their philosophical commitments. They almost seem to judge Muḥammad by the standards laid down by Plato and Aristotle, whereas it should have been just the other way round.

Concluding Remarks. Al-Ghazāli insists with all the emphasis at his command that all philosophical assumptions, speculations and hypotheses should be judged and verified with reference to facts, for otherwise they would be empty and meaningless, and that, among facts, religious facts, based on the indubitable experience of prophetic revelation, are as inescapable as any other. Philosophers *qua* philosophers should not deny the positive facts and experiences of religion, nor should they try to interpret and evaluate them externally from the point of view of their preconceived systems of philosophy, but internally with reference to themselves. This is the *sine qua non* of any really critical or empirical philosophy within the context of a particular religion or all religions in general, as has been firmly established in our own times by such able authors as H. Siebeck, A. Sabatier, A. Widgery, D.E. Trueblood and other exponents of empirical philosophies of religion.

In addition al-Ghazāli seems to look askance at all attempts at the so-called reconciliation between philosophy and a positive religion so characteristic of al-Fārābi and Ibn Sīna and in fact of almost all the subsequent Muslim philosophers. He does not at all mean that reconciliations between religion and philosophy are altogether impossible or even futile. Many reconciliations between philosophy and religion may be possible and they are most welcome, but oppositions should not be overlooked and wherever found should be distinctly recognized, realistically faced, and boldly but justly met. What is most interesting and significant to note is that al-Ghazāli lays down and even implicitly formulates a method or criterion to do a perfect deal of justice in all such cases of opposition: indeed he himself has honestly and faithfully followed and practised this method or criterion throughout his 'Disputations' with the philosophers in the *Tahāfut*. He says: Do not reject a religious truth till it is proved that the acceptance of it is a logical impossibility, and do not accept a philosophical truth till it is proved that the rejection of it is a logical impossibility. Apparently this is a double-faced method to judge variously the truths of religion and philosophy, but really it is grounded in sound logic. Truths of religion are positive facts inasmuch as they are based upon a positive experience and as such cannot be denied. As to the truths of philosophy, to our surprise, al-Ghazāli seems to say that really speaking there are no philosophical truths at all. Philosophy does not have any truths of its own to offer; whatever truths it parades as its own it actually borrows from other disciplines or branches of knowledge, more precisely other areas of experience such as sensory, moral or religious. All that philosophy can justifiably claim for its own is a logic or methodology, i.e., merely a formal system which is neither true nor false. In practice, however, philosophers do claim to propound systems of truths but these are truths only in name; in reality they are assumptions, hypotheses, speculations, conjectures and even logomachies and sheer nonsense. All these do not have any claim to our acceptance except when their rejection becomes a logical impossibility, and this, if we are careful on our part, is in itself no more than another impossibility. This is al-Ghazāli's total rejection of metaphysics in no way less trenchant than that of Kant.

The above method of al-Ghazāli, in spirit at least, comes very close to the method now in vogue in the contemporary movements of philosophy, viz. philosophical analysis and logical positivism, yet al-Ghazāli's religious empiricism, with its emphatic refusal to reject the positive facts and experiences of religion except when their acceptance involves us in logical impossibilities, exposed him to the charge of fundamentalism in a bad sense of that term. Al-Ghazāli certainly was a fundamentalist, but it has become almost a fashion, particularly with Western scholars, to label al-Ghazāli as an anti-intellectualist and anti-liberalist and even as an obscurantist. It is alleged that his vigorous attack on the metaphysics current in his own day created a dread of all future philosophical and scientific inquiry. But we must note that al-Ghazālī's rejection of speculative philosophy did not at all mean the rejection of reason or intellect. MacDonald, otherwise an admirable scholar of al-Ghazālī, certainly makes a very misleading and unhappy statement in his article on al-Ghazālī in the *Encyclopaedia of Islam* when he says: 'al-Ghazālī taught that intellect should only be used to destroy trust in itself.' True, reason for al-Ghazālī is a humble search for truth and not a proud self-assertion, yet in the *Mishkāt al-Anwār*, a work of his last period, al-Ghazālī explicitly refers to the infinite possibilities immanent in reason through the dynamic self-unfolding by which it has the capacity to transcend itself and capture the Absolute.[11] Even in the *Tahāfut* he makes it clear that though the absolute will of God and His omnipotence is unconstrained by any external law or incumbency, yet it is confined within (self-imposed) reason's law of contradiction. It is unfortunate and painful that Iqbal seems to miss these aspects of al-Ghazālī's thought when he makes a critical estimation of him in *The Reconstruction of Religious Thought in Islam* (Oxford, 1934, pp. 4–6).

It is certainly very hard to agree with the very unsafe and sweeping statement of P.K. Hitti in his *History of the Arabs* (Macmillan, London, 1949, p. 432)—and with some such similar statements made by other Orientalists—that al-Ghazālī constructed such a scholastic shell for Islam that all its future progress became arrested within it. If the progress of the West consisted, as is said, in breaking a similar shell within the context of its own religions, then quite a few hammer strokes therein were wrought by the hands of the Muslim thinkers, the uppermost hand being that of al-Ghazālī. This anybody might see for himself by making a close study of al-Ghazālī's influence on the West.

[11] Cf. *Mishkāt al-Anwār*, English translation by W.H.T. Gairdner, Lahore, 1952, pp 83–91. This section in the *Mishkāt* is yet the more striking because of the general opinion of the Ghazālian scholars that this important treatise was written by al-Ghazālī at a time very close to the writing of *al-Munqidh*: a period in the spiritual history of al-Ghazālī during which he came to advocate the supremacy of intuition over reason as against an earlier phase, say, that of *Iḥyā'* (see specially Part I, Book I, section 7) when he ranked reason equal to intuition in the knowledge of ultimate things.

Al-Ghazālī's Influence on Jewish and Christian Scholasticism and on Modern European Philosophy. It is interesting and very significant to note that al-Ghazālī's influence which made itself felt outside Islam, i.e., on Jewish and Christian thinkers, moved very largely, though not exclusively, in the direction of spreading and stimulating philosophical thought. So far as the Jewish thinkers are concerned, it is necessary to recall that most of them from Saadia Gaon (Saʿīd al-Fayyūmi, 279–331/892–942) to Maimonides (530–601/1135–1204) pursued philosophical inquiry in a Muslim *milieu*: they derived their knowledge of Greek philosophy from Arabic translations and Muslim commentaries and wrote in Arabic for Muslims as well as Jews. The scene for the reception of al-Ghazālī's teaching with regard to philosophy was already set by Saadia, who may well be described as the al-Ashʿari of Eastern Judaism, for he not only followed the methods of the Ashʿarites but even the details of their arguments.[12] But the man who first took the role of al-Ghazāli himself in Jewish scholasticism was his contemporary, Jehuda Halevi, born in Toledo about 479/1086. Like al-Ghazāli he keenly felt, with regard to the developments then taking place within Judaism, that philosophy was undermining religion, not merely by questioning dogma, or ignoring it, or interpreting it metaphorically, but by substituting argument for devotion. So he took it upon himself to write a refutation of the philosophers in his work commonly known as *Kitāb al-Khazari*, or simply *Khazari* (c. 535/1140).[13] This work written in Arabic, though using the Hebrew alphabet, has been described as one of the most interesting books of medieval philosophy. Jehuda Halevi in the *Khazari* closely followed al-Ghazāli's method and arguments against the philosophers' thought in a popular form, i.e., without his logical skill and philosophical penetration.[14] Later working in a different age

[12] Cf. I. Husik, *History of Medieval Jewish Philosophy*, New York, 1930, p. 24.

[13] The original title of this work is *Kitāb al-Ḥujjah w-al-Dalīl fi Nuṣr al-Dīn al-Dhalīl* (Book of Argumentations and Proof in Vindication of the Despised Religion). For its more popular title as *Kitāb al-Khazari*, cf. Hartwig Hirschfeld, *Kitāb al-Khazari* (new revised edition), London, 1931, p. 6., also G. Sarton, *Introduction to the History of Science*, Vol. I, p. 680, note.

[14] For Jehuda Halevi's indebtedness to al-Ghazāli and the resemblance of

another Jewish thinker, Hasdai Crescas (741–813/1340–1410) also drew inspiration from al-Ghazāli's *Tahāfut*, though he gave it far more original expression. Professor A.H. Wolfson of Harvard University, in his edition of *Crescas's Critique of Aristotle* (Harvard, 1929), has, however, denied the possibility of Crescas's indebtedness to al-Ghazāli's work on the plea that its first translation into Hebrew by Zerahiah Levi ben Isaac (Crescas's own pupil, also called Saladin) did not appear before 814/1411, whereas Crescas had died in 813/1410. Nevertheless, he admits some points of similarity between Crescas's and al-Ghazāli's objections against the philosophers.[15] One may point out with due deference to Professor Wolfson that even if Crescas could not make use of al-Ghazāli's arguments directly from the *Tahāfut*, there remains the possibility of knowing them all well through their faithful reproduction in Ibn Rushd's *Tahāfut al-Tahāfut* which had already been translated into Hebrew by Qalonymos ben David the Elder under the title *Happalat Happala*. This translation was certainly made before 729/1328, for it is from this Hebrew translation that Qalonymos ben Qalonymos of Arles then took up, on the request of Robert of Anjou, his own translation of *Tahāfut at-Tahāfut* into Latin, which translation was completed on 18 April 1328.[16] To all this may be added the fact, admitted by Professor Wolfson himself, that Crescas's knowledge of Aristotle was essentially derived from the Hebrew translation of Ibn Rushd's commentaries and that in his own works he drew heavily[17] on al-Ghazāli's *Maqāṣid al-Falāsifah*, which in its Hebraicised form had become quite popular by then.

Al-Ghazāli's works began to be translated before the middle of the sixth/twelfth century, first in Latin but soon after also in Hebrew. The exact number of al-Ghazāli's books and the

Khazari with *Tahāfut*, cf. H. Hirschfeld, op. cit., pp. 5, 28; cf. also Sarton, op. cit., Vol II, pp. 118, 186; *Jewish Encyclopaedia*, 1904, Vol. V, p. 649.

15 Cf. H.A. Wolfson, *Crescas's Critique of Aristotle*, Harvard, 1929, pp. 10–12.

16 Cf. G. Sarton, op. cit., Vol. III, pp. 428, 433. But *Tahāfut al-Tahāfut* of Ibn Rushd might have been translated into Hebrew much earlier than 729/1328 for Qalonymos ben David the Elder in the Preface to his *Happalat Happala* makes mention of an earlier translation of the same work by a rabbi named Isaac Denahana.

17 Ibid., p. 1448.

various dates of their translation are not fully known, but there is every reason to believe that all his major works with regard to philosophy, logic, ethics and mysticism were available to the Christian and Jewish scholars. Of all his books their favourite was *Maqāṣid al-Falāsifah*. It was not only translated a number of times but was also commented upon more than a dozen times and continued to remain the popular text-book for the instruction of philosophy until the end of tenth/sixteenth century.[18] The first Hebrew translation of al-Ghazāli's *Maqāṣid al-Falāsifah* was attempted by the Jewish philosopher, Isaac Albalag, in 692/1292 or about that time, for Albalag died at the beginning of eighth/fourteenth century. This translation, though quite elaborate in the sense that it also contained Albalag's own critical comments, was yet not complete. It dealt only with two parts, i.e., those on Logic and Metaphysics. The third part on Physics was translated by Isaac ibn Polgar (or Pulqar) in 707/1307. A new Hebrew translation of the *Maqāṣid* was undertaken by Judah ben Solomon Nathan before 741/1340 now available in a number of manuscripts, which shows its relative popularity. Interestingly enough Judah ben Solomon replaced all the Qur'ānic quotations in the original by Biblical ones in the translation. *Maqāṣid* was Hebraicised a third time by an unknown translator, a contemporary of Solomon. This third translation has been again found in very many manuscripts together with the commentary on it by the Catalan philosopher and physician, Moses ben Joshua of Narbonne (d. 764/1362), which he composed in about 743/1342. It is interesting to add that Abraham Abigdor (fl. 802/1399), in his rhymed philosophical work *Sefer Segullat Melakim* (Treasure of the Kings) completed in 779/1377, derived his material mainly from the *Maqāṣid*.[19] But the value of this work from the point of view of al-Ghazāli's influence lies only in spreading his name and not his teaching, for the *Maqāṣid* is, in fact, no more than an exposition of the views of the Muslim Peripatetics, such as Ibn Sīna, al-Fārābi and others, rather

[18] Cf. *Jewish Encylopaedia*, Vol. V, pp. 649, 650, and S.M. Zwemer, *A Moslem Seeker after God*, London, 1920, pp. 297–9.

[19] Cf. G. Sarton, op. cit., Vol. II, p. 877; Vol. III, pp. 608, 1374, 1381, and S.M. Zwemer, op. cit., pp. 297, 298.

than the statement of his own original position.

The man who made a thorough study of al-Ghazālī's works, unequalled by any non-Muslim until modern times, and who became a link between Christian Europe and al-Ghazālī, was the Dominican Raymund Martin (d. 684/1285). He was trained in the School of Oriental Studies set up at Toledo in 648/1250 where he received a deep knowledge of Arabic and Hebrew. According to M. Asin Palacios, Raymund Martin was thoroughly acquainted with al-Ghazālī's *Mīzān al-'Amal, Iḥyā', Tahāfut, Maqāṣid al-Falāsifah, Maqṣad al-Asmā'*,[20] *Mishkāt al-Anwār* and *al-Munqidh*. Most of this becomes evident from his two works entitled *Explanatio Simboli Apostolorum* and *Pugio Fidei* (Dagger of Faith), particularly the latter, in the first part of which he reproduces all the arguments of al-Ghazālī's *Tahāfut* along with his own. In both of his books he quotes freely from *Iḥyā'*, *Mīzān al-'Amal* and *Tahāfut* and other works. His views, with regard to the doctrines of *creatio ex nihilo*, God's knowledge of the particulars, immortality of the soul and its ultimate beatitude, run closely parallel to those of al-Ghazālī.[21] Unfortunately, another of Raymund's works, *Summa contra Al-coranum*, is not now extant; had it been available it would have thrown further light on his knowledge of al-Ghazālī's works and his indebtedness to him.

But the greatest of the Christian writers who was influenced by al-Ghazālī, was Raymund's contemporary, St Thomas Aquinas (622–73/1225–74) who had received his education from the Dominican Order in the University of Naples, known for promoting the study of Arabic literature and culture at that time. He knew the philosophical views of al-Ghazālī as well as those of other Muslim philosophers and acknowledged his indebtedness to them. From al-Ghazālī (whom he does not hesitate to quote at times) he learned to understand the truth of religion and defend it against the attack of the philosophers and the sophists. His *Summa contra Gentiles*, akin in

[20] This title is most probably *al-Maqṣad al-Asmā'* or perhaps *al-Maqṣad al-Aqṣā*.

[21] Cf. Sweetman, *Islam and Christian Theology*, London, 1955, Part II, Vol. I, pp. 89–93; also T. Arnold and A. Guillaume (Eds.), *The Legacy of Islam*, Oxford, 1931, p. 273.

spirit to the *Pugio Fidei*[22] of Raymund Martin, aims at refuting the arguments of the philosophers against the dogmas of faith; the refutation of St Thomas can be very well compared with that of al-Ghazāli in the *Tahāfut*. Some of the questions on which St Thomas agrees with al-Ghazāli, we are told, are '... the divine knowledge and the divine simplicity; God's speech *a verbum mentis*; the names of God; miracles, a testimony to the truth of the prophets' utterances; the dogma of resurrection from the dead.'[23] In this work Thomas argues almost entirely from reason though at the end he sadly comes to the conclusion, like al-Ghazāli, that 'this is deficient in the things of God'. Both agree, however, in holding that the truths of religion are not contrary to, but beyond, human reason. Like al-Ghazāli he states the case against his own view with startling candour and force before pronouncing his own judgement on it. This is also true of his *Summa Theologica* (666–73/1267–74: incomplete) which in its intention and scope can be compared with the *Iḥyā'* of al-Ghazāli: both works aim at presenting a reasonable statement of their authors' faith and both are comprehensive enough to include their views on philosophy, law, psychology and mysticism. The similarities between the magnificent systems of these two giants of philosophy and theology have not been fully explored yet and would make a most profitable subject of study, if undertaken, say, by scholars of Thomism and of al-Ghazāli in collaboration with one another. We need only add that these similarities are not merely due to an affinity between their respective faiths or between interests and sympathies in general, but that St Thomas sometimes expresses his views in the very diction and metaphor of al-Ghazāli, for instance those with regard to man's knowledge of the majesty of God and the nature of beatific vision.[24]

A much later thinker in whom we find the influence of al-

[22] Cf. G. Sarton, 'Many passages of it (*Pugio Fidei*) are identical with passages of St. Thomas's *Summa contra Gentiles*,' op. cit., Vol. II, p. 892.

[23] St Thomas Aquinas, *Summa contra Gentiles*, London, 1924, Vol. I, p. 2.

[24] For the indebtedness of St Thomas Aquinas to al-Ghazāli and the comparison of the two, cf. Sarton, op. cit., Vol. II, pp. 914, 915, 968; T. Arnold and A. Guillaume, op. cit., pp. 273, 275, and Will Durant, *The Age of Faith*, New York, 1950, p. 963. G.F. Moore also compares al-Ghazāli with St Thomas Aquinas but then pointedly adds that 'his personal contribution to theology was much more

Ghazāli is the French philosopher, mathematician and scientist, Blaise Pascal (1033–73/1623–62), who afterwards turned to mysticism. His knowledge of al-Ghazāli came to him through his study of Raymund Martin's *Pugio Fidei* in a French edition. Pascal is known to the modern student of philosophy of religion for his famous wager for and against belief in God. Pascal contended that belief in God, if God exists, would bring infinite gain, and if He does not exist it means no loss; on the other hand, unbelief in God, if God exists, means infinite loss and if He does not exist it brings no gain. Now this line of argument of Pascal can already be found in a number of al-Ghazāli's works, viz. *Iḥyā', Kīmiyā' al-Sa'ādah, Kitāb al-Arba'īn*. In the last named work it is presented even in the form of verse.[25]

More striking to note, however, is the fact that there is a considerable affinity between Pascal's theory of knowledge as enunciated in his *Pensées sur la religion* and that given by al-Ghazāli in his *al-Munqidh*. Like al-Ghazāli, Pascal recognizes the validity of the first principles of reason but, like him, he adds that first principles by themselves do not give us any knowledge of the ultimate reality. Reason cannot demonstrate the existence of God, nor the immortality of the soul. Reason, therefore, ends in doubt and leaves unanswered the questions with which we are deeply concerned. But if reason cannot prove the existence of God, the heart can have a direct encounter with Him. 'The heart has its reasons which reason does not know.' Thus Pascal's mysticism like al-Ghazāli's is combined with partial scepticism; both reject pure rationalism and express the conviction that the heart, i.e., mystic experience, is the means to discover God.

The extent of al-Ghazāli's influence on European thought and its significance for modern philosophical thought has not yet been fully gauged and appreciated. It looks a little odd that from Thomas Aquinas and Raymund Martin to Blaise Pascal, i.e., for about four hundred years, his works should have remained unnoticed in the then thinking world of Christianity.

considerable than that of the Christian theologian' (*History of Religions,* Edinburgh, 1948, second impression, Vol. II, p. 457).

[25] See *Kitāb al-Arba'īn,* Cairo, 1328/1910, p. 185.

Attention, however, has been called very recently by Dr S. van der Bergh to the influence of al-Ghazāli on the French theologian. Nicholas of Autrecourt who died in about 751/1350 and came later to be known as the medieval Hume.[26] Like al-Ghazāli he was also sceptical of the reasoning process and was primarily concerned with the saving of religious and moral life from its uncertainties. The only certainties he observed in a Ghazālian fashion are the principle of contradiction and the existence of God. But above all there is a close parallel between his theory of causation and that of al-Ghazāli. For him, as for al-Ghazāli, the relation between cause and effect is not a logical one, for it can be denied without self-contradiction. There is nothing in an event to necessitate an antecedent from which it should follow as a consequent. Further, like al-Ghazāli, he adds that there is no sense in the production of one event by another event. There is no more to cause than this, that we experience the repetition of certain sequences and on the basis of that expect that the occurrence of one event will be followed by the occurrence of certain other events. This striking similarity between al-Ghazāli and Nicholas is not a mere happy coincidence, for Nicholas in his discussion of causal connection, Dr Bergh tells us, 'gives the same example of *ignis* and *stupa*; he seems to hold also the Ash'arite thesis of God as the cause of all actions and he quotes in one place Ghazāli's Metaphysics'.

The most important of all the parallels and the most remarkable is that between al-Ghazāli and Descartes (1005–61/1596–1650), and it deals not only with this or that view or theory of our author but with his very method. In particular there is a remarkable similarity between al-Ghazāli's method of doubt as given in his *al-Munqidh* and the one expounded by Descartes in his *Discours de la méthode* which appeared in 1047/1637.[27] In what follows we shall bring out a close parallel between these two works.

[26] Cf. J.R. Weinberg, *Nicholas of Autrecourt,* Princeton, 1948, pp. 83 *et seq,* 149 *et seq,* and 160 *et seq,* and S. van den Bergh (Tr.), *Tahāfut al-Tahāfut,* pp xxx, xxxi, Also cf. G. Sarton, op. cit., Vol. III, pp. 546, 547, and E. Gilson, *The Unity of Philosophical Experience,* London, 1955, pp. 97–103, 107.

[27] Cf. M.M. Sharif, 'Muslim Philosophy and Western Thought,' *Iqbal,* Lahore, July 1959, Vol. VIII, No. 1, pp. 7–14.

Both al-Ghazāli and Descartes rejected beliefs resting merely upon authority, tradition or custom. Both aimed at discovering the 'original disposition' of man unaffected by all such beliefs, i.e., in its native purity—a formidable task indeed! Both aspired to rebuild the entire edifice of knowledge from the very foundations. Both doubted the testimony of the senses in granting certainty of knowledge and precisely for the same reasons; the language and the examples of the defects of sense-experience given by both were almost identical. Both realized that there was no absolute way to distinguish waking experiences from those in dreaming and so both decided to feign that everything that had entered their minds till then was no more than a dream, 'merely the appearances of things and not things in themselves'. Both devised a new method of discovering the truth and that method was exactly the same for both, formulated almost in the same terms. It consisted in taking nothing as true which did not present itself to the mind clearly and distinctly so much so that there was no occasion to doubt it. Both refrained from dogmatising what they found and suggested modestly that others might well come to find some other method in their search for truth. The resemblance between al-Ghazalis *Munqidh* and Descartes' *Discours* is so overwhelmingly close with regard to their entire plan, the treatment of the subjects discussed therein, the details of arguments and the examples and sometimes even the very language itself, that it is impossible to attribute all this to sheer happy coincidence. It was really with reference to al-Ghazāli's *Munqidh* rather than to his *Iḥyā'* that G.H. Lewes (1817–78) was led to exclaim that 'had any translation of it existed in the days of Descartes, everybody would have cried against the plagiarism'.[28] The internal evidence, however, in the two works is so strong that it leaves no doubt as to al-Ghazāli's influence on Descartes. But the external evidence is not altogether missing. Descartes himself acknowledges the indebtedness of the general plan of his work to 'the example of many fine intellects that had previously had this plan'. He does not mention any one of the 'fine intellects' by name but certainly no one among his

[28] G.H. Lewes, *The Biographical History of Philosophy*, London, 1845–6, Vol. II, p. 50.

predecessors had followed exactly the same plan as al-Ghazāli in his *Munqidh*. Whether or not there existed a translation of *Munqidh* in Latin, the language in which Descartes himself wrote two of his most important works, it is for Latin scholars to tell. It would, however, be very strange if it did not, for we know that Raymund Martin was already very well acquainted with this work and that its influence on the *Pensées sur la religion* of Blaise Pascal is quite palpable.

In the case of Descartes himself the influence of al-Ghazāli's method can be traced as far back as 1138/1628, i.e., when he composed his *Rules for the Guidance of Mind*, for some of the rules laid down therein are just those rules which he later expounded in the Ghazālian manner in the *Discours*. There is no doubt about the extensive and almost revolutionary influence that Descartes' method wrought on modern European thought. But, then, it may be claimed, in the light of what has been said above, that wherever it went it took the influence of al-Ghazāli along with it.

Without any pretensions whatsoever that it has now become possible to trace the influence of al-Ghazāli on Kant, we may be allowed to draw attention to some of the points of similarity between the views and attitudes of these two great luminaries of the world, for they resemble each other so closely.

Al-Ghazāli and Kant. Whereas Kant was aroused from his dogmatic slumber by the scepticism of Hume, al-Ghazāli was aroused by his own scepticism. His 'Destruction of the Philosophers,' in spirit at least, is comparable to Kant's *Critique of Pure Reason*. Like the *Critique* it is destructive of all rational philosophy by a pointed emphasis on the limitations of human reason. Iqbal talks of Kant and al-Ghazāli in the same breath when he charges them both with an inadequate view of reason. Kant and al-Ghazāli agree that through speculation or theoretical reason it is impossible for the philosophers to prove the existence of God and of the soul and its immortality. Al-Ghazāli brings out the incompetency of reason in realms divine as effectively as Kant, if not more. He enumerates as many as twenty problems which the philosophers fail to comprehend through pure reason and solve without falling into a morass of inconsistencies. Kant later, however, through his *Critique of Practical*

Reason and *Religion within the Bounds of Reason*, virtually reinstates many religious positions in a philosophical garb. Al-Ghazāli does the same in all his constructive works in a mystical garb. Both al-Ghazāli and Kant had a distaste for scholastic philosophy. In both, religion in a deeper sense was the basis of the structure of their thought; only in Kant it remained latent whereas in al-Ghazāli it was manifest. In one it was more like Christianity; in the other more like Islam.

In both there was an admixture of rationalism and empiricism. The empiricism of Kant remained at the level of sense-experience and moral consciousness, whereas the empiricism of al-Ghazāli was essentially at the level of mystical experience. Both were in unison in emphasising the essentially moral nature of man and the 'moral will' as the ground or avenue for the knowledge of the 'noumenon' or the ultimate reality. The dictum of both was *volo ergo sum*, rather than *cogito ergo sum*.[29] We may not find any explicit note of voluntarism in the Kantian system. Nevertheless, we cannot deny the presence of some germinal ideas in it which later blossomed forth in the full-fledged voluntarism of Schopenhauer, Hartmann, Nietzsche and others. On the other hand, there is an explicit and marked note of voluntarism in al-Ghazāli who, in opposition to the Aristotelians and the Neoplatonists, understood the ultimate reality in terms of 'will' rather than 'thought'. According to him, the philosophers and the dialecticians with their emphasis on Platonic 'ideas' fail to do justice to the multiplicity which attaches to this world of sense. Much less, however, do such ideas exhaust the heights and depths of our inner being. In al-Ghazāli's words 'that which the friend of God knows intuitively remains hidden for ever from the discursive intellect of the learned'. A very small number who attain to the real heights of spiritual development are the saints, the apostles of God and the prophets. It is the duty of the spirits at the lower level to strive to follow them. The prophet actually inspired by God would be recognized by us by merging ourselves in his peculiar personality through the experience of an inward relationship. According to al-Ghazāli, the truth of prophecy is authenticated by the moral influence it exercises

[29] That is: 'I will; therefore I am' rather than 'I think; therefore I am.'

upon the souls of many. Like Kant, he brings religion and morality very close to each other. According to him, as according to Kant, of the truthfulness of God's revelation in the scriptures we acquire a moral and not a theoretical certainty.

The parallels between the views and method of al-Ghazāli and those expounded in modern philosophy do not end with Kant; they can be found as well in the general temper and outlook of the contemporary developments in philosophy right up to our own time. One may confidently add that with the flourishing of the movement of Neo-Scholasticism and Thomism in Europe and with the rising of the renaissance in Islam which is now wrestling with Western thought as it once wrestled with Greco-Alexandrian ideas, there will be a renewal of interest in the study of al-Ghazāli's works and further openings for the influence of his teaching. An intensive study of al-Ghazāli's works in the contemporary age would certainly bring a new impetus, within the Islamic world at least, to two rather divergent movements of our thought, viz. philosophical analysis and religious empiricism, paradoxical though it may seem.

Chapter Ten

IBN BĀJJAH

Abu Bakr Muḥammad ibn Yaḥya ibn al-Ṣā'igh (*c.* 500–33/1106–38), generally called Ibn Bājjah and known as Avempace or Avenpace both in Latin and English, was a celebrated Spanish Muslim philosopher, commentator on Aristotle, scientist (i.e., physician, mathematician, and astronomer), poet and musician.[1] The significance of the title 'Ibn Bājjah' of which Avempace (Avenpace) is a Latin distortion is unknown. Ibn Khallikān derived it from a Frankish word meaning silver. The Arabic *nisbah* 'Ibn Ṣā'igh' also literally means the son of a goldsmith.

He was born in Saragossa about the end of the fifth century H., i.e., before 1106 A.D.; the exact date of his birth is not known. He practised as a physician in his native city, but after the fall in 513/1118 of Saragossa to the Christians he resided in Seville and Xatina. Later he went to Fez in Morocco where he was made vizier at the Almoravid court. Here he was accused of atheism[2] and was poisoned to death in 533/1138 through the intrigue of his enemies.

The many-sided Ibn Bājjah wrote a good number of small

[1] There is a story given by Ibn Khaldūn in the *Muqaddimah* that once the governor of Saragossa was so moved by some of the verses of Ibn Bājjah that he almost tore his garments and swore that the young philosopher should walk back home upon gold. Ibn Bājjah, fearing lest this should not come off well, put a gold coin in each of his shoes and walked home thus on gold (cf. *The Maqaddimah*, English translation by Franz Rosenthal, New York, 1958, Vol. III, pp. 443–4). Among other subjects Ibn Bājjah composed a poem on hunting: *Tardīyah*; cf. G. Sarton, *Introduction to the History of Science*, Baltimore, 1931, Vol. II, Part I, p. 183. For his eminence as a musician, see H.G. Farmer, *A History of Arabian Music*, London, 1929, p. 222.

[2] Some of the Muslim biographers have not hesitated to label Ibn Bājjah as an atheist; this is mostly because of his ultra-rationalism. Cf. Ibn Khallikān, *Wafayāt al-A'yān*, edited by F. Wustenfeld, Göttingen, 1835–50, Vol. II, p. 372.

treatises on medicine,[3] geometry, astronomy, natural science, alchemy and philosophy. He criticised some of Ptolemy's assumptions in astronomy, thus preparing the way for Ibn Ṭufayl and al-Biṭrūji. We may add that al-Biṭrūjī's criticism of Ptolemy's geocentric views later inspired Copernicus to propound his heliocentric theory.[4] His treatise on music was as much appreciated in the West as al-Fārābī's in the East. Like the latter he was adept in playing on musical instruments, particularly on the *'ūd*, i.e., the lute.

In philosophy he wrote many treatises, a number of them on logic, a treatise 'On Soul,' another 'On the Union of Universal Intellect with Man,' 'A Farewell Letter,' and 'The Regime of the Solitary.'[5] To these may be added commentaries on Physics, Meteorology, Zoology and other works of Aristotle. The most famous of his philosophical treatises, in fact the only ones which have come down to us, are 'The Régime of the Solitary' and 'A Farewell Letter' which he wrote to a friend who was leaving Spain for Egypt. Both these works are, at present, known originally through their Hebrew translations; 'A Farewell Letter,' however, was also translated into Latin.[6] His 'Régime of the Solitary' was perhaps inspired by the adverse circumstances and the uncongenial environment in which he was placed. His were the days of orthodoxy and obscurantism rather than of liberalism and enlightenment. As a philosopher and free-thinker all along he developed a keen sense of

[3] Ibn Bājjah's works on medicine, now almost lost, exerted great influence at least in the Muslim West. Ibn Abi Usaybi'ah counts Ibn Rushd among Ibn Bājjah's pupils; cf. his *'Uyūn al-Anbā' fī Ṭabaqāt al-Aṭibbā'* edited by A. Muller, Königsberg, 1884, Vol. II, p. 63. The greatest Muslim botanist and pharmacist, Ibn al-Bayṭār (d. 646/1248), often quoted from Ibn Bājjah's treatise on materia medica; cf. G. Sarton, op. cit.

[4] It is significant to note that Copernicus quotes among others from al-Biṭrūji in his epoch-making work: *De Revolutionibus Orbium Coelestium.*

[5] The last-mentioned three works are now available in the Arabic original as edited by M. Asin Palacios. This fact may be considered a correction on what we have said about the availability of Ibn Bājjah's works in this paragraph.

[6] It was translated into Latin from Hebrew by Abraham de Blames in the fifteenth century under the title *Epistola Expeditionis.* The Hebrew version of 'The Régime of the Solitary' is only a summary of the original by Moses ben Joshua of Narbonne to be found in his commentary on Ibn Ṭufayl's *Ḥayy Ibn Yaqẓān*; see below, p. 182.

loneliness—hence the title of his work: 'The Régime of the Solitary'.

In his metaphysical views Ibn Bājjah is an attributive pluralist rather than a monist. According to him, there are three kinds of entities that may be considered ultimate, namely, matter, soul and intellect; in modern terminology they correspond more or less to matter, life and mind. To bring out the respective differentia of the three, Ibn Bājjah observes that whereas matter is moved from without, intellect or spirit, unmoved in itself, confers movement upon others and soul occupies a middle position, being that which moves itself. Thus matter is not free: its movements are not explained with reference to itself but with reference to intellect and soul. On the other hand, soul is free in its activities. Both intellect and soul confer movement upon matter but, whereas soul may be moved by itself, intellect itself remains unmoved. There is no change in the latter; it is perfect. Its forms and principles are eternal; there is so to say a higher kind of necessitarianism in their working. Thus on the basis of his ontological views Ibn Bājjah could very well explain the determinism of Nature, the freedom of man's ego and the necessitarianism of reason.

The next problem that Ibn Bājjah considers at length is that of the relation between soul and intellect or spirit. According to him, the form of matter is the spiritual principle of the matter which may subsist apart from matter or material objects. Thus the universals subsist independently of the material particulars; they are separate substances, or spiritual entities.[7] Like the Platonists Ibn Bājjah believes that the contemplation of these abstract forms of universals gives us a contact with the realm of the spirit and assists us in the apprehension of the ultimate reality. The first stage in the development of the spiritual in man depends upon the comprehension of the spiritual, i.e., the rational in the material world. The next stage is to apprehend the *a priori* perceptual forms like those of space and time. Further developed, the ego of man comes to recognize pure reason apart from the sense-experiences and apprehends the *a priori* principles such as, for instance, the fundamental

[7] See, *Tadbīr al-Mutawaḥḥid,* edited by M. Asin Palacios, Madrid, 1946, p. 19.

laws of logic and the axioms of mathematics. According to Ibn Bājjah, the universals in the particulars, the *a priori* forms of sense-experience and the *a priori* principles of Pure Reason, are apprehended through intuition rather than through discursive intellect. The apprehension of these comes from above, i.e., from the active intellect. The highest stage in the development of the spiritual or the rational in man is to have a direct apprehension and contact with the purely rational reality or with the pure thought of the spirit, i.e., the so-called active intellect.[8]

Like most of the Muslim philosophers Ibn Bājjah describes *ittiṣāl* or the union of the human intellect with active intellect of which it is an emanation as a supreme beatitude and the *summum bonum* of man's life. By the operation of the active intellect on the latent intellect in man, the latter is awakened to the spiritual life, but eternal life consists in the complete union of man's intellect with the active intellect.

On the basis of a theory like this, it is alleged, not much hope is left for individual immortality. But, according to Ibn Bājjah, the soul that notifies its existence in separate desires and actions in this world may continue to exist in life after death and may receive rewards or punishments. It is the pure reason or intellect alone which, being the same in all, will be merged into the active intellect in the life hereafter and have no separate existence of its own. The reiteration of similar views is found later in Ibn Rushd.[9]

It is noteworthy that, like the Hegelians, Ibn Bājjah believes that thought is man's highest function. Through thought man comes to comprehend the ultimate reality.[10] In the highest

[8] Ibn Bājjah's is a speculative mysticism and not an ascetic one; union with the active intellect is thus a necessary prerequisite for a mystic's encounter with God. To this theme he devoted a separate treatise, viz. *Kitāb Ittiṣāl al-'Aql bi-l-Insān*.

[9] Ibn Rushd held Ibn Bājjah's above work on the union of the human soul with the active intellect in such high esteem that he wrote a commentary on it.

[10] E.I.J. Rosenthal observes that 'if the attitude of the other *Falasifa* can rightly be termed intellectualism, his [Ibn Bājjah's] is undiluted rationalism'; see his *Political Thought in Medieval Islam*, Cambridge, 1958, p. 163. Ibn Bājjah certainly stands alone among the Muslim philosophers for his over-emphasis on reason as an avenue for the knowledge of ultimate reality, yet one does not fail to find in him, as in Spinoza later, a deep quest for the intellectual love of God.

grade of knowledge, which is self-consciousness, i.e., consciousness of pure reason by itself, thought becomes identical with reality. Like Platonists he adds that our perceptual experiences of the particulars as compared with the purely conceptual experiences of the universals are deceptive. Ibn Bājjah has no special aspiration for mystic ecstasy which for him is an experience of the emotional nature communicable only through imagery and metaphor. He does not hesitate to separate himself from the orthodox theologians and the mystics. He feels sorry that al-Ghazāli should have emphasised mysticism and revelation at the expense of philosophy, for he regards the teachings of revelation as the figurative presentations of the truths which are more completely and clearly comprehended through pure reason.[11] This is quite in line with the Hegelian mode of thinking; no wonder he was poisoned to death on the charge of atheism.

Ibn Bājjah's ethical views can be gathered from his 'Régime of the Solitary'. Moral action, according to him, is the action which belongs to the true nature of man. The action directed by reason is a free action, accompanied with the consciousness of a rational purpose. If somebody, for instance, breaks a stone to pieces because he has stumbled against it, he behaves without purpose like the child or the lower animal, but if he does this in order that others may not stumble against it, his action must be considered manlike and directed by reason.

In his ethics Ibn Bājjah occupied himself mostly with the problem of the relation of man to society and concluded that to act in a rational way a man has to keep himself 'far from the madding crowd' and their lower enjoyments. The wise, however, can associate amongst themselves with mutual advantage.[12] An ideal society of wise men would grow up like

[11] Ibn Bājjah does not deny the validity and great value of prophetic revelation; he, in fact, regards the Qur'ān as God's greatest gift to mankind. Yet he firmly believes in the possibility of man's comprehending the truths of religion in a 'natural way,' i.e., through the natural light of reason. For Ibn Bājjah's conception of prophetic experience, see Saghir Hasan al-Ma'sumi, 'Ibn Bajjah on Prophecy,' [Proceedings of] *Eighth Session, Pakistan Philosophical Congress* [1961], Lahore [1962], pp. 53–9.

[12] Ibn Bājjah seems to subscribe to a kind of intellectual aristocracy in so far as he is interested only in the association of philosophers and exceptional men.

plants in the open air without the need of a gardener's care. It is interesting to note that there is no need of physicians, psychotherapists and judges in a society of the wise. They behave as friends amongst themselves, attached to one another through love. As friends of God, they would find a repose and bliss in their continuous search for the absolute truth.

Rosenthal observes that it is to gain intellectual perfection and not merely 'to secure the necessities of life and live in peace with justice' that Ibn Bājjah would have men of varying natural dispositions join in political associations; op. cit., p. 162.

Chapter Eleven

IBN ṬUFAYL

Abu Bakr Muḥammad ibn ʿAbd al-Malik ibn Muḥammad ibn Muḥammad ibn Ṭufayl al-Qaysi (504 ?-81/1110 ?-85), known simply as Ibn Ṭufayl and in Latin as Abubacer, was a Spanish Muslim philosopher, physician, mathematician, poet, and scientist. He practised medicine at Granada and later became chief royal physician to the Muwaḥḥid ruler, Abu Yaʿqūb Yūsuf (r. 558–80/1163–84) and, according to some reports, even his vizier—a combination of functions not uncommon in a Muslim State.

Ibn Ṭufayl is now famous for being the author of the celebrated philosophical romance: *Ḥayy Ibn Yaqẓān* (The Living One, Son of the Vigilant), one of the most remarkable books of the Middle Ages.[1] This work has been translated into a number of languages. In 750/1349 a Jew, Moses ben Joshua of Narbonne, translated it into Hebrew with a commentary. It was first translated into Latin by Edward Pococke at Oxford in 1671 with the Arabic text as previously edited by his father. It was then translated into most of the European languages such as Dutch (1672),[2] Russian (1920),[3] Spanish (1934), etc.[4] English

[1] Ibn Ṭufayl is reported to have composed many other works on various subjects, notably two treatises on medicine and a commentary on Aristotle's *Meteorologica*, all of which seem to have been lost now. For his works on medicine, cf. Ibn Abi Usaybiʿah, *'Uyūn al-Anbā' fi Ṭabaqāt al-Aṭibbā'*, edited by A. Muller, Königsberg, 1884, Vol. II, p. 78.

[2] It is important to note that I. Bouwmeester, the first to translate *Ḥayy Ibn Yaqẓān* into Dutch, was a friend and associate of Spinoza. This translation became so popular that it was reprinted in 1701.

[3] The Russian translation published from Leningrad in 1920 was rendered by J. Kuzmin. Dr Sayyid Muḥammad Yūsuf, however, refers to two more Russian versions, one of which is so old as to have been published in 1701; cf. his Urdu translation of *Ḥayy Ibn Yaqẓān* under the title *Jīta Jāgta*, Karachi, 1955, Foreword.

[4] One must mention here the German translation by J. Georg Pritius (Frankfort, 1726) and another by J.G. Eichhorn (Berlin, 1782, 1783).

versions were made in 1674 by G. Keith, the Quaker, in 1686 by G. Ashwell and in 1708 by Simon Ockley.[5] For the Arabic reader the best critical edition is that of Leon Gauthier with a French translation published in Algiers in 1900.[6]

The great German philosopher Leibnitz (1646–1716) knew Ibn Ṭufayl's work through the Latin edition of Edward Pococke and is reported to have held it in high esteem. It has been suggested very recently that the central idea of the famous novel *Robinson Crusoe* written in 1719 was borrowed by Daniel Defoe from *Ḥayy Ibn Yaqẓān*, most probably through its translation by Simon Ockley already made in 1708.

The literal translation of *Ḥayy Ibn Yaqẓān* is: 'The Living One, the Son of the Vigilant' or 'the Alive, Son of the Awake.' This title has a great symbolic significance: 'The Living One' stands for man or his intellect and 'The Vigilant' for God or divine intellect. It alludes to a verse of the Holy Qur'ān in which it has been stated about God that 'neither slumber nor sleep overtaketh Him' (ii. 255). Thus the book symbolically represents the theme that human intellect partakes of the divine intellect and hence has the capacity to know reality in its innermost truths, independent of prophetic revelations as recorded in the scriptures. Ibn Ṭufayl uses the word 'intellect' in a very wide sense, almost in the sense of 'the mystic's vision'. This is in alignment with the philosophy of Neoplatonism of which the book has quite a good share.

The book has a sub-title, namely *Asrār al-Ḥikmat al-Ishrāqiyyah*, 'Secrets of the Illuminative Philosophy,' which indeed is the title of a work by Ibn Sīna. *Ḥayy Ibn Yaqẓān* too is the title of a short mystical allegory written by Ibn Sīna. Ibn

[5] Simon Ockley's translation has been reprinted a number of times. It was reissued with a few alterations by E.A. van Dyck from Cairo in 1905. A new revised edition by A.S. Fulton came out in London in 1929; a summarised version by Paul Bronnle also appeared in the Wisdom of the East Series, 4th impression, London, 1910.

[6] It is neither possible nor useful to enumerate all the other Oriental editions, as many as six were published in 1299/1881–2: four in Cairo and two in Constantinople. Mention must be made of the two long-awaited Urdu translations published recently: Ẓafar Aḥmad Ṣiddīqi, *Falsafah-i-Ḥayy Ibn-i-Yaqẓān*, Aligarh, 1955 (Urdu), and Dr Sayyid Muḥammad Yūsuf, op. cit.

Ṭufayl, in fact, has borrowed the names for the characters of his novel, namely, *Ḥayy, Salamān, Absāl* or *Asal* from Ibn Sīnā's rather flat and lifeless story. These names later occurred in similar works written by Naṣīr al-Dīn al-Ṭūsi (597–672/1201–74) and Jāmi (817–98/1414–92).[7]

There are some points of resemblance between Ibn Ṭufayl's book and the *Tadbīr al-Mutawaḥḥid* (The Régime of the Solitary) of Ibn Bājjah. Ibn Ṭufayl, however, drew his inspiration, not only from Ibn Bājjah, but also from the earliest philosophers beginning with al-Fārābi. In the introduction of his work, Ibn Ṭufayl praises his predecessors, notably al-Fārābi, Ibn Sīna, al-Ghazāli and Ibn Bājjah, though he also expresses some disagreement with them.

The story of the novel, *Ḥayy Ibn Yaqẓān*, briefly is as follows:

A boy is born without parents on a lonely tropical island near the Equator (probably the island of Ceylon).[8] A gazelle feeds the boy and becomes his first teacher. Suckled by the gazelle he grows up among the animals and learns their language. Later he arms himself with a stick and recognizes the importance of his hands. He now becomes a hunter. The gazelle that suckled him dies and shortly afterwards Ḥayy begins to dismember its body with a sharp stone, till at last he comes to the conclusion that the heart is the central bodily organ and the seat of the principle of life. He also gets thereby his first notion of some invisible thing that escapes the animal organism after its death. As the body of the gazelle begins to decay Ḥayy learns from the

[7] The romantic frame of *Ḥayy Ibn Yaqẓān* is certainly quite old; it can be traced back to an ancient tale sometimes called 'Alexander and the Story of the Idol'. A similar story was translated from the Greek sources by Ḥunayn ibn Isḥāq (d. 264/877). One can possibly think of its genesis in the Neoplatonic and Hermetistic circles—for the latter version of the story, cf. Henry Corbin, *Avicenna and the Visionary Recital*, New York, 1960, pp. 208–23. Yet, it remains true that Ibn Ṭufayl was the first to infuse a new spirit into the story and exploit it fully for a purely philosophical theme; cf. G. Sarton, *Introduction to the History of Science*, Baltimore, 1931, Vol. II, Part I, p. 354.

[8] The climate of Ceylon was considered to be such as to render spontaneous generation possible, where also, according to the popular form of the legend, Adam was supposed to have had his Fall. The possibility of the spontaneous generation of man, in so far as it clashes with the religious view about the creation of man, has been a controversial issue with Muslim scholars; cf. Dr M. Ghallāb, 'Ibn Ṭufayl,' *Majallah Azhar*, Egypt, 1361/1942.

ravens how to bury it. By chance he discovers dead trees catching fire through the rubbing of their dry branches; he brings the fire to his dwelling place and keeps it going. This discovery induces him to reflect on the invisible fire of the animal warmth which he notices in living creatures; as a result, he dissects other animals.

His skill makes further progress. He clothes himself in skin, learns to spin wool and flax and make needles. Swallows show him how to build a house and he teaches birds of prey to hunt for him and learns the use of eggs of birds and the horns of cattle. Ḥayy studies the animals of the island, its plants and minerals and its atmospheric phenomena, etc., and thus achieves the highest degree of knowledge possessd by the most learned of the natural scientists.[9] Ḥayy then passes from science to philosophy and later from philosophy to mysticism.

He is struck by the multiplicity of natural phenomena and endeavours to find a principle of unity in them all, and finally the all-pervading unity of the world. From his study of physical nature, in every part of which he makes the distinction between matter and the spiritual form, 'he infers the existence of a pure and invariable form as the cause of all that is'. Observing diligently and pondering deep, Ḥayy makes the attempt to know the Deity from His manifestations in Nature. God seems to him to have free-will and to be wise, knowing, merciful, etc.

Ḥayy now proceeds to study his own spirit: the medium through which he has obtained the knowledge even about the attributes of God. He comes to realize that he belongs to a realm above the animal kingdom and that he is akin to the spirit that controls the celestial spheres. It is in respect of his body only that he belongs to the earth; his soul or spirit, which is the highest that is in him, is indubitably of a celestial origin. That by which he has come to recognize the Supreme Being must itself be akin to that Being.

These reflections urge him to lay down the rules for his future conduct. He restricts his bodily wants to what is absolutely necessary. He prefers to eat ripe fruits and vegetables and it is only in case of necessity that he resorts to

[9] This part of the story gives miscellaneous scientific information and, among other things, describes a natural classification of sciences.

animal food, while he fasts as often and as long as possible. He resolves that no species of animal or plant should become extinct on his account. He aims at scrupulous cleanliness and in his walks round the beach of the island, he maintains a certain harmony in all his movements in conformity with those of the heavenly bodies. Through such measures Ḥayy is gradually enabled to raise his true self above the heavens and the earth and thus reach the Divine Spirit. At this stage, in place of his earlier philosophical meditations on the existence of God, he begins to enjoy a 'beatific vision' and mystical union.

After Ḥayy has often enjoyed the raptures of mystical ecstasy, his solitude is interrupted by a visitor. Upon an adjacent island live a people, who, though avowed followers of the Islamic faith, are given to worldly pleasures. A friend of Salamān, the ruler of this island, named Asal [Absāl][10], with a view to devoting himself to study and ethical self-denial, sets out towards Ḥayy's island supposing it to be uninhabited. Here he meets Ḥayy and when the latter at last acquires human language, the two are convinced that the religion of the one in its rational interpretation and the philosophy of the other are substantially the same. With a view to preaching this pure version of the dogma to the credulous multitude, Ḥayy proceeds to the neighbouring island accompanied by Asal. But their mission fails and the two friends are finally convinced that the Prophet acted wisely in giving truth to the people under a veil of figurative language. They, therefore, decide to go back to the uninhabited island so that they may further give themselves to a life consecrated to God.

Philosophical Bearings of 'Ḥayy Ibn Yaqẓān'. Studied closely, Ibn Ṭufayl's philosophical novel gives interesting views about problems of great philosophical import.[11]

[10] These are the two variants of this name, but the true form perhaps is Absāl as in Jāmī's celebrated poem.

[11] For the philosophical interpretation of *Ḥayy Ibn Yaqẓān*, see Ẓafar Aḥmad Ṣiddīqi, op. cit., Dr Sayyid Muḥammad Yūsuf, op. cit., Par I; Khwaja Abdul Hamid, 'The Philosophical Significance of Ibn Tufail's Haiy Ibn Yaqzan,' *Islamic Culture*, 1948, pp. 50–70; B.H. Siddiqi, 'The Philosophy of Hai Ibn Yaqzan;' [Proceedings of] *Fifth Session, Pakistan Philosophical Congress* [1958], Lahore [1959], pp. 327–33; M. Yūnus Farangī-Maḥalli, 'Ibn Tufail,' *Ma'ārif*, Azamgarh, 1922, pp. 18–28, etc.

Is natural religion, i.e., religion without revelation, possible? The novel seems to accord this possibility in the most conspicuous terms. Even if God had not revealed Himself through His prophets, the scientists, mystics and philosophers would have discovered Him through the study of Nature, human self and the universe. By the study of Nature it should be possible even to work out the attributes of God such as His wisdom and love. This is an empirical approach *par excellence* towards the proof and recognition of God. God is verily the unifying principle of the universe and the philosopher should not take long to arrive at this truth. The mystic, by delving deep into himself, obtains the vision of God in the spiritual aspiration of his own soul. For him it is not only the vision, it is a living contact with the Ultimate Reality—a union with God. It becomes evident to him that God and the human spirit are akin to each other; the human spirit verily partakes of the Divine Spirit; hence the title *Ḥayy Ibn Yaqẓān.*

Ibn Ṭufayl in his novel clearly brings out the distinction between the two forms of knowledge: the logical and mediate and the intuitive and immediate. It is only through the latter that we have living contact with the Divine Reality. The former, however, has the advantage of being expressible in words and is thus communicable to others. But there are no means of expressing the latter save by imagery and parables; hence the philosophical allegory.

The central theme of the novel is the avowal of a close affinity between religion and philosophy; the philosopher through his vision comes to recognize the profound truths of the dogmas of religion, clothed though they are in a figurative language. The philosopher who alone comprehends the deep significance of religious truths should, however, desist from an attempt at making the multitude understand the philosophical interpretation of religious dogmas. People are much too engrossed in the social and economic struggle of life and are seldom disciplined enough to comprehend the philosophical subtleties and profundities. Ibn Ṭufayl concludes that the Holy Prophet was right in presenting the truths of religion to the masses in the language of the Qur'ān. It is admittedly true that people in general can be disciplined to a moral and social order only by the religion of parables, miracles and ceremonies and supernatural punishments and rewards; thus alone can they be induced to lead a moral life.

There are three distinct types of men whom Ibn Ṭufayl tries to portray as clearly as possible through the main characters of his novel, namely, (1) Ḥayy, (2) Salamān, and (3) Asal.

(*i*) There is the philosopher who, by natural endowment and through his reflections and self-abnegations, is enabled to receive enlightenment from above. He rises step by step to a mystical union with the active intellect and ultimately with the Divine Being Himself. This is Ḥayy, the hero of the novel.

(*ii*) There is the speculative theologian like Asal who tries to interpret the figurative language of the Qur'ān in terms of reason.

(*iii*) There is the man of orthodox views who subscribes to the traditional beliefs and observes the rituals and ceremonies of conventional religion punctiliously; he is represented by Salamān, the prince of the neighbouring island.

These three types have been mentioned in order of their spiritual gradation; it is with Ḥayy that Ibn Ṭufayl identifies himself. It is significant to note that the eyes of Asal are opened to the profound truths of the Qur'ān only through his association and conferences with Ḥayy. This very clearly brings out the importance of philosophy for religion. At all events the book permits the rather shocking inference 'that man may attain to supreme salvation by the inner light alone, without the aid of prophetic revelation'. Ibn Ṭufayl, following the Neoplatonists, firmly believed in the possibility of acquisition of union with God through mystico-philosophic mediation.

The main strain in the novel is indeed that of Neoplatonism. We also find, however, some elements of Pythagoreanism and even of Jainism and Zoroastrianism.[12] The influence of Pythagoreanism is indicated by Ḥayy's avoidance of flesh, his vegetarianism, abstemiousness, bodily cleanliness and the harmonious turns to all his movements in conformity with those of the heavenly bodies. Like the Jainists or Buddhists, Ḥayy is a

[12] In fact one may find in this remarkable work glimpses of the gradual development of human civilisation: the evolution of mankind 'from its first groping in the dark to the most dazzling heights of philosophical speculation'.

scrupulous vegetarian and has great regard, not only for animal life, but also for plant life. He uses only ripe fruit and further consigns the seeds piously to the soil that no kind may die out through his greediness. Ḥayy's first religious sentiment of wonder is evoked by the phenomenon of fire which he constantly keeps lit. This circumstance recalls to us the Persian religion of fire. All this shows Ibn Ṭufayl's efforts towards syncretism and eclecticism which of course were the leading features of the systems of most of the Muslim philosophers.

Chapter Twelve

IBN RUSHD

Abu al-Walīd Muḥammad ibn Aḥmad ibn Muḥammad ibn Rushd (520–95/1126–98), generally known as Ibn Rushd or Averroes, was the greatest philosopher of the Muslim West in the Middle Ages. Dante in his *Divine Comedy* (Inferno, IV, 144) calls him the Commentator, for he was considered, during Dante's time, the greatest commentator on Aristotle's works.[1] He also attained eminence[2] as a physician and astronomer, but this has been eclipsed by his position as a philosopher.

Ibn Rushd's philosophy represents the culmination of Muslim thought in one essential direction, i.e., in the understanding of Aristotle. From al-Kindi onward it had been the

[1] As a matter of fact, Ibn Rushd was officially charged by Amīr Abu Ya'qūb Yūsuf to write commentaries on Aristotle's various works, whereupon he prepared for each major work of the Stagirite first a summary (*jāmmi'*), then a brief commentary (*talkhīṣ*) and finally a detailed commentary (*sharḥ* or *tafsīr*) for advanced students. Strangely enough, Ibn Rushd was for long known in the Muslim world not for his commentaries but for his *Tahāfut al-Tahāfut* written in refutation of al-Ghazālī's *Tahāfut al-Falāsifah*. His commentaries, however, made a considerable stir in the Jewish and Christian worlds. Hence most of his commentaries have been lost in the original Arabic but preserved either in Hebrew translations or Latin translations from Hebrew.

[2] He was regarded as one of the greatest physicians of his time. According to G. Sarton, he was the first to explain the function of the retina and to note that an attack of smallpox confers subsequent immunity from this disease; cf. his *Introduction to the History of Science*, Baltimore, 1931, Vol. II, Part I, p. 356. As a writer on medicine he composed an encyclopedia entitled *Kitāb al-Kulliyāt fi al-Ṭibb* (Book on the Generalities in Medicine). It consisted of seven books dealing respectively with anatomy, physiology, general pathology, diagnosis, materia medica, hygiene and general therapeutics. This medical encyclopedia translated into Latin soon became a popular text-book on the subject in various Christian universities. He also wrote a commentary on Ibn Sīnā's medical poem *Arjuzah fi al-Ṭibb*. As a writer on astronomy he prepared a summary of Ptolemy's *Almagest* and also composed a work on the motions of the spheres entitled *Kitāb fi Ḥarakāt al-Aflāk*; cf. G. Sarton, loc. cit.

effort of nearly all the Muslim philosophers to understand the system of Aristotle, but most of them could not succeed in this endeavour because of their unfortunate side-tracking into the Stagirite's apocryphal works. All along they had been mistaking various Neoplatonic works for the genuine Peripatetic ones. By the time of Ibn Rushd quite a large number of Aristotle's works had become available in Arabic and the spuriousness of many pseudo-Aristotelian works had come to be recognized. Thus the main difference between Ibn Sīna and Ibn Rushd was that the latter had a purer and more thorough understanding of Aristotle.

Aristotle for Ibn Rushd was the supremely gifted thinker, the greatest philosopher ever born, the sage who was in possession of an infallible truth. New discoveries in science or philosophy would necessitate no substantial alteration or significant change in the thought-system already elaborated by Aristotle. Of course it was possible to misunderstand Aristotle and misjudge his position in the history of human thought but, when rightly understood, his system corresponded to the highest knowledge that man could attain. It is interesting to note that Santayana in our own times has expressed similar views with regard to the great Stagirite.[3] Ibn Rushd was an enthusiastic admirer of Aristotle's logic: 'without it one cannot be happy and it is a pity that Plato and Socrates were ignorant of it'. For his devotion to Aristotle, Ibn Rushd had to pay heavily. He was attacked severely by the orthodoxy for his attempt to bring Aristotle and Islam together. The theologians felt that Ibn Rushd, in order to reconcile Islamic dogmas with Aristotelian philosophy, had reduced the former to a bare minimum; they were very bitter about this and levelled many charges of heresy against him[4]

[3] Cf. his *Life of Reason*.

[4] One result of the attack of the theologians on Ibn Rushd's various philosophical doctrines was that in 591/1194–5 Amīr Abu Yūsuf Ya'qūb al-Manṣūr, then at Seville, ordered the burning of all his works except the few strictly scientific ones on medicine, arithmetic and astronomy. The study of philosophy in general was much resented during Ibn Rushd's time, partly for political reasons. As the political power declined in the Muslim world, the Muslim rulers more and more sought the aid of theologians and the lawyers of orthodoxy. It may be noted that Amīr al-Manṣūr while at Seville not only ordered his subjects

The main doctrines of Ibn Rushd's systems which later brought the charge of heresy upon him concerned the question of the eternity of the world, the nature of God's apprehension and foreknowledge and the immortality of the human soul and its resurrection. On first reading, Ibn Rushd may easily appear heretical with regard to these doctrines, but studied closely one comes to realize that he in no way denies the dogma. He only interprets it and expounds it in his own manner so as to bring it into conformity with philosophy.

As to the doctrine of the eternity of the world he does not deny the principle of creation but only offers an explanation of it which is different from that given by the theologians. Ibn Rushd apparently seems to submit that the world is eternal but at the same time makes the important distinction, as emphatically as he can, between the eternity of God and the eternity of the world. There are two kinds of eternities: eternity with cause and eternity without cause. The world is eternal because of a creative and moving agent eternally working upon it; God, on the other hand, is eternal without a cause. The priority of God over the world does not consist with reference to time; God's existence does not imply time, since He exists solely in timeless eternity. God's priority over the world consists solely in His being its cause and that from all eternity.

For Ibn Rushd there is no creation *ex nihilo* once and for all, but rather a creation renewed from moment to moment. According to his views, a creative power is perpetually at work in the world, moving it and maintaining it. It is easy to reconcile this notion with that of evolution and even with the Bergsonian type of evolution, though with Ibn Rushd it is not so much the creature as the creative power which evolves, the final result being the same.

With regard to the knowledge of God, Ibn Rushd seems to subscribe to the view of the philosophers that God apprehends

to throw into the fire all the philosophical works of Ibn Rushd but also condemned him on the charge of heresy and banished him from Cordova. But when the Amīr returned to Morocco, the decree of exile was revoked and Ibn Rushd restored to favour in the court. This shifting attitude of the Amīr can be explained, among other things, with reference to the fact that the people of Spain were in all probability of more rigid orthodoxy that the Berbers.

His own being only. With the philosophers this supposition is necessary in order that God may retain His unity, for if He should recognize the multiplicity of things He would have multiplicity in His own being. This line of thinking forces God to live entirely within Himself and have knowledge of the existence of His own self only and nothing besides. In this case God's omniscience becomes doubtful. Truly speaking, this was only a twisted interpretation of the doctrine of the philosophers forced upon them by the theologians in order to bring them to an embarrassing predicament.

Ibn Rushd's system, however, has greater elasticity; it vouchsafes that God in the knowledge of His own essence knows all the things of the world, for finally He is the ultimate source and ground of them all. God's knowledge is not like that of man; it is a higher kind of knowledge of which we humans can form no idea. God's knowledge cannot be the same as that of man, for then God would have sharers in His knowledge. Moreover, God's knowledge, like man's is not derived from things, rather things derive their being through God's knowing them. God's act of creating and knowing is the same in the sense that God's knowledge is verily the cause through which things come into existence. Ibn Rushd does not circumscribe God's knowledge merely to the universals. For him it is not legitimate to make the distinction between the particulars and the universals with reference to God's knowledge; this distinction is of human origin and does not apply to God. God's knowledge can be called neither particular nor universal. Hence the accusation of the theologians that the system of Ibn Rushd leaves no scope for God's omniscience or knowledge of the world with its multiplicity of particulars, is altogether unfounded.

Ibn Rushd has been further charged with denying personal immortality to the human soul, for individual souls after death, according to him are alleged to pass into the universal soul. Even though no less a philosopher than Iqbal himself[5] has

[5] Sir Muhammad Iqbal, *The Reconstruction of Religious Thought in Islam*, London, 1934, p. 4. This is quite a widespread misinterpretation of Ibn Rushd made current originally by the Christian scholastics who wanted to banish Averroism from Christendom. No wonder that the Orientalists like MacDonald and de Boer have maintained that there is no scope for the existence of the indi-

renewed this charge, we venture to say that there is some misunderstanding of Ibn Rushd on this point. What Ibn Rushd is supposed to have said about the soul applies merely to intellect. The soul must be distinguished from intellect not only in the system of Ibn Rushd but also in the systems of other Muslim philosophers. Intellect in man is the faculty through which he knows the eternal truths without the media of sense-organs, e.g., the axioms of mathematics, fundamental laws of thought, ultimate values, etc. These come to it from the over-mind of the universe, i.e., the active intellect, which is their real source and origin. During its temporary abode in the body the intellect of man suffers separation from active intellect, but after the body has perished at death, itself being imperishable, it goes back to be merged once again into active intellect to live there in eternity along with other intellects. Thus the immortality of the intellect is not individual but collective, it is not personal immortality but corporate immortality.

This, however, is not the case with the human soul. Soul with Ibn Rushd is a driving force, almost an *élan vital*, which sustains life and effects the growth of organic bodies. It is a kind of energy which gives life to matter.[6] It is not altogether free from matter like intellect but, on the contrary, is closely associated with it. Yet it is independent of the body and can be considered apart from it as form, which is closely associated with matter, can yet be conceptually abstracted from it and conceived independently of it. Thus soul being independent of body may continue to exist after the death of the body in an individual capacity. Ibn Rushd, however, adds very judiciously that

vidual soul after death in the system of Ibn Rushd (cf. D.B. MacDonald, *Development of Muslim Theology...*, London, 1903, pp. 257–8, and T.J. de Boer, *The History of Philosophy in Islam*, London, 1933, p. 196). But not much doubt is left as to what the real position of Ibn Rushd is on the subject by making a first-hand study of his views in his works, e.g. in the *Tahāfut al-Tahāfut*, Cairo, 1303, pp. 139 *et seq.* Cf. also B.H. Zedler, 'Averroes and Immortality,' *New Scholasticism*, 1954, pp. 436–53.

[6] The vitalism of Ibn Rushd is apparent from an argument given by him for the immortality of the soul. The soul forms the body and since it forms it, it does not entirely depend upon it. We cannot, therefore, establish the destruction of the soul from that of the body. Cf. Carra de Vaux, 'Averroes,' *Encyclopaedia of Religion and Ethics*, Vol. II, p. 264*b*.

a convincing proof for the immortality of human soul cannot be given merely through philosophical arguments.

Ibn Rushd's belief in personal immortality is fully confirmed by his views regarding the nature of bodily resurrection. Had he considered personal immortality altogether impossible, as it is alleged, the question of resurrection would not have arisen with him at all. It is a different matter if the theologians have charged him with heterodoxy even on this score and have reproached him with the denial of the resurrection of the body. His is not denial but only an interpretation and exposition of the dogma in a manner different from that of the theologians. The body which we shall have in the next world, according to him, will not be the same as our body now, for what has passed away is not reborn in its identity; it can at best appear as something similar. Life hereafter is not mere endlessness but a perpetual growth and development and a continuation of this very life. Just as the soul is to grow and evolve from one stage to another, so has the body to grow and acquire new attributes. The life hereafter will be of a higher kind than this life; bodies there will be more perfect than they are in their earthly form.[7] What exactly this more perfected form of the body would be he leaves unexplained as anybody's guess. He carefully avoids all mytho-poetic account of life hereafter and disapproves of all popular eschatological representations made merely to feed the imagination.

As Ibn Rushd was subjected to severe criticism by orthodoxy right in his own lifetime he had of necessity to make his position as clear as he could with regard to the relation of religion and philosophy. He expounded his views on the subject substantially in his two able works: (1) 'A Decisive Discourse on the Relation between Religion and Philosophy,' and (2)'An Exposition of the Methods of Argument concerning the Doctrines of Religion'.[8] His first principle is that philosophy must agree

[7] Ibn Rushd quotes in this connection a tradition on the authority of Ibn 'Abbās: 'There is of the other world nothing but names in this world.'

[8] In the original Arabic they are entitled as (1) *Faṣl al-Maqāl wa Tāqrir ma bayn al-Sharī'ah wa-l-Ḥikmah min al-Ittiṣāl* and (2) *Kitāb al-Kashf'an Manāhij al-Adillah fi'Aqā'id al-Millah*. English translation of both these works can be found in Mohammad Jamil-ur-Rehman's *Philosophy and Theology of Averroes*, Baroda, 1921. A more careful translation of the *Faṣl al-Maqāl* with

with religion; this in fact was the belief and hope cherished by all the Muslim philosophers. Like Francis Bacon, Ibn Rushd believed that though a little philosophy might incline a man towards atheism, a deeper study of it would enable him to have a better understanding of religion. Ibn Rushd is believed to have put forward the formula of two truths, so to speak, of two revelations: one, the philosophical and, the other, the religious, both of which must concur in the final analysis. The prophets, in order to appeal to the masses, make use of allegories, parables and metaphors; the philosophers, however, express themselves in a higher and less material form. With regard to the language of the scriptures a distinction must be made between the literal sense and the allegorical sense. If a passage is found in the text of the Qur'ān which appears to contradict the results of philosophy, we may suspect that the passage really has a sense other than the apparent one and so seek a deeper and purer meaning. It is the duty of the multitude to keep to the literal sense: to seek the correct interpretation is the task of the learned. To take a concrete instance the simple-minded would take the statement: 'God is in heaven,' in the literal sense and localise Him somewhere in the skies. The learned, knowing that God cannot be represented as a physical entity in space, would interpret this statement to mean that God is exalted above all that is earthly and human. They would maintain that God is everywhere and not merely in heaven; but if the omnipresence of God be taken again in a spatial sense, this assertion of the learned is also liable to be misunderstood. According to Ibn Rushd, the philosopher who interprets the statement 'God is in heaven' to mean that God is nowhere but in Himself expresses the purely spiritual nature of God much more adequately than anybody else. Instead of 'God is in heaven,' the philosopher would rather say that 'heaven is in God.' Thus it might more justifiably be said that space is in God than that God is in space.

Statements like this are surely mere philosophical conun-

Introduction and Notes has been recently issued by G.F. Hourani under the title: *Ibn Rushd (Averroes) on the Harmony of Religion and Philosophy*, London; cf. also his 'Ibn Rushd's Defence of Philosophy,' *The World of Islam: Studies in Honour of Philip K. Hitti*, London, 1960, p. 145–58.

drums to lay people and are more liable to confuse and mislead than to enlighten and guide. The philosophers should, therefore, make it a practice not to communicate their interpretations of the dogma to the masses.[9] In fact Ibn Rushd has insisted that religious dogmas be explained to the people variously according to the level of their intellectual calibre. He grades people into three classes. The first and the largest is of those who develop a pious faith in the dogmas of religion because of the sermons they receive from the pulpit; they are easily swayed by the mere oratorical effect of speech. This is the class of the unsophisticated orthodox. The second class consists of those whose understanding of religion is based partly upon reasoning but largely on the uncritical acceptance of certain premises from which that reasoning proceeds. Such is the class of the scholastics and the theologians. The third and the last class is the smallest of them all. It includes those who succeed in having a rational understanding of religion: their beliefs are based on proofs proceeding from premisses which have been thoroughly examined and established. These are the philosophers in whom religious understanding reaches its highest development. This grading of the interpretation of the dogma according to the intellectual level of the people only goes to show Ibn Rushd's keen psychological insight.[10] But this was severely subjected to the suspicion of the theologians who charged him with insincerity. This double-faced truth, one for the orthodox and the other for the philosophers, they said, was mere deception and duplicity. Yet he was, undoubtedly, no less sincere or less pious than the best of the theologians.[11] He honestly believed that the same truth could be presented in various forms. Only he was more intelligent and more perspicacious; his deeper vision and greater philosophical ingenuity enabled him to reconcile doctrines which seemed irreconcilable

[9] Cf. Jamil-ur-Rehman, op. cit., p. 50, 51 and 191.

[10] So goes the saying of Ḥaḍrat ʿAli: *Tukallimu al-nāsa ʿala qadr ʿuqūlihim* (Speak to the people according to the level of their understanding).

[11] Ibn Rushd was essentially a Muslim philosopher and perhaps more pronouncedly so than al-Fārābi and Ibn Sīna or as E.I.J. Rosenthal puts it: 'Ibn Rushd was a Muslim first and a disciple of Plato, Aristotle and their commentators second': cf. his *Political Thought in Medieval Islam*, Cambridge, 1958, p. 177.

to less elastic minds. The more narrow and evil interpretation of the theory of twofold truth, however, was expressly rejected by him.[12]

[12] The theory of twofold truth may be rightly attributed to the Averroists but certainly not to Ibn Rushd himself.

Chapter Thirteen

IBN KHALDŪN

Abu Zaid 'Abd al-Rahmān ibn Khaldūn (732–808/1332–1406) was a Muslim historian, philosopher, economist, politician and pedagogue. Above all he was the father of the science of history, and one of the founders of sociology. His position as a philosopher in the professional sense of the term has almost been completely eclipsed by his fame as a sociologist and theorist in history. He was indeed, in a sense, hostile towards philosophy and, like Kant, deemed metaphysics an impossibility. Yet his pronouncements against philosophy are philosophically so significant that no student of philosophy can afford to ignore them. Ibn Khaldūn struck quite an independent and original note in Muslim philosophy by doing away with all the Aristotelian and Neoplatonic borrowings. He was one of the first to make a really critical study of the nature, limitations, and validity of human knowledge. Of the whole array of Muslim philosophers who preceded him he was impressed by none; of the speculative systems of al-Fārābi, Ibn Sīna, Ibn Rushd and others he speaks rather lightly. We can, however, compare him with al-Ghazāli:[1] both had a highly critical attitude towards philosophy, and both strongly maintained that it is not through reason alone but through religious experience that we apprehend the nature of ultimate reality.

It is quite interesting to note that the philosophical views of Ibn Khaldūn are available to us not through any regular and independent work on philosophy[2] but in an introductory

[1] Ibn Khaldūn, in fact, was deeply influenced by al-Ghazāli. Sarton calls him even the follower of al-Ghazāli; cf. his *Introduction to the History of Science*, Baltimore, 1947, Vol. III, Part II, p. 1775.

[2] According to Ibn al-Khatīb (713–76/1313–74), the Spanish Muslim historian and physician and a friend of Ibn Khaldūn, he did compose a number of independent works on philosophy among which were the summaries (*talkhīṣ*) of some of the works of Ibn Rushd and of the *Muḥaṣṣal* (a treatise on metaphysics) of Fakhr al-Dīn al-Rāzi and also treatises on logic. All these works seem to have been lost now or at least forgotten. One must also take into account a deep sense

volume 'on the methods of history' called *Muqaddimah*, i.e., 'Prolegomena,' which he wrote before he launched upon his voluminous history of the world. It is a 'prolegomena not to all future metaphysics' like that of Kant, but to all future history, yet, significantly enough, it serves the former purpose as well as the latter; a student of philosophy would benefit from its study no less than a student of history.

As a preliminary it would be necessary to determine his position with regard to the science or philosophy of history and sociology, and mention some of his views about these and other cognate branches of study before we give an exposition of his standpoints in epistemology or ontology. That he is the father of the philosophy of history and the founder of sociology is now an established fact. We would do well to note in this connection the following observations made by Arnold Toynbee, a great British historian, Robert Flint, a British philosopher, and George Sarton, an American historian of science, respectively. These indeed are just a few of the many commendatory remarks sincerely bestowed upon Ibn Khaldūn by the great thinkers of the world.[3]

(1)... in the *Muqaddama*[4] to his Universal History he has conceived and formulated a philosophy of history which is undoubtedly the greatest work of its kind that has ever yet been created by any time or place.... In his chosen field of intellectual activity he appears to have been inspired by no predecessor

of gratitude that Ibn Khaldūn ever had for his teacher in philosophy, Muḥummad ibn Ibrāhīm al-Abīli, known as 'an authority on metaphysics' during his time.

[3] The importance of Ibn Khaldūn was not realized in his own lifetime and not until the seventeenth century did the Muslim scholars take any notice of him; the first to do so were the Turks. The European writers discovered him only in the last century and the first fully to recognize his greatness was Hammer-Purgstall who called him in 1812 'an Arabic Montesquieu'.

[4] Whether the word should be spelled *Muqaddamah* or *Muqaddimah* is a debatable grammatical point: the former is a passive while the latter is an active participle. As the vowel has not been indicated in the original Arabic manuscripts it is up to the writer himself to decide whether he would like to give the word a passive or an active form. Most of the scholars now use the word in the latter form and the matter seems to have been clinched in favour of this choice with the recent publication of Franz Rosenthal's three-volume English translation of *The Muqaddimah*, New York, 1958.

(Arnold Toynbee, *A Study of History*, Vol. III, p. 322).

(2)... As regards the science or philosophy of history Arabian literature was adorned by one most brilliant name. Neither the classical nor the medieval Christian world can show one of nearly the same brightness as Ibn Khaldun.... As a theorist in history he had no equal in any age or country.... Plato, Aristotle, Augustine were not his peers and all others were unworthy of being even mentioned along with him.... He was admirable alike by his originality and sagacity, his profundity and his comprehensiveness (Robert Flint, *History of the Philosophy of History*, p. 86).

(3) Ibn Khaldun was a historian, politician, sociologist, economist, a deep student of human affairs, anxious to analyze the past of mankind in order to understand its present and future... one of the first philosophers of history, a forerunner of Machiavelli,[5] Bodin, Vico, Comte and Cournot (George Sarton, *An Introduction to the History of Science*, Vol. III, p. 1262).

We would appreciate the genius of Ibn Khaldūn better by recalling to our mind that all these praises have been lavished on him in respect of that part of his *opus magnum* which he wrote by way of an introduction. His major work *Kitāb al-'Ibar*[6]

[5] For the comparison of Ibn Khaldūn with Machiavelli, see Mohammad Abdullah Enan, *Ibn Khaldūn, His Life and Work*, Lahore, 1941, Book II, Chapter V; E.I.J. Rosenthal, *Political Thought in Medieval Islam*, Cambridge, 1958, pp. 106–9.

[6] The full title of Ibn Khaldūn's universal history is: *Kitāb al-'Ibar wa Dīwān al-Mubtada w-al-Khabar fi Ayyām al-'Arab w-al-'Ajam w-al-Barbar wa man 'Asarahum min Dhawi al-Sulṭān al-Akbar* (Book of Instructive Examples and Register of Origins and Information concerning the History of the Arabs, Persians and the Berbers and the Supreme Rulers who were Contemporary with Them). Though the first complete edition of this, one of the greatest monuments of Arabic literature, was published in 1876 at Būlāq in seven volumes, it was originally divided by the author into three parts. The first part consisting of Vol. I is the Introduction (*The Muqaddimah*); the second covering Vols. II to V is the main body dealing with the Arabs and neighbouring peoples and the third contained in the last two volumes sketches the history of the Berbers and the Muslim dynasties of North Africa. Volume VII also includes the history of his own family and of himself and is the best source of his life. Though the part dealing with the Arab and Berber tribes of the Maghrib is one of our very valuable sources for the history of those people, according to many critics, it is not so well written as could be expected from a person who knew so much and

is a universal history written in seven volumes; the introduction to this work entitled *Muqaddimah*, extensive enough to take the whole of the first volume, was written to explain the author's views with regard to the nature and methods of history. As if almost accidentally the *Muqaddimah* gave rise to new subjects, viz. science or philosophy of history and sociology, and in such a way that it almost overshadowed the rest of his work. It seems as if Ibn Khaldūn had aspired to become a great historian and instead became a great theoretician of history. The *Muqaddimah* is really a treasure-house of information—a sort of encyclopedia in a handy form. We get interesting and often quite instructive information on all subjects in this work, viz. astronomy, meteorology, geography, climatology, history, politics, economics, ethnology, anthropology, pedagogy, literature, philology, logic, dialectics, metaphysics, mysticism, propheticism, psychology, parapsychology (clairvoyance, telepathy, divination, dreams),[7] medicine, midwifery, music, agriculture, alchemy, astrology, magic,[8] etc.

Method of History. Ibn Khaldūn opens his 'Prolegomena' by discussing the purpose or value of history, its different kinds, and the errors into which historians fall while recording and

was one of the greatest theoreticians of history. Perhaps Ibn Khaljūn was overwhelmed by the very mass and bewildering variety and even contradictoriness of the information at his disposal. Yet it remains true that the greatest theoretician of history is not also one of the greatest historians. Account must also be taken of the fact that throughout his life Ibn Khaldūn was torn between a career as a practical statesman and as a scholar. About 1374 A.D. he actually had to withdraw himself to a Berber castle, Qala'at ibn Salama (now called Ta'ughzut) in the Mina mountains, east of Tilimsan in Northern Algeria and remain there for four years to work at his history. It was in that retreat that he wrote his *Muqaddimah* and part or whole of his universal history. According to Sarton, the first draft of his masterpiece, the *Muqaddimah*, was outlined during the months from May to October 1377; op. cit., p. 1769.

[7] Ibn Khaldūn's treatment of the phenomena of abnormal psychology, psychopathology, parapsychology, etc., forms one of the most original parts of the *Muqaddimah* (English translation by Franz Rosenthal, Vol. I, pp. 184–245). For Ibn Khaldūn's views on mysticism, see Miya Syrier, 'Ibn Khaldun and Islamic Mysticism,' *Islamic Culture*, 1947, pp. 264–302, and for those on propheticism, F. Rahman, *Prophecy in Islam*, London, 1958, pp. 115–8.

[8] Ibn Khaldūn did consider magic to be a part of science, yet he made a careful distinction between what was legitimate and illegitimate in magic. As for alchemy and astrology he had little interest if any and much denunciation.

reporting events. The purpose of history for him is not to arouse the curiosity of the reader, much less to feed his imagination; it is to analyse the past of man in order to understand his present and future. The aim of history for him is not merely to narrate the stories of kings and dynasties or prepare the chronicles of wars and pacts, but to describe the story of human civilisation. It is essentially the record of human society, its growth and decay, under different geographical, economic, political, religious and other cultural conditions.[9]

While discussing the scientific method of historical research, Ibn Khaldūn calls attention to a number of pitfalls into which historians are liable to stumble: partisanship towards a creed or an opinion, over-confidence in one's resources, mal-observation, poetic exaggeration, inability to place an event in its proper context, temptation to win the favour of royal or high-ranked personages, drawing analogies on superficial resemblances, etc., etc. An historian is expected by Ibn Khaldūn to have developed an insight into the laws governing the structure of human society and its transformations. He should have a scientific approach towards the understanding of historical changes. These should not be explained away as had been done in the past merely by alluding to accidents of Nature such as earthquakes, floods, sandstorms, epidemics, etc., important though they may be. Nor should the great changes in history be explained away with reference to divine interventions. Ibn Khaldūn seems to have no faith in *deus ex machina*. The historian should be biased by no speculative or theological prepossessions. He is required to base his explanations strictly on some empirical evidence, i.e., his own observations and experiences and those of others. While searching for the causes of historical changes he should carefully look into the climatic, territorial, occupational, economic, social, religious and other cultural conditions of the people under study. History and sociology are considered by Ibn Khaldūn to be cognate sciences; the study of sociology is a necessary prelude to the study of history. He has a keen realization of sociological laws govern-

[9] Cf. Buddah Parkash, 'Ibn Khaldūn's Philosophy of History,' *Islamic Culture*, 1954, pp. 492–508; 1955, pp. 104–19, 184–90, 225–36; 1956, pp. 225–36.

ing the course of history. Indeed it may be safely maintained that Ibn Khaldūn was the first to state these laws clearly and show their concrete application.[10]

Laws of Sociology. Social phenomena seem to obey laws which, though not so absolute as those governing natural phenomena, are sufficiently regular to cause social changes and follow well-developed patterns and rhythms. Hence a grasp of these laws would enable the sociologist to understand and predict the direction of social processes around him.

Secondly, these laws operate with regard to masses only and would not be significantly determined with reference to single individuals, for the individuals' own attitudes and beliefs are considerably conditioned by the social environment in which they are placed. The 'leaders' by themselves, without the social forces already immanent in the structure of a society, cannot bring about any substantial social change.

Thirdly, these laws can be determined only by gathering social data on a very large scale and by working out their concomitants and patterns. The social data may be gathered from either of the two sources, viz. faithful records of the past events and careful observations of the present ones.

Fourthly, much the same set of laws operate in societies with similar structures and antecedents, howsoever widely separated they may be in place or time.

Fifthly, societies are essentially dynamic like living organisms.[11] Social forms change and evolve. The factor which, more than any other, determines this change, Ibn Khaldūn

[10] Ibn Khaldūn was undoubtedly a sociologically-minded historian. He was conscious of the originality of his work and claimed himself to be the discoverer for the first time of the laws of national progress and decay; see *The Muqaddimah*, English tanslation, Foreword, pp. 10 *et sq.*

[11] Ibn Khaldūn conceived of the growth, development and decline of nations, societies and cultures as similar to those of the human organism in 'that a period of progress is necessarily followed by a period of regress and extinction'. In this Sarton considers Ibn Khaldūn to be the forerunner of Oswald Spengler (1890–1936), op. cit., p. 1770. It may be noted that Ibn Khaldūn witnessed during the span of his own life the coming to power and fall of various dynasties and found the gradual giving way of the old order to new patterns of political, economic and spiritual forces. All this must have helped him realize the regular rise, growth and fall of societies and cultures according to the inevitable laws of causality.

holds almost in the McDougallean fashion, to be the contact between different peoples or groups and the consequent mutual imitation and assimilation of cultural traditions and institutions.

Finally, the above laws, he adds emphatically, have their own unique nature, i.e., they are specifically sociological laws and not merely reflections of biological impulses or physical forces. Ibn Khaldūn sees this point clearly and, although he makes allowance for environmental factors such as climate and food, he gives much greater importance to such social factors as cohesion of interests, occupation, religion, education, etc. A careful study of the *Muqaddimah* reveals many more points where Ibn Khaldūn anticipates modern sociologists: for example, in his use of mechanistic concepts such as the balance of forces or the radiation of energy; his understanding of social morphology and its growth and decay almost in biological terms; his keen realization of the economic factors influencing the structure and growth of society, etc.

Philosophy, Its Dangers and Limitations. Ibn Khaldūn's philosophical views and his attitude towards philosophy may be gathered from the few sections scattered in his 'Prolegomena' entitled 'Science of Logic,' 'Dialectics,' 'The Dangers and Fallacies of Philosophy,' 'Metaphysics,' etc.

(a) Logic. Ibn Rushd gave logic the highest place in the domain of knowledge and felt sorry that Socrates and Plato could not be aware of Aristotle's logic. Ibn Khaldūn pulls logic down from this high place, calls it merely an auxiliary or instrumental science and feels sorry that so much time in the educational institutions should be given to the study of this subject. Logic at its best sharpens the mind of a student.[12] but more often than not it makes him only clever and pedantic and not a genuine seeker after truth. Its function is essentially a negative one: it helps us only in knowing what is not true, but not what is true. Logic does not give us any positive knowledge with regard to a particular branch of study; for this we have to resort to observations and experiences, our own and those of others. A genius or a man endowed with scientific talent would generally think logically enough without any formal training

[12] *The Muqaddimah*, English translation, Vol. III, p. 257.

in logic. On the other hand, a scholar, in spite of his discipline in logic, may commit many logical fallacies in his actual thinking. Even a professional logician may not be immune from them, and here the modern reader may easily be reminded of the example of J.S. Mill.

(b) Dialectics. Dialectics is the use of reason and rhetoric to establish the truth of the dogmas of religion and thus amounts to a sort of scholastic philosophy. Dialectics too, like logic, according to Ibn Khaldūn, is only an instrumental science and performs merely a negative function. Tracing the history of *'Ilm al-Kalām* in Muslim thought, Ibn Khaldūn observes that it originated only as a weapon of defence against the atheists and the non-Muslims who attacked the doctrines of Islam.[13] Ibn Khaldūn does not doubt its serviceability as 'a weapon of defence'. But he adds that though dialectics can very well disprove the arguments against the doctrines of religion, it can hardly offer any conclusive arguments to establish the truth of these doctrines. With dialectics we may silence the sceptic and yet fail to convince him and make him religious-minded. Dialectics should not be supposed to prove truths of religion, for that is beyond the scope of logical argumentation. Besides, dialectics is often reduced to mere rhetoric of the worst kind. A dialectician is often lost in the subtleties and sophistries of words and thus tracks off the path of truth. He is generally tempted to show off his own mastery of, and skill in, words rather than seek the truth; truth thus becomes concealed under the overdressings of the verbal foliage with him.

(c) Dangers and Fallacies of Philosophy.[14] Right in the beginning of this section in the 'Prolegomena' Ibn Khaldūn declares philosophy to be dangerous to religion. The dangers of philosophy, according to him, are mainly due to the various presumptions and prepossessions of the philosophers; these indeed are false or at least unfounded, yet they do much harm. Some of them he mentions as follows:

(*i*) Philosophy is competent enough to understand and interpret the truths of religion and is thus capable of

[13] Ibid., pp. 154–5.

[14] Cf. E.I.J. Rosenthal, 'Ibn Jaldun's Attitude to the Falasifa,' *Al-Andalus*, Vol. XX, No. 1, 1955.

being reconciled with it.

(*ii*) The salvation of the human soul is possible merely through abstract philosophical cogitation.

(*iii*) In the graded series of emanations from God to the world, God is directly related only to the first item of that series, namely, the First Intelligence.

(*i*) Reconciliation of philosophy and religion has been the hope and aspiration of almost all the Muslim philosophers. Philosophy and religion, according to them, give us the same truth with the difference that in the former it is given in abstract terms and in the latter clothed in figurative language so as to be intelligible to the people at large. They have maintained that a philosopher is not only competent to understand the truths of religion but further that he comprehends them in a purer and better way. Now all this is highly presumptuous on the part of the philosophers, according to Ibn Khaldūn. Like Kant, he warns the philosophers to be aware of the limitations of their method which after all is nothing but that of concept-formation and abstract reasoning. Through this method, Ibn Khaldūn holds, the philosophers can never reach the ultimate truth independently of religion. Further, there arises no question of reconciling the religious truth with the philosophical truth, for the philosophers have none to offer; their claim that they too possess truth remains unsubstantiated in the final analysis. They further cannot fully comprehend the religious truth which is more a matter of inner intuition, i.e., living experience, than abstract conceptualisation and wordy argumentation. Because of the limitations of their method, the philosophers can succeed in reconciling the doctrines and religion with those of philosophy only by a lifeless and distorted interpretation of the former; this is how philosophy is dangerous to religion.

(*ii*) Following the Greek masters, Plato and Aristotle, the Muslim philosophers were of the opnion that true happiness and salvation of the human soul lies in abstract philosophical contemplation. But this, according to Ibn Khaldūn, is contrary to actual experience: philosophy is a perpetual quest leading nowhere; the more you study it, the greater the confusion and doubt that it brings. Instead of bringing happiness and salvation it might bring misery and damnation, the latter because it more often than not takes us away from religion. Many students piously devote themselves to the study of the *Shifā'* and *al-Najāt* of Ibn Sīna hoping to effect the healing and deliverance of their souls, but, instead, their souls become sickened with confusion and get imprisoned in doubts from which there is no escape. It is a pity that many scholars waste their lives in reading the commentaries of Ibn Rushd which entangle them in the impossible task of disentangling the knots of philosophy.[15]

(*iii*) The theory of the emanation of a number of intellects and souls from the being of God in an hierarchical fashion as expounded by al-Fārābi, Ibn Sīna and others, Ibn Khaldūn strongly suspects to be without any logical or empirical base. It seems to him to be a sort of philosophical cobweb, a gossamer which can be blown away by raising some very innocent objections. According to this theory, God is directly related only to the First Intelligence, i.e., the first item of the entire series of emanations between God and the world. On the other hand, the world is directly related only to the last item of that series. This creates a wide gulf between God and the world. If such is the view subscribed to by the Muslim Neoplatonists, they may easily be shown to be advocating a curious brand of materialism. To say that the world is not directly the result of God's act of creation but an emanation from the last item of the series of emanations, is to concede that the world has evolved from primal matter.

(*d*) *Metaphysics.* Like Kant, Ibn Khaldūn believes metaphysics to be an impossibility. The force of his arguments against the possibility of metaphysics lies in bringing out the limitations of human knowledge, and this he does in a number of ways. The knowledge of the phenomenal world in the last analysis is based on perceptual experiences. But the knowledge of a percipient is limited by the number and capacity of his sense-organs. The blind man has no idea of visual experiences nor the deaf of auditory ones. Should they deny the reality of these experiences, we would simply feel pity for them. But we should learn to feel humble regarding our own knowledge of the

[15] *The Muqaddimah*, English translation, Vol. III, p. 254.

phenomenal world, for, after all, the number and the range of our own perceptual experiences are also much limited.[16] There may be beings in the universe better equipped for the knowledge of things, both in range and quality, than we are.

The possibility for the existence of such beings Ibn Khaldūn suggests by alluding to the process of biological evolution of which he gives a clear and detailed account. There is a gradual but continuous evolution from minerals to plants, from plants of a lower grade to those of a higher grade, from the latter to the lower animals, from the lower animals to higher animals, and from the higher animals, the highest of which is the ape, to man. But this is only what we know of the process of evolution as it works on this planet. There may be beings of an order higher than we are. And as there are grades of being so there are grades of knowledge. Our knowledge, as compared to the knowledge of the higher beings, may be analogous to the knowledge of the animals as compared to ours. Would that the philosophers recognized the limitation of their knowledge and had the realization that human reason is incapable of comprehending all the deep-lying mysteries of the universe.

Ibn Khaldūn describes reasoning as a faculty through which we form concepts out of a number of percepts and consequently move from the less general concepts to the more general ones. It is through the processes of analysis and synthesis that we form a general concept from the particular percepts; through the same process we move from the less general concepts to the more general ones—thus, for example, we move from the idea of the species to that of the genus. But the more general a concept is, the simpler it is, for, as the denotation of a term increases, its connotation decreases. Finally, we reach the most general and the simplest of the concepts, viz. being, essence or substance. Here human reason comes to its limits; it cannot go beyond these ultimate concepts, nor can it explain their mystery.

At another place Ibn Khaldūn remarks that reasoning is a faculty through which we find the causal connection between things and trace a chain of causes and effects. The more intelligent a person is the greater the number of things or events that he connects through a causal nexus. For instance, in the game

[16] Ibid., pp. 37, 38; see also p. 154.

of chess a more intelligent player can calculate a greater number of possible moves to be made one after the other than a less intelligent one. The whole universe is an architectonic whole and things are bound together through the chain of causes and effects. As we run through this entire gamut of causal connections we come ultimately to the notion of the first cause, for the series of causes cannot go on regressing infinitely. But one fails to understand the nature of the first cause; here reason comes to its limits once again. Philosophers identify the first cause with God and so far so good; but their incompetence becomes apparent when they try to explain the nature and attributes of God. To do this through reason is an impossible task; it is like trying to weigh a whole mountain with the help of a goldsmith's pair of scales.[17] Would that the philosophers knew that they could not know everything through reason.

[17] Ibid., p. 38

SELECT BIBLIOGRAPHY

The books under each head except the last have been listed in two parts: the first deals with the primary sources and the second with modern works.

Muʿtazilism and Ashʿarism

al-Ashʿari, Abu al-Ḥasan, *Al-Ibānah ʿan Uṣūl al-Diyānah* (The Elucidation of Islam's Foundation), Eng. tr. by W.C. Klein, New Haven, American Oriental Society, 1940; *Kitāb al-Lumaʿ* and *Risālah fi Istiḥsān al-Khawd fi ʿIlm al-Kalām*, ed. and tr. into Eng. by Richard J. McCarthy: *The Theology of al-Ashʿari,* Beirut, Imprimerie Catholique, 1953.

al-Baghdādi, ʿAbd al-Qāhir ibn Ṭāhir, *Kitāb al-Farq bayn al-Firaq,* Eng. tr. of the first half by K.C. Seelye: *Moslem Schisms and Sects,* New York, Columbia University Press, 1920; tr. of the second half by A.S. Halkin, Tel Aviv, 1935.

al-Fuḍali, Muḥammad, *Kifāyat al-ʿAwwām fi ʿIlm al Kalām,* Eng. tr. of al-Fuḍalī's creed from the *Kifāyah* by D.B. MacDonald in his *Development of Muslim Theology ...,* London, 1903, pp. 315-51.

Ibn Ḥazm, *Kitāb al-Fiṣal fi'l-Milal wa'l-Niḥal,* Urdu tr. by Mawlāna ʿAbdullah ʿImādi: *al-Milal wa'l-Niḥal,* Hyderabad (Deccan), Dār al-Ṭabaʿ Jāmiʿah ʿUthmānīyah, 1945, 3 Vols.

Ibn Qudāmah, *Taḥrim al-Naẓar fl Kutub Ahl al-Kalām,* ed. and tr. into Eng. by G. Makdisi: *Ibn Qudāmah's Censure of Speculative Theology,* London, Luzac, 1965.

al-Nasafi, Najm al-Dīn, *ʿAqā'id,* Eng. tr. from the *ʿAqā'id* by D.B. MacDonald in his *Development of Muslim Theology ...,* London, 1903, pp. 308-15.

al-Shahrastāni, ʿAbd al-Karīm, *Kitāb Nihāyat al-Iqdām fi ʿIlm al-Kalām,* ed. and tr. into Eng. by A. Gillaume, London, O.U.P., 1934.

al-Taftazāni, Saʿd al-Dīn, *Sharḥ ʿAqā'id-i Nasafi,* Eng. tr. with intro. and notes by E.E. Elder: *A Commentary on the Creed of Islam,* New York, Columbia University Press, 1950.

al-Ṭaḥāwi, Abu Jaʿfar Aḥmad, *Bayān al-Sunnah wa'l-Jamāh,* Eng. tr. by E.E. Elder in the *MacDonald Presentation Volume,* Princeton, University Press, 1933, pp. 129-44.

Arberrry, A.J, *Revelation and Reason in Islam,* London, George Allen and Unwin, 1957.

Badr-ud-Din 'Alavi, Syed M., *Fatalism, Free Will and Acquisition as Viewed by Muslim Sects,* Lahore, Orientalia, 1956.

Iqbal, Shaikh Muhammad, *The Development of Metaphysics in Persiā,* London, Luzac, 1908; Lahore, Bazm-i Iqbal, n.d.; *The Reconstruction of Religious Thought in Islam,* London, O.U.P., 1934; Lahore, Ashraf, 1960, etc.

MacDonald, D.B., *Development of Muslim Theology, Jurisprudence and Constitutional Theory,* London, George Routledge & Sons, 1903; Lahore, Premier Book House, 1960.

Majid Fakhry, *Islamic Occasionalism,* London, G. Allen & Unwin, 1958.

Maudūdi, Sayyid Abul 'Ala, *Mas'alah-i Jabr-o Qadar,* Pathankot, Maktabah Jamā'at-i Islāmi, n.d. (Urdu).

Muzaffar-ud-Din Nadvi, *Muslim Thought and Its Source,* 2nd edition, Lahore, Ashraf, 1946.

Najm al-Ghani, *Madhāhib-i Isālmiyyah,* Rampur, 1924 (Urdu).

Rosenthal, Franz, *The Muslim Concept of Freedom Prior to Nineteenth Century,* Leiden, Brill, 1960.

Seale, M.S., *Muslim Theology,* London, Luzac, 1964.

Shibli Nu'māni, *'Ilm al-Kalām,* 4th edition, A'zamgarh, Matba' Ma'arif, 1341/1923 (Urdu).

Tritton, A.S., *Muslim Theology,* London, Luzac, 1947.

Watt, W.M., *Free Will and Predestination in Early Islam,* London, Luzac, 1948; *Islamic Surveys I: Islamic Philosophy and Theology,* Edinburgh, University Press, 1962.

Wensinck, A.J., *The Muslim Creed,* Cambridge, University Press, 1932.

Sufism

'Abd al-Karīm al-Jīli, Insān-i Kāmil, Urdu tr. by Zahir Aḥmad Ẓahīr, Ferozpur, Madani Kutub Khānah, n.d.

'Abd al-Qādir al-Jilāni, *Futūḥ al-Ghayb,* Eng. tr. by M. Aftāb-ud-Dīn Aḥmad, Lahore, Ashraf, 1967. Many Urdu translations.

'Aṭṭār, Farid al-Dīn, *Manṭiq al-Ṭayr,* Eng. tr. by S.C. Nott: *Conference of the birds,* London, Janus Press, 1954; *Tadhikirat al-Awliyā',* Urdu tr. by 'Ināvat Ullah, Lahore, Malik Dīn Muḥammad, n.d.

al-Hujwīri, 'Ali ibn 'Uthmān, *Kashf al-Maḥjūb,* Eng. tr. by R.A. Nicholson, 3rd edition, London, Luzac, 1959. Many Urdu translations.

Ibn 'Arabi, Muḥyi al-Dīn, *Fuṣūṣ al-Ḥikam,* Urdu tr. by Mawlawi Muḥammad 'Abd al-Qādir, Hyderabad, Jāmi'ah 'Uthmāniyah, 1942; *Rarjumān al-Ashwāq,* ed. with a literal Eng. tr. along with an abridged tr. of Ibn 'Arabī's *Kitāb al-Dhakhā'ir al-'Alaq* by R.A. Nicholson, London, Royal Asiatic Society, 1911.

Ibn al-Farīd, 'Umar ibn 'Ali, *Al-Ta'iyyāt al-Kabra,* Eng. tr. of 574 verses out of a total of 761 by R.A. Nicholson in his *Studies in Islamic Mysticism.* Cambridge University Press, 1921, pp. 170-91; also by A.J. Arberry, *The Mystical Poems of Ibn al-Farīd,* Dublin, 1956.

Ibn Jawzi, 'Allāmah, *Talbis Iblis,* Urdu tr. by Abu Muḥammad 'Abd al-Ḥaqq,

Karachi, Nūr Muhammad al-Matabi' Kārkhānah Tijārat-i Kutub, 1959. (Against Sufism.)
'Irāqi, Fakhr al-Dīn, *'Ushshāq Nameh,* Eng. tr. by A.J. Arberry: *The Songs of Lovers,* London, O.U.P., 1939.
Jāmi, 'Abd al-Raḥmān, *Lawā'ih,* Eng. tr. by E.H. Whinfield and Mirza M. Kazvini, London, Royal Asiatic Society, 1928.
al-Kalabādhi, Abu Bakr, *Kitāb al-Ta'arruf li Madhhab Ahl al-Taṣawwuf,* Eng. tr. by A.J. Arberry: *The Doctrine of the Sufis,* Cambridge University Press, 1935.
al-Kharrāz, Aḥmad ibn 'Īsa, *Kitāb al-Ṣidq: The Book of Truthfulness,* ed. and tr. by A.J. Arberry, London, O.U.P., 1937.
al-Niffairi, 'Abd al-Jabbār, *The Mawāqif and Mukhaṭabāt with Other Fragments,* ed. with tr., commentary and indices by A.J. Arberry. London, Luzac, 1935.
al-Rūmi, Jalāl al-Din, *Diwān-i Shams-i Tabriz: Selected Poems from the Divāni Shams-i Tabriz,* ed. and tr. by R.A. Nicholson, 2nd edition, Cambridge University Press, 1952; *Fihi mā Fihi: Malfuẓāt,* Urdu tr. by 'Abdul Rashīd Tabassum: *Malfūẓāt-i Rūmi,* Lahore, Idārah-i Thaqāfat-i Islāmīyah, 1956; Eng. tr. with notes by A.J. Arberry: *Discourses of Rumi,* London, John Murray, 1961; *Mathnawi,* critical edition of the text, Eng. tr. and commentary by R.A. Nicholson in the Gibb Memorial New Series, London, Luzac, 1925-40, 8 Vols. Many partial translations and selections in English; also many translations and commentaries in Urdu; *Tales from the Masnavi,* London, G. Allen and Unwin, 1961. *More tales from the Masnavi,* London, G. Allen and Unwin, 1963.
al-Sarrāj, Abu Naṣr, *Kitāb al-Luma':* Selections tr. into Eng. by A.J. Arberry: *Pages from the Kitāb al-Luma',* London, Luzac, 1947.
Shabistari, Sa'd al-Dīn Maḥmūd, *Gulshan-i Rāz,* Eng. tr. with intro. by F. Lederer: *The Secret Rose Garden,* London, John Murray, 1920 (Wisdom of the East Series).
al-Shādhili, Abu al-Mawāhib, *Risālah Ḥikam al-Ishrāq,* Eng. tr. with Intro. and notes by E.J. Jurji: *Illumination in Islamic Mysticism,* Princeton, University Press, 1938.
al-Suhrawardi, Abu Ḥafṣ 'Umar, *Kitāb 'Awārif al-Ma'ārif,* Eng. tr. by H.W. Clarke, Calcutta, 1891; Urdu tr., Lucknow, Newal Kishore, 1926.
al-Suhrawardi Maqtūl, *Kitāb Ḥikmat al-Ishrāq,* Urdu tr. by Mirza M. Hadi, Hyderabad, Jāmi'ah 'Uthmānīyah; also by Yāsīn 'Ali, Lahore, A.R. Company, 1925 (3 Parts); *Three Treatises [of al-Suhrawardi] on Mysticism.* ed. and tr. by O. Spies and S.K. Khattak, Sttutgart, 1935.

'Abd al-Mājid, *Taṣawwuf-i Islām,* 3rd edition, A'zamgarh, Maṭba' Ma'ārif, 1365/1946 (Urdu).
Affifi, A.E., *The Mystical Philosophy of Muḥyid Dīn-Ibnul 'Arabi,* Cambridge University Press, 1939.
Afzal Iqbal, *The Life and Work of Rumi,* Lahore, Institute of Islamic Culture.
Arberry, A.J., *Sufism,* London, G. Allen and Unwin, 1950; 2nd edition, 1956.
Gibb, H.A.R., *Mohammedanism: An Historical Survey,* London, O.U.P., 1949.

Cf. chapters 8 and 9.

Hakim, Khalīfah 'Abdul, *Ḥikmat-i Rūmi,* Lahore [Institute of Islamic Culture], 1955, (Urdu); *Metaphysics of Rumi,* 2nd edition, Lahore, Institute of Islamic Culture, 1959; *Tashbīhāt-i Rūmi,* Lahore [Institute of Islamic Culture], 1959 (Urdu].

Husaini, S.A.Q., *Ibn 'Arabi,* Lahore, Ashraf, 1962.

Iqbal, M., *The Development of Metaphysics in Persia,* London, Luzac, 1908; Lahore, Bazm-i Iqbal.

Landau, Rom, *The Philosophy of Ibn 'Arabi,* London, G. Allen & Unwin, 1959.

Lings, Martin, *Moslem Saints of Twentieth Century: Shaikh Aḥmad al-Alauri,* London, G. Allen & Unwin, 1961.

Nicholson, R.A., *Idea of Personality in Sufism,* Cambridge University Press, 1923; *Mystics of Islam,* London, G.G. Bell & Sons, 1914; *Rumi: Poet and Mystic,* New York, Macmillan, 1950; *Studies in Islamic Mysticism,* Cambridge University Press, 1921.

Rice, C, *The Persian Sufis,* London, G. Allen & Unwin, 1964.

al-Sakakini, Sayyidah Dāda, *Rābi'ah Baṣri,* Urdu tr. by 'Abd al-Ṣamad, Lahore, Maktabah-i Jadīd, 1960.

Smith, Margaret, *An Early Mystic of Baghdad: Ḥārith al-Muḥāsibi,* London, 1935; *Al Ghazāli: The Mystic,* London, Luzac, 1944; *Rābi'ah: The Mystic and Her Fellow-Saints in Islam,* Cambridge University Press, 1928; *Readings from the Mystics of Islam,* London, Luzac, 1950; *The Sufi Path of Love: An Anthology of Sufism,* London, Luzac, 1954; Valliuddin, Mīr, *Qur'ān awr Taṣawwuf,* Delhi, Nadwat al-Muṣannifīn, 1956 (Urdu); *The Quranic Sufism,* Delhi, Motilal Banarsidas, 1959.

Zaehner, R.C., *Hindu and Muslim Mysticism,* London, Athlone Press, 1960.

Ẓahūr-ud-Dīn Aḥmad, M.M., *An Examination of the Mystic Tendencies in Islam in the Light of the Qur'ān and Traditions,* Bombay, published by the author, Pali Road, Bandra, 1932.

Ikḥwān al-Ṣafā'

Ikhwān al-Ṣafā', *Al-Ḥayawān wa'l-Insān,* Eng. tr. by J. Platts; *Dispute between Man and the Animals,* London, W.H. Allen & Co., 1869; *Rasā'il Ikḥwān al-Ṣafā'* ed. by Khayr al-Dīn Zirikli, Cairo, al-Maṭba'at al-'Arabīyah, 1347/1928, 4 vols. Hindustani tr. by Mawlawi Ikrām 'Ali, revised by Duncan Forbes and Chr. Rieu, London, 1861; Urdu tr. by Mawlawi Ikrām 'Ali: *Ikḥwān al-Ṣafā',* Delhi, Anjuman-i Taraqqi-i Urdu, 1939 (Sections); Eng. tr. from the Hindustani by John Dawson: *Ikḥwān al-Ṣafā',* London, 1869 (sections).

Lane-Poole, Stanley, *Essay on the Brotherhood of Purity,* Lahore, Orientalia, 1954 (reprint from *Studies in a Mosque,* London, Trübner, 1883, Chapter VI).

Levy R., *The Social Structure of Islam,* Cambridge University Press, 1957; cf. pp. 471–96.

Al-Kindi

Al-Kindi, *Rasā'il al-Kindi al-Falsafiyah*, ed. by Muḥammad Abd al-Hādi Abu Ridah, Cairo, Dār al-Fikr al-'Arabi, 1369/1950, 384 p. (Text of fourteen treatises, etc., with an introduction: pp. 1–80); Vol. II: 1372/1953, 152 p. (Text of eleven treatises with an Intro.; pp. 3–4) (Arabic).

Atiyeh, George N., *Al-Kindi: The Philosopher of the Arabs*, Rawalpindi, Islamic Research Institute, 1966.

Levy, Martin, *The Medical Formulary of al-Kindi*, University of Wisconsin Press, 1966.

Rescher, Nicholas, *Al-Kindi: An Annotated Bibliography*, University of Pittsburgh Press, 1965.

Al-Rāzi

al-Rāzi, Zakrïya, *Al-Ṭibb al-Rūhāni*, ed. by Paul Kraus in the *Rhagensis [Razis] Opera Philosophica* (Cairo, 1939, Vol. I, pp. 1–96; this is the only edition of al-Rāzi's extant philosophical treatises and fragments. Eng. tr. of the *al-Ṭibb al-Rūhāni* with an introduction by A.J. Arberry: *The Spritual Physick of Rhazes*, London, John Murray, 1950 (Wisdom of the East Series).

Al-Fārābi

Al-Fārābi, *Falsafah Arisṭūṭālïs*, tr. into Eng. by Muḥsin Mahdi: *Al-Farabi's Philosophy of Plato and Aristotle*, Glencoe (Illinois), 1962; *Fuṣūl al-Madani: Aphorisms of the Statesman*. ed. with an Eng tr., Intro. and notes by D.M. Dunlop, Cambridge University Press, 1961; *Kitāb Ārā'Ahl al-Madinat al-Fāḍilah*, ed. by 'Id ['Abd] al-Wāṣif Muḥammad al-Kurdi 2nd edition, Cairo, 1368/1948 (Arabic); *Kitāb al-Siyāsat al-Madaniyah*, Hyderabad, Dairatul-Maarif-il-Osmania, 1346 H. (Arabic); *Kitāb Tahḥṣīl al-Sa'ādah*, Hyderabad, Dairatul-Maarif-il-Osmania, 1345 H. (Arabic); *Rasā'il al-Fārābi, Hyderabad,* Dairatul-Maarif-il-Osmania, 1340–9 H Parts in 4 Vols. (Arabic); *Al-Thamarat al-Marḍïyah fi Ba'd al-Rasā'il al-Fārābïyah* (Philosophische Abhandlungen), ed. by F. Dietrici, Leiden, 1890 (Arabic text of eight opuscules, etc.).

'Aqqād, 'Abbās Maḥmūd, *Al-Fārābi*, Urdu tr. by Ra'īs Aḥmad Ja'fri: *Abu Naṣr Fārābi ke Ḥālāt*, Karachi, al-Maṭbu'āt, 1953.

Farmer, A.G., *Al-Fārābī's Arabic-Latin Writings on Music in the Iḥṣā' al-'Ulūm*, Glasgow, Civic Press, 1934. The texts ed. with tr. and commentaries.

Hammond, Rev. Robert, *The Philosophy of Alfarabi and Its Influence on Medieval Thought*, New York, Hobson Book Press, 1947.

Lerner, R, and Muhsin Mahdi *Medieval Political Philosophy: A Source Book*, Free Press, 1963.

Rescher, Nicholas, *Al-Farabi: An Annotated Bibliography*, University of Pittsburgh Press, 1962.

Ibn Sīna

Ibn Sīna, *Ḥayy Ibn Yaqẓān*, Eng. tr. along with that of the Persian commentary on it (attributed to Juzjāni) in Henry Corbin's *Avicenna and the Visionary Recital*, New York, 1960, pp. 137–50, 279–380; *Kitāb al-Ishārāt wa'l-Tanbihāt*, ed. by Sulaymān Duniya, Cairo, Dār al-Iḥyā' al-Kutub al-'Arabīyah, 1367/1948. 3 Vols. (Arabic): *Kitāb al-Nafs* (Avicenna's *De Anima*, being the Psychological Part of *Kitāb al-Shifā'*), ed. by F. Rahman, London, O.U.P., 1937; *Kitāb al-Shifā'*, Teheran, 1924, 2 Vols. (Arabic); *Majmu' Rasā'il al-Shaykh al-Ra'īs*, Hyderabad, Dairatul-Maarif-il-Nizamia, 1353 H (Arabic); *al-Najāt*, ed. by Muḥyi al-Dīn Ṣabri al-Kurdi, 2nd edition, Cairo, 1938, Eng. tr. of Book II, Chapter VI, with Historico-Philosophical notes and textual improvements on the Cairo edition by F. Rahman: *Avicenna's Psychology*, London, O.U.P., 1952—see also A.J. Arberry's *Avicenna on Theology; Risālah fi Māhiyyat al-'Ishq*, Eng. tr. by E.L. Fackenheim: "A Treatise on Love by Ibn Sina," *Medieval Studies*, Vol. VII, 1945, pp. 208–28; *Risālah al-Ṭā'ir*, Eng. tr in *Three Treatises on Mysticism* by O. Spies and S.K. Khattak, Stuttgart, 1935; also in Henry Corbin's *Avicenna and the Visionary Recital*, New York, 1960, pp. 186–92; *Tis' Rasā'il fi al-Ḥikmah wa'l-Ṭabī'iyat*, Cairo, Maṭba' Hindīyah, 1326/1908; also Constantinople, 1298 H. (Arabic).

Afnan, Soheil M., *Avicenna: His Life and Works*, London, G. Allen and Unwin, 1958.

Arberry, A.J. (Tr.), *Avicenna on Theology*, London, John Murray (Wisdom of the East Series), 1951. (Extracts from *al-Najāt* with an account of Ibn Sīnā's life.)

Corbin, H., *Avicenna and the Visionary Recital*, New York, Pantheon; London, Routledge & Kegan Paul, 1960.

Faḍl Ḥaqq, Muḥammad, *Tajallīyāt-i Ibn Sina*, Lahore, Rifāh-i-'Ām Steam Press, 1928 (Urdu).

Indo-Iranian Society, *Avicenna Commemoration Volume*, Calcutta, 1956.

Rahman, F., *Prophecy in Islam; Philosophy and Orthodoxy*, London, G. Allen & Unwin, 1958. Cf. chapters I and II.

Wickens, G.M. (Ed.), *Avicenna: Scientist & Philosopher; A Millenary Symposium*, London. Luzac, 1952.

Al-Ghazāli

al-Ghazāli, *Ayyuh al-Walad*, text and Eng. tr. by G.H. Scherer, Beirut, 1936 (Doctorate thesis); *Bidāyat al-Hidāyah*, Eng. tr. by W.M. Watt, in his *Faith and Practice of al-Ghazali*, London, 1953, pp. 86–152; *Al-Ḥikmah fi Makhlū-*

qāt Allah, Urdu tr. by Muḥammad 'Ali Luṭfi, Karachi, 30 New Karachi Housing Society, 1960; *Iḥyā' 'Ulūm al-Din*, Urdu tr. by Muḥammad Aḥsan Ṣiddīqi: *Madhāq al-'Ārifin*, 7th edition, Lucknow, Maṭba' Tejkumar, 1955, 4 Vols.; *Kimiyā'-i Sa'ādat*, Urdu tr. by M. 'Ināyat Ullah, revised edition, Lahore, Din Muhammadi Press, n.d.; *Kitāb al-'Ilm*, Eng tr. by Nabih Amin Faris: *The Book of Knowledge*, Lahore, Ashraf, 1962; *Makātib* (Letters), Urdu tr. by 'Abudl Wahhāb Ẓuhūri: *Makātib-i Imām Ghazāli*, Karachi, Nafis Academy, 1949; *Maqāṣid al-Falāsifah*, Urdu tr. by Muḥammad Ḥanif Nadwi: *Qadim Yūnāni Falsafah*, Lahore, Majlis-i Taraqqi-i Adab, 1959; *Minhāj al-'Ābidin*, Urdu tr. by Muḥammad Munīr: *Sirāj al-Sālikin*, Lucknow, Newal Kishore, 1927; *Mishkāt al-Anwār* (*Niche of Lights*), Eng. tr. with Intro. by W.H.T. Gairdner, London, Royal Asiatic Society, 1924; Lahore, Ashraf, 1952; *Mīzān al-'Amal*, Urdu tr. by Naṣr Ullah Khān, Pindi Bahauddin [W. Pakistan], Sufi Printing and Publishing Company, n.d.; *Al-Munqidh min al-Ḍalāl*, Eng. tr. by W.M. Watt: *The Faith and Practice of al-Ghazāli*, London, G. Allen & Unwin, 1953, pp. 19–85; also by Claud Field: *Confessions of al-Ghazzāli*, London, John Murray, 1909 (Wisdom of the East Series); Lahore, Ashraf, n.d.—many Urdu translations, *Murshid al-Amin*, Urdu tr. by 'Abd al-Quddūs Hāshimi, Karachi, Urdu Manzil, 1955 (summary of *Iḥyā'*); *al-Risālat al-Ladunniyah*, Eng. tr. by Margaret Smith in the *Journal of Royal Asiatic Society*, 1938, pp. 177–200, 353–74; *Risālat al-Ṭā'ir*, Eng. tr. by N.A. Faris: "Ghazzālī's Epistle of the Bird," *The Muslim World*, Vol. XXXIV, 1944, pp. 47–53; *Tahāfut al-Falāsifah*, Eng. tr. by Ṣabīh Aḥmad Kamāli: *Incoherence of the Philosophers*, Lahore, The Pakistan Philosophical Congress, 1958.

Bagley, F.R.C. (Tr.), *Al-Ghazāli's Book of Council for Kings*, Leiden, Brill, 1964.

Calverley, E.E., *Worship in Islam* (being a translation with commentary and introduction of al-Ghazzālī's Book of the *Iḥyā'* on worship), London, Luzac, 1957, 2nd edition with corrections.

Fakhry, Majid, *Islamic Occasionalism*, London, G. Allen and Unwin, 1958. Cf. Chapter II.

Faris, Nabih Amin, *The Foundations of the Articles of the Faith* (tr. of the *Kitāb Qawā'id al-'Aqā'id* of *Iḥyā'*), Lahore, Ashraf; 'Al-Ghazzāli' in *The Arab Heritage*, ed. *idem*, Princeton University Press, 1946, pp. 142–58.

Field, Claud, (Tr.), *The Alchemy of Happiness*, Lahore, Ashraf, n.d. (reprint from Wisdom of the East Series).

Isma'il R. el-Faruqi (Tr.), *Our Beginning in Wisdom* (translation of al-Ghazālī's *Min Hunā' Na'lamu*), Washington, American Council of Learned Societies, 1953.

MacDonald, D.B., *Development of Muslim Theology* ..., London, 1903. Cf. Part III, pp. 215–42.

Mackane, William (Tr.), *Al-Ghazzāli's Book of Fear and Hope*, Leiden, Brill, 1962.

Nadwi, Muḥammad Ḥatīf, *Afkār-i Ghazāli*, Lahore, Idārah-i Thaqāfat-i Islamīyah [Institute of Islamic Culture], 1956 (Urdu); (Tr.) *Sargudhasht-i Ghazāli*, Lahore, Idārah-i Thaqāfat-i Islāmīyah, 1959 (Urdu tr. of *al-*

Munqidh with introduction); *Ta'limāt-i Ghazāli*, Lahore, Idārah-i Thaqā-fat-i Islāmīyah, 1962 (Urdu).

Nawab Ali, Syed, *Some Moral and Religious Teachings of al-Ghazzali*, Lahore, Ashraf, 1946.

Nūr al-Ḥasan Khān (Tr.), *Ghazāli ka Taṣawwur-i Akhlāq*, Lahore, Maktabat al-'Ilmīhah, 1956 (Urdu).

Sayyid, Ḥasan Qādiri Shor, *Imān Ghazāli ka Falsafah-i Madhhab-o Akhlāq*, Delhi, Nadwat al-Muṣannifīn, 1380/1961 (Doctorate thesis in Urdu).

Shehdai, F., *Ghazāli's Unique Unknowable God*, Leiden, Brill, 1946.

Smith, Margaret, *Al-Ghazāli: The Mystic*, London, Luzac, 1944.

'Urmaruddin, M, *The Ethical Philosophy of al-Ghazzāli*, Aligarh, Published by the author, 1949–1951, 4 Parts; also in one volume, Aligarh, 1962; *The Idea of Love in the Philosophy of al-Ghazzali*, Alibarb, Muslim University Press, 1941; *Some Fundamental Aspects of Imam Ghazzali's Thought*, Aligarh, Irshad Book Depot, 1946.

Watt, W.M., *Muslim Intellectual: A Study of al-Ghazali*, Edinburgh University Press, 1963.

Wensinck, A.J., *On the Relation between Ghazali's Cosmology and His Mysticism*, Amsterdam, 1933.

Zolondek, L. (Tr.), *Al-Ghazali's Conduct of State*, Leiden, Brill, 1963.

Ibn Bājjah

Ibn Bājjah,... *al-'Aql al-Fa''āl:* Text with Eng. tr. under the title: 'Ibn Bājjah on Agent Intellect' in the *Journal of Asiatic Society of Pakistan* (Dacca), Vol. V, 1960; *Kitāb al-Nafs*, ed. with notes and intro. by Dr M. Ṣaghīr Ḥasan al-Ma'ṣūmi, Damascus, Al-Majma' al-'Ilm al-'Arabi, 1960 (Eng. tr. to be published by the Historical Society, Karachi); *Risālah al-Ghāyah al-Insāniyah*: text with Eng. tr. under the title: 'Ibn Bājjah on Human End,' in the *Journal of Asiatic Society of Pakistan* (Dacca), Vol. II. 1957; *Tadbir al Mutawaḥḥid*, ed. by M. Asin Palacios, Madrid-Granada, 1946 (Arabic).

Ibn Ṭufayl

Ibn Tufayl, *Ḥayy Ibn Yaqẓān*, Eng. tr. by Simon Ockley: *The Improvement of Human Reason Exhibited in the Life of Hai Ebn Yakdhan*, London, 1708; new edition by A.S. Fulton, London, 1929, also by Paul Brönnle; *Awakening of the Soul*. London, John Murray 1910, 4th impression (Wisdom of the East Series), Urdu tr. by Dr Sayyid Muḥammad Yūsuf: *Jīta Jāgta*, Karachi, Anjuman-i Taraqqi-i Urdu Pakistan, [1955?], and Ẓafar Aḥmad Ṣiddiqi: *Ḥayy Ibn-i Yaqẓān*, Aligarh, 1955.

Ibn Sina, *Ḥayy Ibn Yaẓān* (with Juzjānī's commentary on it), Eng. tr. in Henry Corbin's *Avicenna and the Visionary Recital*, New York, 1960, pp. 137–50, 279–380.

Jāmi, ʿAbd al-Raḥmān, *Salamān-u Absāl*, Eng. tr. by A.J. Arberry in *Fitzgerald's Salaman and Absal*, Cambridge University Press, 1956.
Ṣiddīqī, Ẓafar Aḥmad, *Falsafah-i Ḥayy Ibn-i Yaqẓān*, Aligarh, 1955 (Urdu).

Ibn Rushd

Ibn Rushd, *Bidāyat al-Mujtahid...*, Urdu tr.: *Hidāyat al-Muqtaḍid*, Rabwah, Idārat al-Muṣannifīn, n.d.; *Faṣl al-Maqāl...*, Eng. tr. by Jamilur Rehman, in his *Philosophy and Theology of Averroes*, Baroda, 1921, pp, 13–80, also by G.F. Hourani with intro, and notes: *Ibn Rushd (Averroes) on the Harmony of Religion and Philosophy*, London; *Kitāb al-Kashf ʿan Manāhij...*, Eng. tr. by Jamilur Rehman in his *Philosophy and Theology of Averroes*, Baroda, 1921. pp. 83–308; *Sharḥ Jamhūrīyah Aflāṭūn*, ed. with an intro., tr. and notes by E.I.J. Rosenthal: *Averroes' Commentary on Plato's "Republic,"* Cambridge University Press, 1956; *Tahāfut al-Tahāfut: The Incoherence of the Incoherence* Eng. tr. with intro. and notes (Vol. II) by Simon von den Bergh, Oxford, Gibb Memorial Trust, 1954, 2 Vols:; Urdu tr. in preparation by the Board for the Advancement of Literature, Lahore.

Fakhry, Majid, *Islamic Occasionalism and Its Critique by Averroes and Aquinas*, London, George Allen & Unwin, 1958.
Hourani, G.F., *The Life and Thought of Ibn Rushd*, Cairo, American University.
Renan, E., *Averroes et l'averroisme*, Urdu tr. by Mawlwi Maʿshūq Ḥusain: *Ibn-i Rushd wa Falsafah-i Ibn-i Rushd*, Hyderabad, Dār al-Ṭabaʿ Uthmānīyah, 1347/1929.
Yūnus Farangi Maḥalli, M., *Ibn Rushd*, Aʿẓamgarh, Maṭbaʿ-i Maʿārif, 1342/1923 (Urdu).

Ibn Khaldūn

Ibn Khaldūn, *Kitāb al-ʿIbar...*, ed. by Naṣr al-Hūrīni, Bulaq, 1284 [1867–8], 7 Vols., many Urdu tr. but of parts only; *Muqaddimah*, Beirut, 1900 (vocalised edition); Urdu tr. by ʿAbdur Raḥmān: *Muqaddimah-i Ibn Khaldūn*, Lahore; also by Saʿd Ḥasa Khān Yūsufi: *Muqaddimah-i Ibn Khaldūn*, Karachi, Nūr Muḥammad Kār-Khānah Tijārat-i Kutub, n.d.; Eng. tr. by Franz Rosenthal: *Ibn Khaldūn: The Muqaddimah; An Introduction to History*, New York, Pantheon (London, Routledge and Kegan Paul), 1958, 3 Vols.; also by Charles Issawi, *An Arab Philosophy of History: Selections from the Prolegomena of Ibn Khaldūn of Tunis (1332–1406)*, London, John Murray, 1950 (Wisdom of the East Series), etc.; *Al-Taʿrif bi Ibn Khaldūn...* (Autobiography), Eng. tr. with commentary by W.J. Fischel: *Ibn Khaldūn and Tamerlane: Their Historic Meeting in Damascus A.D. 1401 (803 A.H.)*, Berkeley and Los Angeles, 1952.

'Abd al-Qādir, Muḥammad, *Ibn Khaldūn ke Mu'āsharti, Siyāsi awr Mu'āshi Khayālāt*, Hyderabad, Idārah Ishā'at-i Urdu [1943], 32 p. (Urdu).

'Abd al-Salām Nadwi, *Ibn Khaldūn*, A'zamgarh. Maṭba'-j Ma'ārif, 1359/1940 (Urdu tr. of Ṭāḥa Ḥusain's doctorate thesis in Arabic).

Enan, M. Abdullah, *Ibn Khaldūn: His Life and Work*, Lahore, Ashraf, 1946 (translated from Arabic).

Farrukh, Omar A., *'Abqariyat al 'Arab fi al-'Ilm wa'l-Falsafah*, Eng. tr. by B. Hardie: *The Arab Genius in Science and Philosophy*, Washington, The American Council of Learned Societies, 1954 (Near Eastern Translation Program, Publication No. 10).

Muhsin Madi, *Ibn Khaldūn's Philosophy of History*, London, G. Allen and Unwin, 1957.

Nadwi, M. Ḥanīf, *Afkār-i Ibn-i Khaldūn*, Lahore, Idārah-i Thaqāfat-i Islāmīyah [Institute of Islamic Culture], 1954 (Urdu).

Nikhat Shāhjahānpūri, *Ibn Khaldūn ki 'Aẓmat awr 'Ulamā'-i Yūrap [Europe]*, Bombay, Maṭba'-i Muḥammadi, 1944 (Urdu).

Schmidt, N., *Ibn Khaldūn: Historian, Sociologist and Philosopher*, New York, 1930.

Reference and General Works

'Abd al-Salām Nadwi, *Ḥukamā-i Islām*, A'ẓamgarh, Maṭba'-j Ma'ārif, 1953, Vol. I; 1956, Vol. II (Urdu).

Ali Mehdi Khan, *The Elements of Islamic Philosophy*, Allahabad, 1947.

Arnold, T.W., and A. Guillaume (Eds.), *The Legacy of Islam*, 7th edition, London, O.U.P., 1952.

de Boer, T.J., *The History of Philosophy in Islam*, 7th edition, London, Luzac, 1961. (Arabic translation with critical notes by M. 'Abd al-Hādi Abu Rīdah: *Tārikh al-Falsafah fi al-Islām, Cairo.*)

Donaldson, D.M., *Studies in Muslim Ethics*, London, S.P.C.K., 1953.

El-Ehwani, Ahmed Fouad, *Washington Lectures: Islamic Philosophy*, Cairo, 1937.

Encyclopaedia of Islam, The, ed. by W.Th. Houtsma and others, Leiden, Brill, London, Luzac, 1908–38, 4 Vols. and *Supplement*. New edition by B. Lewis and others in preparation, 1954—; 26 parts published: Vol. I comprises first 22 Parts. *The Shorter Encyclopaedia of Islam*, ed. by H.A.R. Gibb and J.H. Kramers, Leiden, Brill, 1953 (reprint with revisions of the articles on religion and law in the *Encyclopaedia of Islam*). Urdu translation of the *Encyclopaedia of Islam* with revision and improvements edited by Mawlwi Muḥammad Shafī, Lahore, Urdu Encyclopaedia of Islam, University of the Panjab (in preparation).

Encyclopaedia of Religion and Ethics, ed. by James Hastings, New York, Scribner, 1908–27, 2nd impression: 1952, 13 Vols.

Hitti, P.K., *History of the Arabs*, 4th edition, revised, London, Macmillan, 1949.

Iqbal, S.M., *The Development of Metaphysics in Persia: A Contribution to the*

History of Muslim Philosophy, London, Luzac, 1908; Lahore, Bazm-i Iqbal, n.d.

Levi, R., *The Social Structure of Islam*, Cambridge University Press, 1957 (the second edition of the *Sociology of Islam*).

Luṭfi, Jum'ah Muḥammad, *Tārīkh-i Falasafat-ul-Islām*, Hyderabad, Dār al-Ṭaba', Jāmi'ah 'Uthmānīyah, 1360/1941.

MacDonald, D.B., *Development of Muslim Theology*..., New York, Scribner, 1926; Lahore, Premier Book House, 1963 (reprint).

Nasr, Seyyed Hossein, *An Introduction to Islamic Cosmological Doctrines: Conceptions of Nature and Methods Used for its Study by the Ikhwān al-Ṣafā', Al-Birūni and Ibn Sina*, Cambridge (U.S.A.), Belknap Press of Harvard University Press, 1964; *Islamic Studies*, 1968; *Three Muslim Sages: Avicenna, Suhrawardi, Ibn 'Arabi,* Harvard University Press, 1964.

Nicholson, R.A., *A Literary History of the Arabs*, 2nd edition, Cambridge University Press, 1930.

O'Leary, De Lacy, *Arabic Thought and Its Place in History*, 3rd edition, London, Routledge and Kegan Paul, 1954; *How the Greek Science Passed to the Arabs*, 2nd edition, London, Routledge and Kegan Paul, 1951.

Osman Amin, *Light on Contemporary Muslim Philosophy*, Cairo, 1958.

al-Qifṭi, *Tārikh al-Ḥukamā'*, Urdu tr. by Dr Ghulām Jīlāni Barq, Delhi, Anjuman-i Tarraqqi-i Urdu, 1945.

Rahman, F., *Prophecy in Islam: Philosophy and Orthodoxy*, London, G. Allen and Unwin, 1958.

Rescher, Nicholas, *The Development of Arabic Logic*, University of Pittsburgh Press, 1964; *Studies in Arabic Philosophy*, University of Pittsburgh Press, 1968; *Studies in the History of Arabic Logic*, University of Pittsburgh Press, 1963.

Rosenthal, E.I.J., *Political Thought in Medieval Islam*, Cambridge University Press, 1958.

Sarton, G., *Introduction to the History of Science*, Baltimore, Williams and Wilkins, 1927–48, 3 Vols.

Sharif, M.M. (Ed), *A History of Muslim Philosophy with Short Accounts of Other Disciplines and the Modern Renaissance in Muslim Lands*, 2 Vols., Wiesbaden Otto Harrassowitz, 1963, Vol. I; 1966, Vol. II; *Muslim Thought: Its Origin and Achievements*, 2nd edition, Lahore, Ashraf, 1959.

Shushtery, A.M.A., *Outlines of Islamic Culture*, 2nd edition, Bangalore City, Bangalore Printing & Publishing Co, 1955 (2 volumes in one).

Stephan and Nandy Ronart, *Concise Encyclopaedia of Arabic Civilization*, Amsterdam, Djambatan, 1959.

Waḥīd al-Dīn, Dr Sayyid (Tr.), *Qurūn-i Wasaṭa ka Islāmi Falsafah*, Hyderabad (Deccan), Jami'ah 'Uthmānīyah, 1363/1944 (original by Ignaz Goldziher).

Walzer, R., *Greek into Arabic: Essays on Islamic Philosophy*, Oxford, Bruno Cassirer, 1962.

Watt, W.M., *Islamic Surveys—I: Islamic Philosophy and Theology*, Edinburgh University Press, 1962.

INDEX

Abbasids, 4–5, 33
'Abd al-Salām Nadvi, 52 n.
Abdul Hamid, Khwaja, 58 n., 127 n.
'Abdullah ibn Ḥārith, 4
'Abdul Malik, Caliph, 2
Abigdor, Abraham, 108
al-Abīli, Muḥammad ibn Ibrāhīm, 141 n.
Abraham de Blames, 118 n.
Absāl, 125, 127 n.; *see also* Asal
Absolute Man, Ikhwān al-Ṣafā's idea of, 39
Absolute, the, 46
Abubacer (Ibn Ṭufayl), 123
Abu Bakr, 28
Abu Ḥanīfah, Imām, 20 n.
Abu Hāshim (the Mu'tazilite), 15
Abu al-Ḥudhayl, 5, 15; on beatific vision, 8
Abu Sahl Balkhi, 52
Abu Sa'īd, 2
Abu Ya'qūb Yūsuf (al-Muwaḥḥid), 123, 131 n.
acquired intellect, 48, 49
acquisition, doctrine of, 19, 20; *see also kasb*
active intellect/intelligence, 48, 64, 74, 76, 77, 119, 129, 135; Aristotle's notion of, 47 n.
'Adalites, 2
Adam, Fall of, 125 n.
al-'adl, 4, 6
aḥad, 9
Ahl al-Ḥadīth, 3 n.
Aḥmad ibn Dāwūd, Qāḍi, 5
'Ā'ishah (Prophet's wife), 1, 9
Albalag, Isaac, 108
Albert the Great, 58, 62
Aleppo, 57
Alexander of Aphrodisias, 42, 47 n., 51
Algiers, 183, 124
'Ali (Ḥaḍrat), 1, 28, 138 n.
'Alīm, God as, 6
Almagest (Ptolemy), 131 n.
Almoravid, 117
Alpharabius (al-Fārābi), 57
amicable numbers, 34 n.
Amīn (the Abbasid Caliph), 27
amr bi'l-ma'rūf wa'l-nahy 'an al-munkar, 6
'Amr ibn 'Ubayd, 3, 4
Anaxagoras, 51, 52
Antinomies of Pure Reason, 77, 81, 82
'aql bi'l-fi'l, 48
'aql fa''āl, 48
'aql hayyūlāni, 48
Aquinas, St Thomas, 109, 110 n., 111; and al-Fārābi, 58, 62; and al-Ghazāli, 110, 111
Aqwāl al-Dhahbīyah (Kirmāni), 55
Arabs, 1, 22
Arberry, A J., 56 n.
Aristotelianism, 45, 57
Aristotelian/s, 54, 55, 100, 115
Aristotle, 24, 35, 42, 44, 44 n., 45, 47 n., 54, 57, 60, 64, 67, 68, 70, 92 n., 100, 117, 118, 131, 132, 138 n., 142, 146, 148; conception of God in, 92; Ibn Rushd's estimation of, 132; souls and intelligences of spheres in, 75
Arjuzah fi al-Ṭibb (Ibn Sīna), 131 n.
Armenia, 4

Armstrong, A.H., 75 n.
Asal (Absāl), 125, 127, 129
al-Ash'ari, 14, 15, 16, 17, 18, 19, 19 n., 20 n., 88, 106; on beatific vision, 17; doctrine of acquisition of, 19; freedom of will in, 19; on God's seating Himself upon the throne, 18; and pre-established harmony, 20; *Maqālāt Islāmiyīn*, 19 n.
Ash'arism, 14, 19 n.; beginnings of, wrapped in obscurity, 14
Ash'arites, 27, 82, 106, 112; on the createdness or uncreatedness of the Holy Qur'ān, 15, 16; on God's seating Himself upon the throne, 18; on the possibility of beatific vision, 17, 18; on relation of God's attributes with His essence, 14, 15
Ashwell, G., 124
Asin Palacios, M., 109, 118 n.
Asrār al-Ḥikmat al-Ishrāqīyyah (Ibn Sīna/Ibn Ṭufayl), 124
Assassins, 33
'Aṭā' ibn Yassar, 2
Augustine, St, 85, 90, 142
Avempace/Avenpace (Ibn Bājjah), 117
Aven Sina (Ibn Sīna), 67
Averroes (Ibn Rushd), 131, 136 n.
Averroism, 134 n.
Averroists, 139 n.
Avicenna (Ibn Sīna), 67
al-'Awfi, 33
Ayyub (the Mu'tazilite missionary), 4

Bacon, Roger, 43
Bactria, 25
Badruddīn 'Alavi, M., 19 n.
Baghdad, 32, 35, 57
'Balance,' 10
Balkh, 25
baqā', 25
al-Bāqilānī, 14
Bashshār ibn Burd, 27
Basra, 3, 32
Bāṭinites, 27
battle of Badr, 30
beatific vision, 127; possibility of, according to the Ash'arites, 17; according to the Mu'tazilites, 8–9; proof from the Hadīth, 9, 17; proof from logic, 17; proof from the optical sciences, 9; proof from the Qur'ān, 8, 17
Bergh, S. van den, 112
Bergson, 77
bila kayfa wala tashbihah, 15
al-Bīrūni, 26; and al-Rāzi, 54, 55
al-Biṭrūji, 118
Blumberg, H., 67 n.
bodily resurrection, dispute between al-Ghazāli and the philosophers with regard to, 95, 103; according to Ibn Rushd, 135, 136 n.; according to the Mu'tazilites, 10; philosophers' denial of, 96 f.
Bodin, 142
de Boer, T. J., 41 n., 52, 72 n., 135
Book of Apple (pseudo-Aristotelian), 35
Bouwmeester, J., 123 n.
'Bridge,' 10
Briffault, 42, 43 n.
Bronnle, Paul, 124 n.
Browne, E.G., 21, 50 n.
Buddha, 25
Buddhism, 25, 26
Buddhists, 25, 129
Bukhāri, 9
al-Burhān (*Second Analytics*), 68

Carra de Vaux, 69, 135 n.
Casanova, P., 33
categories, Aristotelian, 44; Ibn Sīnā's conception of, 70
Categories (Aristotle), 67
causality, al-Ghazālī's theory of, 97
Ceylon, 125
Christianity, 21, 22, 23, 111, 115; and Sufism, 21
Christians, 56, 117
cogito ergo sum, 79, 87, 115
command and creation (God's), 7, 16
Companions (of the Prophet), 1

Comte, 142
Copernicus, 118
Corbin, 125 n.
corporate immortality, 65, 134
cosmological argument, 78, 80
cosmology, al-Fārābī's, 63, 64; Ikhwān al-Ṣafā's, 38–9; al-Kindī's, 43, 44
Cournot, 142
Courtois, V., 67
creatio ex nihilo, 83, 102, 109; according to al-Ghazāli, 92; Ibn Rushd's view of, 133; according to Ibn Sīna, 83
Crescas's Critique of Aristotle, 107
Crescas, Hasdai, 107
Critique of Practical Reason (Kant), 114
Critique of Pure Reason (Kant), 114

Dante, 131
De Anima (Aristotle), 47, 92 n.
De Caelo (Aristotle), 75 n.
Defoe, Daniel, 124
Democritus, 51, 52, 53
Denahana, *see* Isaac
Descartes, 49, 77, 78, 79, 85, 86 n., 87, 112, 113, 114; *see also* al-Ghazāli and Ibn Sīna
'Destruction of the Philosophers' (al-Ghazāli's *Tahāfut al-Falāsifah*, s.v.), 87, 114
dhikr, 23
Discours de la méthode (Descartes), 86 n., 113, 114
Divine Comedy (Dante), 131
divine justice, Mu'tazilites' doctrine of, 10–12
divine unity, Mu'tazilites' doctrine of, 6, 10
Donaldson, D.M., 40 n.
Dozy, 21
Dunlop, D.M., 67 n.
Durant, Will, 110 n.
Dyck, E.A. van, 124 n.

eclecticism, 36, 37, 40, 140
Egypt, 4, 118
Eichhorn, J.G., 123 n.
emanation, doctrine of, 24
emanation/ism, theory of, and causality, 97, 101; criticism of, 76–7; in al-Fārābi, 63–5; al-Ghazālī's criticism of, 74–7; Ibn Khaldūn's criticism of, 149 f.; in Ibn Sīna, 73–7; in Ikhwān al-Ṣafā', 39; in al-Kindi, 4, 5–7; reasons for Muslim philosophers' acceptance of, 73–7
Emanul Haq, 26 n.
Empedocles, 51, 52
Enan, Muhammad Abdullah, 142 n.
Encyclopaedia of Islam, 105
'Encyclopedia' (Ikhwān al-Ṣafā'), 33–6
Enneads (Plotinus), 24, 35
essence and existence, separation between, 59 n.
eternity of the world, al-Ghazālī's criticism of, 89–92; in Ibn Sīna, 82–4; Ibn Rushd's view of, 133
ethics, Ibn Bājjah's views on, 121; Ikhwān al-Ṣafā's, 39–40; al-Rāzī's, 55–6
Euclid, 55
Explanatio Simboli Apostolorum (Raymund), 109

fallacy of ontologism, 78; *see also* ontological fallacy
fanā', 25
Fārāb, 57
al-Fārābi, 34, 36, 43, 49, 57–66, 67 n., 72, 74, 76, 85, 88, 89, 103, 108, 118, 125, 140, 149; and Albert the Great, 53, 62; on the attributes of God, 62–3; and Ibn Sīna, 57; on the immortality of the soul, 64; ontology of, 58–60; political philosophy of, 65–6; on the proofs for the existence of God, 61–2; and St Thomas Aquinas, 58–62; on teaching philosophy, 57 f.; theory of emanation in, 63–4; *Fuṣūṣ al-Ḥikam*, 60; (*Kitāb Ārā' Ahl*) *al-*

Madīnat al-Fāḍilah (A Treatise on the Opinions of the People of the Ideal City), 65, 66 n.; *Kitāb al-Siyāsat al-Madanīyyah* (Political Economy), 65 n., 66 n.
farḍ al-'ayn, 13
farḍ al-kifāyah, 13
Farmer, H.G., 43, 117 n.
Farqad Sabakhi, 23
Faṣl al-Maqāl . . . (Ibn Rushd), 136 n.
Fatimids, 33
al-Fauz al-Aṣghar (Ibn Miskawayh), 57
Fermat, 34 n.
Fez, 117
Field, Claud, 86 n.
al-Fihrist (al-Nadīm), 24
First Analytics (Aristotle), 68
Flint, Robert, 141, 142
freedom of man, according to the Ash'arites, 19–20; according to the Mu'tazilites, 11
Fulton, A.S., 124 n.
Fuṣūṣ al-Ḥikam (al-Fārābi), 60

Gairdner, W.H.T., 105 n.
Galileo, 75
Gauthier, Leon, 124
genetic fallacy, 22
Ghallāb, Dr M., 125 n.
Ghaylān al-Dimashqi, 2
al-Ghazāli, 14, 35, 46 n., 64 n., 85 ff., 86 n., 110 n., 121, 125, 131 n., 140; and Blaise Pascal, 111; on bodily resurrection, 95; on causality, 97 ff.; charge of anti-intellectualism against, 104–5; on the composite nature of cause, 99; and contemporary philosophy, 103, 115, 116; criticism of the theory of emanation by, 91–2; and Descartes, 85–8, 112, 114; on the eternity of the world, 89–92; on God's knowledge of the particulars, 92–5; and Hasdai Crescas, 107; and infidelity of the philosophers, 88; influence of, on Christian scholasticism, 109–11; on Jewish scholasticism, 105–8; on intellect/reason, 104; and Jehuda Halevi, 106; and Kant, 88, 114–6; Latin and Hebrew translations of the works of, 107–8; method of, in the *Tahāfut*, 104–5; and Nicholas of Autrecourt, 112; plurality of causes in, 99; and Raymund Martin, 109–10; on reconciliation between philosophy and religion, 103–5; and St Thomas Aquinas, 109–11; voluntarism of, 95, 98, 115; *Ihyā'* ('Ulūm al-Dīn), 105 n., 109, 110, 113; *Kīmiyā' al-Sa'ādah*, 87 n., 111; *Kitāb al-Arba'īn*, 111; *Maqāṣid al-Falāsifah*, 108, 109; *Maqṣad al-Asmā' (Asnā' Aqsā')*, 109; *Mishkāt al-Anwār*, 105, 109; *Mīzān al-'Amal*, 109; *al-Munqidh*, 109, 111; *Tahāfut al-Falāsifah*, 88, 92 n., 96, 104, 105, 107, 109, 110, 131 n.
Ghoraba, Hammouda, 19 n.
Gilson, E., 112 n.
God, attributes of, in Al Fārābi, 62–3; beatific vision of, 8–9, 17–18; command and creation of, 7, 16; justice of, according to the Mu'tazilites, 10–12; knowability of, 60 f.; and the knowledge of the universals and particulars, 92–5, 134 ff.; proofs for the existence of 61–2, 78, 79; relation of attributes of, with His essence, 6–7, 14–5; seating Himself upon the throne, 18 ff.; ṣūfi love of, 29–30; unity of, in Mu'tazilites 6–9; will of, 99, 100
Goldziher, 25, 32
Granada, 123

Ḥadīth, 9, 14, 17; and Sufism, 30
Ḥafṣ ibn Salīm, 4
Ḥajjāj, 2
Haldane, E. S., 86 n.
Hammer-Purgstall, 141 n.
Hammond, Robert, 58 n.
Happalat Happala (Qalonymos ben

David), 107
Harran, 52
Harranians, 52
Harranians, 52
Hartmann, 115
al-Ḥasan al-Baṣri, 2, 3
Ḥasan ibn Zakwān (the Mu'tazilite missionary) 4
hayula, 73
Ḥayy, 124, 125, 126, 127, 129, 130
Ḥayy, God as, 6
Ḥayy Ibn Yaqẓān (Ibn Ṭufayl), 124 n, 125 n., 125–8, eclecticism of, 130; Leibnitz's estimation of, 124; and Neoplâtonism, 124, 129; philosophical bearings of, 125 n. 127, 129; and *Robinson Crusoe*, 124; the romantic frame of, 125 n; story of, 125–7; symbolic significance of the title, 124, 128; translation into various European languages of, 123–4; Urdu translations of, 124 n.
Hegelians, 7, 120
hell and paradise, Mu'tazilites' view of, 10, 12; philosophers' conception of, 96 f.
Hermeneutica (Aristotle), 68
Ḥimād ibn Salm, 23
Hippocrates, 55
Hirschfeld, Hartig, 106 n.
Hishām ibn Malik (the Umayyad Caliph) 2
historicism, fallacy of, 22
History of the Arabs (Hitti) 105
History of the Philosophy of History (Flint) 142
Hitti, Philip K., 105, 136 n.
Hiyal al-Mutanabbiyīn (al-Rāzi) 51, 54
Hobbes, 66
Holmyard, 51
Hourani, G.F., 136 n.
ḥuduth, 80, 90
al-Hujwîri, 27
Hume, 85, 98, 112, 114
Ḥunayn ibn Isḥāq, 125 n.
Husik, I., 35, 51 n., 106 n.

Iamblichus, 34 n.
al-'Ibārah (Hermeneutical). 68
Ibn 'Abbās, 136 n.
Ibn Abi Usaybi'ah, 118n.
Ibn al-'Arabi, Muhyi al-Dīn, 123 n.
Ibn Ashras (the Mu'tazilite) 15
Ibn Bājjah (Avempace) 117, 120, 122; ethical views of, 121; on immortality of the soul, 120; metaphysical views of, 119; as a poet, 117 n.; rationalism of, 120; works of, 118; *Kitāb Ittisāl al-'Aql bi'l-Insān*, 120 n.; 'The Régime of the Solitary,' 118–121, *Tadbir al-Mutawaḥḥid* (The Régime of the Solitary), 119 n.; *Tardiyah*, 117n.
Ibn al-Bayṭār, 118 n.
Ibn al-Farīd, 26
Ibn Gabirol, 35
Ibn Ḥazm, 55
Ibn Khaldūn, 140–151; compared with Oswald Spengler, 145 n.; criticism of the theory of emanation, 149 f.; on the dangers and fallacies of philosophy, 147; on dialectics, 147; the discovery of the greatness of, 142 n.; estimations of, 140–2; on evolution, 150; as an historian, 141 n., 145 n.; laws of sociology, 145–6; on the limitations of metaphysics, 149–50; on logic, 146; and magic, 143 n.; on methods of history, 143–5; philosophical works of, 140 n.; on philosophy and religion, 148–9; *Kitāb al-'Ibar* . . ., 142; *Muqaddimah (Muqaddama/h:* 'Prolegomena'), 141, 143, 146, 147
Ibn Khallikān, 57, 117
Ibn al-Khaṭīb, 140 n.
Ibn Mas'ūd, 1
Ibn Miskawayh, 57
Ibn al-Qifṭi, 32, 35 n.
Ibn Rushd (Averroes) 35, 49, 107, 120, 131–9, 146, 149; and Aristotle, 131; charge of heresy against, 132 n.;

132; as a commentator on Aristotle, 132, difference between soul and intellect in, 135; on the eternity of the world, 133; on God's knowledge, 133–4; on the immortality of the soul, 135–6; on philosophy and religion, 136–7; and the theory of twofold truth, 137; *Faṣl al-Maqāl...*, 136 n.; *Kitāb fi Ḥarakat al-Aflāk*, 136 n.; *Kitāb al-Kashf ʿan Manāhij...*, 136n.; *Kitāb al-Kulliyāt fi al-Ṭibb*, 131 n.; *Tahāfut al-Tahāfut (Incoherence of Incoherence)*, 107, 134 n.
Ibn Ṣā'igh (Ibn Bājjah) 117
Ibn Sīna 46 n., 49, 50, 57, 62 n., 67–84, 88, 90, 92, 100, 103, 108, 124, 131 n., 132, 140, 149; arguments for the existence of God, 79, 80; on the createdness and the eternity of the world, 83–4; *cogito ergo sum* in, 78, 80; and Descartes, 78–80; and Kant's Antinomies of Pure Reason, 80–82; on logic, 67–70; on metaphysics, 72–77; and modern philosophy, 77–83; on psychology, 70–72; on God and world, 84; and the theory of emanationism, 73–76; *Arjuzah fi al-Ṭibb*, 131 n.; *Asrār al-Ḥikmat al-Ishrāqīyyah*, 124; *al-Ishārāt*, 67, 68; *al-Najāt*, 67, 119; *al-Shifā'*, 93, 140; *Tisʿ Rasā'il fi al-Hikmah wa'l-Ṭabiʿ-iyyat*, 67 n.
Ibn Ṭufayl, 118, 123–30; *see Ḥayy Ibn Yaqẓān*
Ibn Waḥshīyah, 52
Ibrāhīm ibn Adham, 25
Iḥyā' (al-Ghazāli), 105 n., 109, 110, 111, 113
ikhtiyār, 19
Ikhwān al-Ṣafāʿ (Brethren of Purity), 32–41; cosmology of, 38–9; eclecticism of their philosophy, 35, 36, 40; and emanation, 39; ethics of, 39–41; idea of *Insān-i Kāmil* in, 40; the origin and explanation of the name, 32; religio-philosophical leanings of, 33; resurrection, major and minor, in, 39; theory of knowledge, 37–8; 'Encyclopedia' (*Rasā'il Ikhwān al-Safā'*): collaborators in compiling, 33; influence of, 34–5; Jesus Christ in, 36; place in world literature, 33; al-Sijistānī's criticism of, 35; treatises and subject-matter of, 34–6; transmission of, to Spain, 35; *Jāmiʿah*, 33
iktisāb, 19 n.
ʿilm al-kalām, 147
Imām al-Ḥaramayn, 14
immortality of the soul, corporate, 65, 134; in al-Fārābi, 64–5; al-Ghazālī's discussion of, 95–103; in Ibn Bājjah, 120; in Ibn Rushd, 134–6; philosophers' view of, 95–7
Imrā' al-Qays (the poet), 22
India, 25
insān-i kāmil, 31, 40
intellect, Aristotle's theory of, 47 n.; al-Kindī's fourfold division of, 48–9
intelligence, first, 92, 148, 149
Introduction to the History of Science (Sarton) 50 n., 67, 107 n., 117 n., 125 n., 131 n., 140 n., 141, 142
Iqbal, 21 n., 27 n., 105, 114, 134
Isaac Denahana, 107 n.
Isagoge (Porphyry), 36, 67
al-Ishārāt (Ibn Sīna), 67, 68
Ishrāqi Taṣawwuf, 30
Ismā'īlites, 27, 33, 55
Iʿtazalah ʿanna, 3
ittiṣāl, 120

al-Jadl (Topics), 68
al-Jāḥiẓ, 15
Jainism/Jainists, 129
Jāmi, 125, 127 n.
Jāmiʿ ah (Ikhwān al-Ṣafā'), 33
Jamil-ur Rehman, M., 136 n.
Jazīrah, 4
Jehuda Halevi, 35, 106
Jesus Christ, 18, 23, 36, 40

al-Jīli, 'Abd al-Kariīm, 31 n.
John Philoponos, 51
al-Jubba'i, 5
Judah ben Solomon Nathan, 108
Judaism, 106
Jurji, E.J., 30 n.
Justinian, 25

Kalām Allah (the Qur'ān), 7, 16
Kalām-i Ilāhi (al-Rāzi), 51, 52
Kalilah wa Dimnah (The Fables of Bidpai), 32
Kamali, S.A., 64 n., 92 n., 96 n.
Kant, 11, 48 n., 80, 85, 96, 104, 148, 149; Antinomies of Pure Reason, 77, 81–3; and al-Ghazāli, 88, 114–6; and Ibn Khaldūn, 140, 141; and Ibn Sīna, 80–82
Kanṭians, 10, 12
al-Karmāni (Spanish mathematician), 35
kasb, doctrine of, 19; and *iktisāb*, 19 n.; the originality of, 19 n.
Keith, G., 124
Khārijites, 1
al-Khaṭabah (Rhetoric), 68
al-Khayyāṭ, Abu al-Ḥusayn, 5
Khurasan, 4
Kimiya al-Sa'ādah (al-Ghazāli), 81 n., 111
al-Kindi, 36, 42–9, 48 n., 57, 64, 131; cosmology of, 43–4; the father of Arabic philosophy, 49; on five essences, 45; on fourfold division of intellect, 48–9; on nature and destiny of human soul, 46–7; and Neoplatonism, 45; and quantitative methods, 42; on religion and philosophy, 43; and theory of philosophy, 43; and theory of emanation, 45–6; and Weber-Fechner Law, 43; 'On the Five Essences' (*Risālah fi al-Jawāhir al-Khamsah*), 44; 'On the Intellect' (*Risālah fi al-'Aql*), 47–9
Kirmāni, Ḥamīd-ud-Dīn, 55
(Kitāb Arā' Ahl) al-Madīnat al-Fādilah (al-Fārābi), 65, 66 n.
Kitāb al-Araba'in (al-Ghazāli), 111
Kitāb fi Ḥarakat al-Aflāk (Ibn Rushd), 131 n.
Kitāb al-'Ibar . . . (Ibn Khaldūn), 142
Kitāb Ittiṣāl al-'Aql bi'l-Insān (Ibn Bājjah), 120 n.
Kitāb al-Judari wa'l-Ḥasbah (al-Rāzi), 50 n.
Kitāb Kashf 'an Manāhij . . . (Ibn Rushd) 136 n.
Kitāb al-Khazari (Jehuda Halevi), 106
Kitāb al-Kulliyat fi al-Tibb (Ibn Rushd), 131 n.
Kitāb al-Mitāl wa'l-Niḥal (Ibn Ḥazm/al-Shahrastāni), 24, 55
Kitāb al-Siyāsat al-Madaniyyah (al-Fārābi) 66 n.
Kraus, Paul, 51, 52
Kremer, von, 21, 22
Kufa, 4
kun (fa yakūn), 7, 16
Kuzmin, J., 123 n.

Lane-Poole, Stanley, 36
latent (potential) intellect, 48–9
Leibnitz, 20, 69, 84, 124
Levonian, L., 36 n.
Levy, Reuben, 32
Lewes, G.H., 113
logic, Ibn Khaldūn's criticism of, 146; in Ibn Sīna, 67–70
Logos, 16, 48

al-Ma'arri, Abu al-'Alā, 27
Ma'bad al-Juhani, 2
MacDonald, D.B., 10, 11 n., 19, 20, 23 n., 57 n., 85, 88, 105, 134 n.
Machiavelli, 142
al-Maghālit (Sophisticii), 67
maḥall, 19
Maimonides, 106
al-Majrīṭi, Maslamah ibn Aḥmad, 35
Making of Humanity (Briffault), 42
Manichaeans, 54
al-Māmūn, 5, 13, 27

al-Manṣūr, Amīr Abu Yūsuf Ya'qūb, 132 n.
Manṣūr (the Abbasid Caliph), 4
manzilaḥ bayn al-manzilatayn, 3 n., 6
Maqālāh fi ma ba'd al-Ṭabi'ah (al-Rāzi), 51
Maqālāt Islāmiyyin (al-Ash'ari), 19
Maqāṣid al-Falāsifah (al-Ghazāli), 108, 109
Maqāṣid al-Asmā' / Asnā' / Aqsā (al-Ghazāli), 109
al-Maqtūl, Shihāb al-Dīn al-Suhrawardi, 30
al-Māqūlāt (The Categories), 68
Martin, *see* Raymund
Mary, 19
al-Mas'ūdi, 3 n.
Ma'sūmi, Dr Ṣaghīr Ḥasan, 121 n.
Māṭūrīdi, 14
Merx, 21
Metaphysica (Aristotle), 44, 47 n., 65 n., 75 n., 92 n.
metaphysics, Ibn Bājjah's views on, 119–21; Ibn Khaldūn's criticism of, 149–50; Ibn Sīnā's, 72–7; al-Rāzī's, 51–4
Meteorologica (Aristotle), 123 n.
Meyerhof, Max, 50, 52 n.
miḥnah (inquisition), 13
al-Mihrajāni, Abu Ahmad, 33 n.
Mill, J.S., 147
miracles, 95
Mishkāt al-Anwār (al-Ghazāli), 105, 109
Mizān al-'Amal (al-Ghazāli), 109
Moore, G.F., 110 n.
Morocco, 117
Moses, 8, 17, 23
Moses ben Joshua of Narbonne, 108, 118 n., 123
Mu'ādh ibn Jabal, 1
al-mu'allim al-thāni, 57
Muḥammad, 11, 94, 103; *see also* Prophet
Muḥammad Yūsuf, Dr Sayyid, 123 n., 127 n.
Muḥaṣṣal (Fakhr al-Dia al-Rāzi), 140 n.
mujāddid, 85
mukhālafah lil-ḥawādith, 15
Mukhāriq al-Anbiyā' (al-Rāzi), 51, 54
al-Munqidh (al-Ghazāli), 105 n., 109 113; and *Discours de la méthode* of Descartes, 86 n., 112, 113
al-Muqaddasi, Abu Sulaymān . . ., 33
al-Mūqaddimah (*Muqaddima/h* Ibn Khaldūn's), 119 n., 141, 143, 146
muqāmāt, 25
Murji'ites, 3 n.
Murūj al-Dhahab (al-Mas'ūdi), 3 n.
al-Mustanjid (the Abbasid Caliph), 35
al-Mu'taṣim, 5
mutawātir, 9
Mu'tazilism, 13, 33, 42; historical development of, 1–5; *see* next
Mu'tazilites, (Mu'tazilah) 3 n., 12, 13, 14, 16, 17, 18, 19, 27; on the beatific vision, 8–10; on the uncreatedness of the Qur'ān, 7, 15; on divine justice, 10, 11; on divine unity, 6–10; doctrines of, 6–10; origin of the name, 3 n.; sceptical tendencies in, 15, 27
Muwaḥḥid, 123

al-Nadim (bin abi Ya'qūb), 24
al-Nahrajūri, Muḥammad ibn Aḥmad, 33
al-Najāt (Ibn Sīna), 67, 149
Naples, 109
Nāṣir Khusraw (Persian poet), 55
al-Naẓẓām, 5, 7, 10
Neoplatonism, 21, 24, 25, 42, 44, 45, 124, 129.
Neoplationists, 24, 25, 38, 74, 76, 115, 129
Neo-Pythagoreanism, 42
Newton, 54
Nicholas of Autrecourt, 112
Nicholson, R. A., 21 n., 25, 26 n., 33 n.
Nietzsche, 66, 115
nirvana, 25
Nous, 48
Nushīrwān, 25

Ockley, Simon, 124
O'Leary, De Lacy, 44, 72
'On the Five Essences' (al-Kindi), 44–5
On the Smallpox and Measles, A Treatise (al-Rāzi), 50
ontological fallacy, 91
Organon (Aristotle), 67, 68
Orientalists, 16, 21, 22, 105

Parkash, Buddah, 144 n.
Parmenides, 59
Pascal, Blaise, 111, 114
Pensées sur la religion (Pascal), 111, 114
People of the Bench, 1
people of unity and justice, 6
Peripatetics, 45, 48 n., 69, 76, 89, 108
Persia, 25
Phaedo (Plato), 35
Philo, 48
Philoponos, *see* John
philosophy and religion, in al-Ghazāli, 103–5; in *Ḥayy Ibn Yaqẓān* (Ibn Ṭufayl), 128–30; in Ibn Bājjah, 120–1; in Ibn Khaldūn, 148; in Ibn Rushd, 136–9; in al-Kindi, 43; in al-Rāzi, 54–5
Physics (Aristotle), 45
Plato, 32, 35, 37, 42, 46, 48, 51, 53 n., 54, 66, 103, 132, 133 n., 142, 146, 148
Platonism, 45, 57, 115
Platonists, 119
Plotinus, 24, 35, 38, 45, 48, 51 88; *see also* Neoplatonism
Plutarch, 51
Pococke, Edward, 123, 124
Poetics (Aristotle), 68
Polgar (Pulqar?), Isaac ibn, 108
Porphyry, 24, 36, 51, 67
Posterior Analytics (Aristotle), 36; *see also Second Analytics*
pre-Socratics, 51, 53
Pringle-Pattison, 84
Prior Analytics (Aristotle), 36; *see also First Analytics*
Pritius, J. Georg, 123 n.
Proclus, 51
'Prolegomena' (*Muqaddimah*), 141, 146, 147
Prophet, the Holy, 1, 7, 9, 11, 17, 18, 23, 28, 30, 31, 97, 102, 127, 128; *see also* Muḥammad
Ptolemy, 75, 118, 131 n.
Pugio Fidei (Raymund), 109, 110, 111
Pythagoras, 38, 51, 52
Pythagoreanism, 45, 129
Pythagoreans, 34 n., 42

qadar, 2, 4
Qadarites, 2, 11
Qādir, God as, 6
Qalonymos ben David (the Elder), 107
Qalonymos ben Qalonymos of Arles, 107
Qārmaṭians, 27, 33
qidām, 80, 90
al-Qifṭi, *see* Ibn
al-Qiyās (First Analytics), 68
qudrah, 19
Qur'ān the, 3, 7, 8, 9, 10, 11, 12, 13, 15, 16, 17, 18, 19 n., 28, 29, 93, 94, 96, 101, 102, 121 n., 124, 128, 129, 137; createdness/uncreatedness of, 7, 15 ff.; Muʿtazilites on the anthropomorphic verses of, 9; as the speech of God, 7, 15; and Sufism, 28 ff.
al-Qushayri, 27

Rābiʿah al-Baṣri, 30
Rābiʿah: The Mystic (M. Smith), 30 n.
Rahman, F., 49 n., 65 n., 135 n.
Rasā'il Ikhwān al-Ṣafā', 33, 35, 36 n.
Raymund, Martin, 109, 110, 111, 114
Rayy, 50
al-Rāzi, Abu Bakr, 50–6, atomism of 53 f.; condemnation of heretical views of, 55; empiricism of, 50–1; ethics of, 55–6; metaphysics of, 51–4; as a physician, 50; and pre-Socratics, 51; and the Sabians of Harran, 52; on science, philosophy

and religion, 54–5; on space and time, 53; 'Discourse on the Five Eternal Elements,' 51; *Hiyal al-Mutanabbiyīn*, 51, 52; *Kalām-i Ilāhi*, 51, 52; *Kitāb al-Judari wa'l-Ḥasbah*, 50 n.; *Maqālah fi ma ba'd al-Tabi'ah*, 51; *Mukhāriq al-Anbiyā'*, 51, 54; *On Smallpox and Measles, A Treatise*, 50; *al-Sirat al-Falsāfiyah*, 56; *The Spiritual Physick of Rhazes*, 56n.
al-Rāzi, Fakhr al-Din, 14, 52, 140 n.
Reconstruction of Religious Thought in Islam (Iqbal), 105, 134 n.
'Régime of the Solitary' (Ibn Bājjah), 118–22
Regulae ad Directionem Ingenii (Descartes), 86 n.
Religion within the Bounds of Reason (Kant), 115
Rhetoric (Aristotle), 68
Robert of Anjou, 107
Robinson Crusoe (Defoe), 124
Rosenthal, E. I. J., 74 n., 120 n., 121 n., 142 n., 143 n., 147 n.
Ross, G.R.T., 86 n.
Ross, W.D., 44 n., 65 n., 75 n.
Rousseau, 58, 66
Rules for the Guidance of Mind (Descartes), 114

sa'ādah, 65 n.
Saadia Gaon, 106
Sabatier, A., 103
Sabians, 52
Saffarids, 27
Sa'rd al-Fayyūmi, *see* Saadia Gaon
Saladin (pupil of Crescas), 107
salaf, 14
Salamān (in *Ḥayy Ibn Yaqẓaān*), 125, 127, 129
Salmon, D., 58 n.
Samanids, 27
Samarqand, 14
Santayana, 132
Saragossa, 117
al-Sarakhsi, Abu Tayyab, 52
Sarton, G., 33 n., 35 n., 67, 106 n., 108 n., 110 n., 112 n., 125 n., 131 n., 140 n., 141, 142, 145
Sayf al-Dawlah al-Hamdāni, 57
Schopenhauer, 115
Second Analytics (Aristotle), 68
Sefer Segullat Melakim (Abigdor), 108
Seville, 114
al-Shahrastāni, 24, 52
ṣhaqā', 65 n.
Sharī'ah, 32
Sharḥ, 131
Sharif, M.M., 48 n., 112 n.
al-Shaykh al-Ra'is, 67
Shaykh Yūnāni, 24
Shibli Nu'māni, 4 n.
al-Shifā (Ibn Sīna), 93, 149
Shī'ism, 33
Shī'ites, 1
al-Shi'r (Poetics), 68
Shirk, 16
Shu'ūbiyah controversy, 27
Siddiqi, B.H., 127 n.
Ṣiddīqi, Ẓafar Aḥmad, 124 n., 127 n.
Siebeck, H., 103
Ṣifātiyah, 6
al-Sijistāni, Abu Sulaymān al-Manṭiqi, 35
Sinai, desert of, 22
al-Sīrat al-Falsāfiyah (al-Rāzi), 56
Smith, Margaret, 30 n.
Socrates, 37, 42, 132, 146
Sophisticii (Aristotle), 68
space, in al-Kindi, 45; in al-Rāzi, 54
Spain, 14, 35, 118
Spencer, Herbert, 58, 66
Spengler, Oswald, 145 n.
spheres, order of, 73 n.
Spinoza, 58, 120 n., 123 n.
Spiritual Physick of Rhazes (al-Rāzi), 56 n.
Stagirite, the, 132
Stern, M., 33 n.
Studies in a Mosque (Lane-Poole), 36 n.
Study of History (Toynbee), 141

ṣūfi, 23
Ṣūfī(s), 23, 25, 26, 31, 87
Sufism, 21–31, 57; Aryan reaction, theory of, 26; and Buddhism, 25–6; and Christianity, 22–4; and divine love, 23, 29; and Indian religions and culture, 25; and Neoplatonism, 24–5; and the Prophetic traditions, 30–1; and the Qur'ān, 28–30; socio-politico-cultural conditions for the growth of, 26–7
Summa contra Alcoranum (Raymund), 109
Summa contra Gentiles (Aquinas), 109, 110 n.
Summa Theologica (Aquinas), 110
Sunnah, 14
Sweetman, J.W., 23 n., 36 n., 109 n.
syncretism, 42, 130
Syrier, Miya, 143 n.

Tadbir al-Mutawaḥḥid (Ibn Bājjah), 119 n., 125
Tadhkirahs, Ṣūfi, 23
tafsir, 131 n.
al-Tafsir (Hermeneutica), 68
Tahāfut al-Falāsifah (al-Ghazāli) 64 n., 88, 92 n., 104, 105, 107, 109, 110, 131 n.
Tahāfut al-Tahāfut (Ibn Rushd), 107, 134 n.
al-Ṭaḥāwi, 14
Ṭāhirids, 27
talkhiṣ, 131 n., 140 n.
tanzih, 15
Tara Chand, 26 n.
Tardīyah (Ibn Bājjah), 117 n.
Tā'rikh al-Ḥukamā' (al-Qifṭi), 32
ṭariqah, 25
tawakkul, 23
al-tawḥid, 6
tā'wil, 10
Tehran, 50
Teicher, J.L., 77
Theaetetus (Plato), 56 n.
Theology of Aristotle (pseudo-Aristotelian), 24, 35, 45
Thilly, Frank, 53 n.
Thomism, 110, 116
Tibawi, A.L., 33 n.
Timaeus (Plato), 53 n.
time, in al-Ghazāli, 94; in al-Kindi, 45; in al- Rāzi, 54
Tirmidhi, 9
Tis' Rasā'il fi al-Ḥikmah wa'l-Ṭabī'iyyat (Ibn Sīna), 67 n.
Toledo, 106, 109
Topics (Aristotle). 68
Toynbee, A., 141
Tradition (of the Holy Prophet), 97, 102
Transoxiana, 25
Trueblood, D.Æ., 103
al-Ṭūsi, Nāṣir al-Din, 125
twofold truth, theory of, 137–139

'ūd, 118
Umayyads, 2, 27

Valla, G., 50 n.
Valiuddin, Mir, 26 n., 28 n.
Vedantism, 21
Vico, 142
volo ergo sum, 115

al-wa'd wa'l-wa'id, 6
wāhib al-ṣuwar, 74
Wā'idites, 3 n.
Wali-ur-Rahman, Mu'tazid, 64 n., 70 n.
Ward, James, 83
Wasij, 57
Wāṣil ibn 'Aṭā', 4
al-Wāthiq, 5
Watt, W. Montgomery, 20 n.
Weber-Fechner Law, 43
Weinberg, J.R., 112 n.
Weltanschauung, 96
Wensinck, A.J., 20 n.
Whitehead, 84
Wickens, G.M., 74 n., 77 n.
Widgery, A., 103
Wilson, C.E., 28 n.
Witelo, 43

Wolfson, A.H., 107
World-soul, 39

Xatina, 117

Yazīd ibn Walīd, 4
Yūnus Farangi-Maḥalli, M., 127 n.

Zād al-Musāfirin (Nāṣir Khusraw), 55
al-Zanjāni, Abu al-Ḥasan 'Ali ibn Hārūn, 33
Zayd ibn Rifā'ah, 33
Zedler, B.H., 134 n.
Zeno, 81
Zerahiah Levi ben Isaac (Saladin), 107
Zoroastrianism, 129
Zwemer, S.M., 108 n.